CAUGHT IN
THE WEB

CAUGHT IN THE WEB

INSIDE THE POLICE HUNT TO RESCUE CHILDREN FROM ONLINE PREDATORS

JULIAN SHER

CARROLL & GRAF PUBLISHERS
NEW YORK

CAUGHT IN THE WEB
Inside the Police Hunt to Rescue Children from Online Predators

Carroll & Graf Publishers
An Imprint of Avalon Publishing Group, Inc.
245 West 17th Street
11th Floor
New York, NY 10011

AVALON
publishing group incorporated

First Carroll & Graf edition 2007

The author wishes to gratefully acknowledge the Michener-Deacon Fellowship
of Canada and Her Excellency, Governor General Michaëlle Jean, for a generous
grant to complete research on this book.

Library of Congress Cataloging-in-Publication Data is available.

ISBN-13: 978-0-78671-888-7
ISBN-10: 0-7867-1888-9

9 8 7 6 5 4 3 2 1

Printed in the United States of America
Distributed by Publishers Group West

For my father, Ben Sher,
1921–2006
who inspired me to write

CONTENTS

"HEAR THE CHILDREN CRY"

The cage was not big, even if it had been for a dog. For a small six-year-old, it was cramped. The girl, though, was used to it. Shivering—more from fear than from cold—she crouched in her pen.

She was naked, except for a small orange wristband on her right arm. Her soft brown hair fell over her shoulders. On her face, no tears ran down her cheeks.

The man did unspeakable things to her, hurting her, touching her, penetrating her private parts. And then took digital pictures, movies. All the time.

Click. The camera catches her peering through the bars.

Click. Another shot shows her sprawled on a bed, naked.

Click. She grasps a hunting knife far too large for her tiny hand, its blade touching her skin. Scrawled across her chest, the words scream out: "Cut me. Hurt me."

There are tens of thousands of children trapped like her around the world right now, but we know the names of only a handful. In 2002, the National Center of Missing and Exploited Children (NCMEC—pronounced *nick-mick*) outside Washington, D.C.—the central clearinghouse in the United States for victims of online abuse—had "identified" about two hundred children, meaning that their full identities were known and they had been rescued. By the end of 2005 the number was five hundred; by 2006, it had climbed to more than eight hundred children from around the world.

Still, those numbers represent only the proverbial drop of water in the online ocean. No one knows precisely how many children are victims of Internet porn—the crime is amorphous, often anonymous and always hard to pin down. The National Child Exploitation Co-ordination

Centre in Ottawa, run by the Royal Canadian Mounted Police (RCMP), cited one study that estimates there are fourteen million Web sites displaying child abuse images, and more than twenty thousand new or recycled images posted on the Web each week. Five years ago, the CyberTipline run by NCMEC was receiving reports of child pornography at the rate of 24,000 a year; by 2006, that number had increased more than fourteen times to over 340,000.

Behind each of those pictures is a child's solitary nightmare. Children like Shy Keenan, who was abused for years in England and saw her abuse pictures widely circulated on the Web before becoming one of the country's leading children's rights advocates as an adult. "When I was a kid, I used to try to send 'Help me' messages with my eyes,"she says. "It didn't take too long to figure out that no one good was looking at these pictures. And no one was looking at my eyes."

Even as a child, Keenan realized that ultimately it was not about the pictures. The visual images are, in effect, crime scene photos: crimes of humiliation and torture of the most vulnerable members of society. Crimes committed not just by those who took the pictures. "It made no difference to me whether the abuser was under the covers or behind the lens or behind the computer," says Keenan. "I was there because they wanted to be amused by the corruption and degradation of me."

In fact, those who are downloading, viewing and trading the pictures are all too often much more than just voyeurs but active hands-on abusers themselves. Far from being down-and-out loners and isolated computer geeks, the creators and consumers of such images are teachers, priests, doctors, politicians, police and Boy Scout leaders. They are your relatives, your neighbors and your civic leaders. In just the first six months of 2006, the roster of Americans arrested on child porn charges included the former publisher of the New York newspaper *Newsday,* who also served on the city's education policy board; a police chief in North Carolina; and the deputy press secretary for the Department of Homeland Security, who pled guilty to using the Internet to seduce someone he thought was a teenage girl.

Mark Foley, the Republican congressman who was forced to resign in the fall of 2006 after revelations of sexually explicit e-mail messages he'd sent to teenage male Congressional pages, was co-chairman of the Congressional Missing and Exploited Children's Caucus. He had been fond of telling cable TV talk shows that sex offenders were "animals" who would persist "unless stopped."

"They come from all walks of life," says Emily Vacher, an agent with the FBI's Innocent Images program, "from all socio-economic backgrounds, educational backgrounds, sexual orientation—it doesn't matter. And that's what makes it even more difficult for law enforcement to catch them and for people to protect their kids."

It's not hard to find images of abuse on that computer sitting on your desk or in your child's bedroom. One in seven young Web surfers has encountered unwanted sexual material or online harassment, according to the latest "Online Victimization of Youth" study commissioned by the U.S. Department of Justice. Only one in three American families protect their children's Internet surfing with filters or blocking software. Even among those parents who do monitor their youngsters' Web activities, 71 percent stop after the children turn fourteen.

Few people will ever witness a cocaine deal or a murder. But online child abuse is the crime that can reach out and touch anyone.

This book tracks the efforts of police and prosecutors around the world to find and save children being exploited by sexual predators—often at tremendous personal cost to themselves. It tells the harrowing tales of children rescued—and those still being abused online; it reveals the courage of some who have spoken out and the crippling trauma for some who will never recover. It follows the money trail of the shrewd entrepreneurs who have made millions by peddling child pornography, and it looks at how the top executives at banks and credit card companies are realizing that they have for too long neglected how their financial institutions are entangled in this Web of exploitation.

Because the crime is global, so is this book. Instead of focusing on a single country, I concentrate on the United States, the United Kingdom and Canada—where the predators and their pursuers are the most active—along with recounting forays into Europe, Australia and Asia.

All the cases documented in this book are real, but to protect the identities of the children involved and to ensure that they are not revictimized, their names have been changed. Such names are followed by an asterisk the first time they appear. In cases where the offender is a family member, the surnames have also been modified, except in a few rare instances where the convicted abuser's name has been already widely publicized. Every other detail of the abuses documented in the following pages is taken—unaltered and uncensored—from interviews, court testimony, police records and Internet logs. In the course of investigating this story, no child abuse images were purchased or downloaded; none were viewed except in the presence of a law enforcement officer at work. Descriptions of any images come from court records, police accounts or from the writings of the accused.

Because the term "child pornography" is so current in American, Canadian and other court systems and in the media, it is regrettably but unavoidably used at times in this book as well. As we shall see, many investigators in this field prefer the phrase "child abuse images" or "child exploitation material." They insist that the term "child pornography"—and the even more demeaning phrase "kiddie porn"— is a contradiction, since pornography is usually defined as sexually explicit material featuring consenting adults. But children are neither adults nor can they give legal consent. To label these pictures "pornography" is to suggest they are like "adult pornography" except with an age difference. Nothing could be further from the truth. In most adult pornography—at least in professional productions—the participants are paid, and consumers make a moral or esthetic choice to enjoy it or not. Child abuse images are the evidence of the torture and mistreatment of society's most defenseless members, and the images cannot be justified by any claim to individual preference or morality.

It is time for the children's stories, too often hidden in the dark corners of the Web, to be told. Their torment has been etched in their memories—and the memories of the police officers dedicated to rescuing them. It is what scars the investigators. But it is also what spurs them on.

"Police departments spend more money tracking down stolen cars than we do policing Internet porn. Why is it more important to retrieve property that's already insured anyway than to rescue kids?" asks Det. Sgt. Paul Gillespie of the Child Exploitation Section of the Toronto Police's Sex Crime Unit. It was his team that scrambled madly to try to identify and rescue the girl in the cage when they saw her pictures online. They dropped everything to find her, because they know that behind every picture or video is a frightened little child. Gillespie can't shake the lingering effects of seeing some of the worst videos of shackled children:

"Sometimes," he says, "you can hear the children cry."

PART ONE THE WILD, WILD WEB

One

SAVING JESSICA

We didn't know if this girl was at great risk—or dead. So we had to move fast.

—Det. Const. Bill McGarry,
Toronto Police Sex Crimes Unit

At least while she was in her cage, the man could not hurt her. But how could she ever hope someone could come and save her? Because no one knew she even needed rescue. Jessica* was imprisoned in her own home; her abuser was not some stranger who had kidnapped her.

Her tormentor was her father.

The irony was that as far as victims of abuse went, Jessica's plight was hardly unknown. In fact, she was famous, in a way. Tens of thousands, if not hundreds of thousands, of people had seen the pictures of her. In her cage. In her bedroom. At her computer. Outside, playing in the street.

But the men who gazed at her day in and night out were not about to rescue her. Jessica was a hot item, and her photos traded like baseball cards by pedophiles who couldn't get enough of her torture.

Jessica's father, Burt Thomas Stevenson,* was a software engineer at one of the many firms in the region's high-tech hub. He frequently worked at home; Jessica's mother, on the other hand, put in long days at a local telecommunications firm. Earning a comfortable $91,000 a year, Stevenson was typical of the new face of child abuse in the twenty-first century: not dirty old men in parks but tech-savvy young professionals from suburbia. An analysis of arrested child porn possessors by the University of New Hampshire's respected Crimes Against Children Research Centre (CCRC) showed that 73 percent were employed and 27 percent earned a decent salary over $50,000; in fact, one in ten, like Stevenson, were making more than $80,000. His family tie to his primary victim was also not exceptional: the cases registered in NCMEC's database show that 45 percent of the arrested molesters were parents or other family members.

Stevenson was as computer literate as they come: he had programmed his own encryption software, and he had networked his house so he could move seamlessly from computer to computer. He had at least five computer hard drives, plus the latest in digital video hardware. For fifteen years, Stevenson collected more than 100,000 pornographic images of children being sexually abused. Then in October of 2002 he decided to make his own albums of abuse.

"I decided to get rid of the obsolete idea of morality," he later told the FBI.

Within a few months, graphic pictures of his daughter's torture were flooding the Web. Jessica's pictures initially got wide dissemination on the Internet in 2003. By June of that year, a man named "Trasher," with a Russian e-mail address, posted many of them in a Usenet discussion group—one of the Web's ubiquitous e-mail exchange forums that are free and open for anyone to join. Eventually, the series ballooned to include almost four hundred coveted photographs in close-up and wide angle, the girl grimacing as she is forced to perform sexual acts with her father.

Stevenson had first released the images to a restricted group on a secure underground part of the Web called the Freenet. He was even confident enough to distribute a few photographs showing clearly a side of his own face in the same frame as his daughter. When Stevenson discovered the pictures had made it onto the wider Internet, he sent an e-mail to his pedophile buddies to replace the identifying photos with ones in which he had blurred his face. They complied.

But not everyone who was looking at the pictures of his daughter was taking pleasure from sharing in his abuse of her. In three countries across two continents, Jessica's pictures had grabbed the attention of police investigators, desperate to identify, find and rescue the girl in the cage.

*   *   *

It was the last Sunday in November 2003, that gray and dreary month in Toronto when autumn is too weak to hang on much longer but the winter hasn't made up its mind yet to arrive with its full force. It was still pitch dark at 4:30 A.M. when Paul Gillespie walked into his third-floor office at the downtown police headquarters, not much looking forward to the day ahead. A police officer for almost three decades, Gillespie had joined the force as an eighteen-year-old cadet, moving through intelligence work on organized crime and international jewel thieves to keeping the peace in the caldron of one of the city's toughest inner-city neighborhoods. A father of three, he had taken over the Child Exploitation Section of the Sex Crimes Unit of Canada's largest city's police force on Christmas Day 2000. Now, three years later, he had a promotional exam to write in a few hours. He was hoping to make inspector. By habit, he first turned on his computer to check his messages on a secure Web-based police message board.

Even for a cop used to stomach-turning pictures, Gillespie was horrified by what he saw—graphic images on his computer sent by a police colleague in England, showing a young girl, naked and being tortured.

"Does anybody know this series?" asked Paul Griffiths, an investigator at the National Crime Squad's Pedophile Online Investigation Team (POLIT) in London who was one of the pioneers of image analysis. The girl in the series was one the police would later learn was Jessica, but for now she was just one of the nameless sufferers online.

"I couldn't take my eyes off them," Gillespie says. "There was some really nasty stuff there—really bad pictures. But as bad as they were you could see the clues in them. I worked on this for five hours."

Gillespie was applying some of the lessons he had learned when he had first met Griffiths several months earlier on a trip to Europe to look at what was emerging as a promising field in police work: online image analysis to track down clues in child abuse pictures. For some time now, police forces in North America and Europe had been busting the men who manufactured and traded pornographic images of children, but scant resources had been devoted to actually trying to identify and rescue the victims.

Child sex crimes police in Canada, the U.K. and elsewhere had recently set up a Web-based chat network to exchange information using Groove, a software program secure enough that even the American military used it in Iraq. Groove created a common work space instantly available on the computer desktops of a select group of investigators who knew and trusted one another. With tens of thousands of child abuse images floating around the Web, the police hoped they could exchange leads and tips on a select few, make sure they were not wasting time on old, resolved cases and perhaps isolate the most urgent cases to crack. The "Jessica" series would be one of the first tests of this loose-knit Groove network. Online predators had been cooperating for years, exchanging not just photos but security tips, encryption software and warnings. Could the police create the same kind of Web to catch the porn merchants at their own game?

Paul Griffiths was blessed with a photographic memory; he could see bathroom tile in one picture and then—after viewing thousands of other images—identify a shot with tile that matched. When he first saw the Jessica pictures, three things struck him right away: "I knew they were not from the U.K., I knew that they were new and I knew that there were clues there," he said. He uploaded encrypted copies of some of Jessica's pictures to the police's Groove bulletin board back in June, with this e-mail note:

> I have just added some new files to the work space. Let's
> test out the new system to see if we can get some useful
> cooperation started in identifying the victim.

Griffiths was not sure at first if the police would make any headway. "I picked the images up from a fairly obscure newsgroup," he said. "Very often you have five or ten photos, and you don't think you can do anything with them. Then another investigator comes up with more photos, and if you put all of them together, maybe you get something."

Indeed, a German police officer soon discovered more than three hundred images on a computer seized in his country and realized that they were part of the same series that Griffiths had circulated. By the time Paul Gillespie was looking at the series on that Sunday morning in November, there were more than four hundred pictures of Jessica.

In one, she's asleep in her bed, but in her hands has been placed a picture of a blond girl—another victim in a well-known series of child pornography. The setup is code for an exchange: Jessica's father was signaling to the consumers of his daughter's online abuse that if they sent him more pictures of the blond girl, he'd send them more of Jessica.

"There are some very popular series out there that every bad guy has to have," said Gillespie. The Toronto cop never did get back to his studies on that dreary Sunday, and he blew his promotional exam. But that was okay. He had a much more important test to pass: he and his team had to find that little girl.

For Jessica, her home—and her prison—was in a tree-lined suburb where the streets have bucolic names and quaint bridges cross over winding streams. A wealthy-enough neighborhood where the yards are so large that there are no sidewalks. Basketball hoops in the driveways. Birds chirping noisily in the nearby forests.

"This area is observed by Community Watch citizens," says a sign posted on several streets. No citizens were there to observe what went on behind the closed doors of the pretty two-story home at the end of a cul-de-sac.

Jessica had an older and a younger brother, but among her siblings she was the only target of her father's obsessions. When he had Jessica all to himself, Burt Thomas Stevenson was as twisted as they come. He drugged his daughter. He boasted in his chat logs about the things he would make her do. "Society's morals are all wrong," he later told police.

"I believe he would have killed Jessica eventually, because he was into the bondage and really strange stuff," said the senior FBI agent who worked on the case.† "Pain. He liked hypodermic needles. He was into the master/slave thing."

The worst pictures of Jessica in his collection confirmed that: her wrists were tied behind her back with cord, her feet bound

---

† She cannot be named because it would help identify the victim and her father.

behind her back with thick black Velcro, her eyes closed tightly, tears streaming down her cheeks as she gritted her teeth in pain.

Back in Toronto, Paul Gillespie had spent several hours alone on Sunday hunting for clues in the Jessica pictures, without much luck. Her bedroom, with the Pokemon bedspread, had that well-appointed middle-class look. The furniture in the home, the casual clothes she and her brother wore in some of the everyday outdoor shots, even the cars in the distance behind her in one outside shot all pointed to a North American location.

But where?

For Gillespie, rescuing such children had long since stopped being just his job. It was his all-consuming mission. And now he wanted to find *this* girl.

Gillespie spoke in a staccato burst of energy as he railed against the Internet industry that seems willfully blind to the abuse that travels on the network. He wrote messages to himself on his BlackBerry as thoughts popped into his head about new laws, new tools, new ways to persuade politicians, the public and the press to take this new crime seriously. He was forever bolting out of his office into the squad room, barking suggestions to his detectives, nagging them about progress on one case or the other.

Always wired, Gillespie seemed particularly on edge at 7 A.M. on Monday, December 1, 2003, when the rest of his team filed in to work. Most of their computers were far from the latest models, and their surroundings were typical police drab. The gray carpet was stained from age. On a crowded coffee table, an empty coffee maker fought for space with a big open jar of peanut butter. One entire wall was covered with a large whiteboard detailing their mountain of assignments. Green tape marked off the rows and boxes: Active Investigations, Courts-Trials and Priorities.

This morning, there was a new priority. "I just saw this new series. It's horrendous," Gillespie told his team. "We can't walk away from this." He gave his people simple marching orders: drop whatever you're doing; we are concentrating on nothing else but examining these four hundred pictures and cracking the clues.

"You could tell he was pretty disturbed," Det. Const. Bill McGarry remembered. A father of four, McGarry had joined the unit two years earlier, having spent several years working on domestic violence and child abuse cases. "I can still remember the look of shock. Everybody forgot about any current investigations. Our parental and humane instincts took over. Every time you see these abuse pictures, a little bit of your heart gets torn out."

More quiet and reserved than many of his boisterous fellow cops, McGarry seemed almost out of place in the bustling squad room. In an office cluttered with paperwork and discarded computer parts, his work space was as neat and organized as his thinking was methodical. The only distraction was a family photo, showing his children laughing on the back of a pickup truck. McGarry, who had a college education in graphic arts and had worked for several computer imagery companies before joining the police, now hoped he could direct his talents to the hunt for victims.

Gillespie also reached out to Special Agent Emily Vacher at the FBI's Innocent Images task force in Calverton, Maryland, one of the first law enforcement centers dedicated to online child abuse. Gillespie had first met Vacher when he sent his new team down to the FBI to get training. At the time, the young agent was one of the emerging experts at undercover Web work—police officers who posed as young victims to lure pedophiles on the Internet. Vacher had also become adept at image analysis and victim identification. Gillespie sent the FBI agent some of the pictures right away, and they spent some time on the phone analyzing them.

McGarry and his colleagues feared that time was running out for Jessica. The more than four hundred pictures of her spanned at least two years of her childhood; the police could roughly date them from the time they were first posted on the Web. But as the girl aged, the images were becoming increasingly violent. "There was consensus in our office that if this child wasn't dead, she was going to be soon," McGarry said. Indeed, one of his first tasks was to start checking North American death records to see if a girl of about six had been murdered recently.

Death was very much on the mind of Burt Thomas Stevenson—but not the death of Jessica. Stevenson was planning the murder of her mother and perhaps her brothers, presumably to give him unrestricted access to his daughter. He first sent sex toys worth $1,000 to a German man and then $300 to a British man to carry out the killings. Both Web correspondents took the bribes but not the job.

Stevenson hoped he would have better luck with a South Carolinian fan of his handiwork. According to instant-message conversations later found by Vacher, Stevenson asked this man to commit the crime in March 2003, when he was out of town. He sent photos of his house, the fusebox and power lines and a copy of his wife's work schedule. Then Stevenson hid duct tape, knives and rope under the house—along with twenty compact disks filled with his entire collection of child abuse images as a reward.

He wasn't particular about what the man should do with his sons: he could take the boys and sell them into slavery or kill them, he told Spies, but he was not to hurt Jessica. The murderer could have sex with his daughter—but that was all. However, Stevenson spelled out in gruesome detail the fate he had planned for his wife. "He wanted her to be tortured before she died," says the FBI supervisor. "It was to be a long, long killing."

There was one very special request made: "He wanted the hit man to show his wife an image of Stevenson abusing Jessica before she died," said FBI agent Emily Vacher, who would later uncover details of the murder plot on Stevenson's computer. "He wanted an image of her husband sexually abusing her daughter to be the last image in her head here on earth."

The adage that a picture is worth a thousand words haunted the Toronto cops. The pictures could speak to them, if only they could decipher the clues.

For starters, they had a lead on her abuser—albeit a slim one.

Stevenson had tried to withdraw from the Web the shots that had shown his face unblurred. John Menard, however, one of Gillespie's more talented high-tech experts, had found his way into an obscure Freenet chat group and secured the original, clean shot of the side of the face of Jessica's abuser—it showed that the perpetrator was white, middle-aged, with a receding brown hairline, a mustache and a scar on his neck. Not enough to create a mug shot but sufficient for a match if they ever arrested someone.

Another clue was the girl's room, which had distinctive wallpaper with a strip running along the middle of the wall with fire trucks and firemen in yellow outfits. Again, not enough to pin down a location but useful to confirm the crime scene—if and when the cops could ever locate the bedroom.

With hundreds of photos, there were bound to be hundreds of false leads. Look at that pop can in the background: is that a Coke? Is it a Canadian Coke can or an American one? Can the company give us a region for that product's sales? A doll in one snapshot—let's run down that doll. A large dog plays with the girl in another photograph—contact kennel clubs, see where that leads. In another picture, Jessica holds up a piece of paper with strange letters scrawled over it. Is it a secret message? A code? The cops blow it up and even try reversing it in a mirror shot. Nothing.

Hours and hours of wasted time. Hours the cops feared the little girl did not have.

The first big break came with a close examination of the orange band Jessica had on her right wrist in several of the photos. It had some indistinct letters on it. Was it a medical bracelet? A charm? McGarry used several computer graphic programs to blow it up. After several hours of work, he was able to make out almost all of the letters and guess the rest:

F-U-N-W-E-R-K-S

A quick Google search revealed that a chain of children's amusement parks was operating under that name in five southern and western American states. Some of the publicity shots of the firm's Web site showed laughing kids wearing the same kind of orange admission bracelet that the girl in the cage had. A call to the company revealed that the wristbands were distributed to large groups of children who visited the park on school trips or group outings.

The next break came from several photos of the girl wearing a Brownie uniform. The American flag in the background left no doubt that the girl was somewhere in the States. Part of her troop badge was visible in one picture; her hair fell over one number, and her abuser had been cautious: he had intentionally blurred the other numbers.

McGarry zoomed in, cropped the image, turned it around and—though they were fuzzy—it looked as if the first two digits of her troop number could be 1 and 7. At the FBI's Innocent Images headquarters, Emily Vacher was coming to the same conclusion. "Okay, what number do you think this is?" Vacher asked Paul Gillespie as they kept staring at the pictures: 1 and 7 were the likeliest combination.

A call to the Girl Scouts of America revealed that though there were several hundred groups across the country whose numbers began with 1 and 7, three of them happened to be in one southern state. That didn't eliminate the other states, but suddenly one of them was looking more and more likely. The circle was closing.

By then, the FBI had ten field agents working the case. "The agents from other squads dropped everything and tried to help us find if this little girl was there," said the senior FBI supervisor for the state.

Gillespie had been posting his team's progress regularly on the Groove network for investigators around the world to see. "We're taking ownership of this, and we're going to try to find out where she is," he told them. "Once they found out we were working on clues, it energized the whole group."

More help came from a civilian team of investigators at the National Center for Missing and Exploited Children (NCMEC) headquartered in Alexandria, Virginia. A powerful nonprofit organization with strong connections—and financial backing—from both Capitol Hill and the corporate world, NCMEC had originally been set up to help find missing and abducted children. A small team of image analysts was gaining an expertise in identifying children from online child abuse images. "We had seen the pictures of that girl for some time," says Michelle Collins, head of NCMEC's Exploited Child Unit. "Now it looked like there were real clues and a chance to find her."

By this time it was late Monday afternoon. In Toronto, Gillespie's team had been working flat out for hours. "It appeared as though we were running out of clues," McGarry recalled. He made the long train commute to his home that night, drained and disappointed. It only made matters worse that the girl he was trying to rescue reminded him of one of his own children. "There is one picture of her that looks identical to my daughter," he said.

McGarry didn't sleep much that night.

The morning of December 2 brought a fresh perspective and hope to the Sex Crimes Unit. They had tried to grab a few hours of rest and some needed time away from their computer monitors. Sometimes the best way to crack a case is to step away for a while. It's like looking at a painting in a museum: you step back and see it from a different angle. "This is where you have to have an open mind," Bill McGarry said. "You start looking at the pictures for the non-obvious stuff."

In several of the photos the team had pored over the day before, Jessica was wearing a simple green dress. So far, the Toronto investigators had largely ignored the dress to look for other, seemingly more useful, clues in the same picture—the dog tag on her pet or an object on the coffee table behind her. "Just when we had thought we had exhausted everything about this photo, we had to slow down and think out of the box," said McGarry.

There was nothing identifiable or remarkable about the dress, though. It had a simple cut, with a belt, pleats and a collar that did make it look a little formal. Then it hit the cops: what if that meant something? Could it even be a school uniform?

McGarry and the others started researching the Web for American-based companies that manufactured school clothes. There were hundreds. So the team decided to take a chance and limit the search to the one southern state—since so far, at least, that's where the Girl Scout and amusement park clues had pointed. On one Web site, McGarry was able to find a dress that appeared to have all the same details.

At 8:40 A.M., McGarry picked up the phone and called the store. "I had to convince the manager that I was actually a police officer and not some nut," he says. By 8:58, McGarry had fired off a detailed e-mail to the manager, attaching a cropped photograph of the girl in the dress with her face obliterated.

"A young girl is being severely sexually abused and tortured," he wrote. "Could you please look at the photograph and confirm whether or not this dress matches your 'Chapel Dress'?"

By 11:50, the manager phoned back to explain that his company was right in the middle of the Bible Belt, and he would do everything in his power to help stop the abuse of a child. Yes, he said, the dress appeared to be from his line of clothing. What's more, his company sold that particular dress to several schools across the country—but only to two schools in the largest city of that state.

Both schools, fortunately, had Web sites. The Toronto cops started looking for pictures of children, thinking they might even find a class photo with a match for their victim. No such luck. One of the schools—a Catholic institution that served children from kindergarten to high school—had only one picture that featured children at all, and they were all older than Jessica. But the police noted that many of the boys and girls were wearing green T-shirts. There appeared to be a small logo over the left breast area. The cops went back into the hundreds of photos they had of Jessica and remembered that in a few of them, she and her older brother were wearing the same kind of T-shirt. And the abuser had taken the trouble to blur the logo on their clothes. "Now why would he do that? He's not going to delete it if it's a Nike swoosh," said team leader Paul Gillespie.

The team knew they were on to something; they had seen many pictures of the girl in the same kind of green outfit, but how could that help them? Then one officer remembered—from among the hundreds of photographs—catching sight of a picture of Jessica in her dress with the top part of the logo just barely visible above the bottom of the photograph. McGarry isolated the picture: part of three letters could be discerned on the dress.

McGarry's pulse was racing. "All of a sudden you get filled with this energy. All I could do was type as fast as I can to try to pull this stuff in. We always say, 'Don't get too excited—it might be wrong.'"

He went back to the school Web site and grabbed a shot of the official logo on the main page. He then rotated the graphic and reduced it to superimpose it over the outline of the three letters on Jessica's dress.

It was a perfect match. They had the city and the school—and that meant the girl could not be far away.

"I'll bet you my mortgage that this is the right thing," McGarry said.

It had taken all of ten minutes from the time he had gotten the call back from the uniform supplier. By noon, he was on the phone to the local FBI special agent in the city they had identified. By 12:17, McGarry had sent him an e-mail with all the clues the Toronto squad had gathered, as well as cropped photos of Jessica's face, her school uniform and the unblurred photo of the man seen in the pictures abusing her.

It was, technically, a breech in international police protocol. Usually, to pass on sensitive information in a criminal investigation, the Toronto cops would start by going through a liaison officer at the American consulate or the appropriate official at the headquarters of a law enforcement agency in Washington, D.C. "But that could take months; it was clear in this instance that we didn't have that kind of time," says McGarry.

By 2:14, McGarry had sent seven more e-mails to the FBI, eventually supplying them with the entire set of images.

Then he waited. His phone kept ringing, but the calls were not the ones he was waiting for from the FBI.

At 3:50, the black phone on McGarry's desk rang one more time. His fellow officers fell silent as they watched him pick up the phone.

"You're kidding, right?" they heard him say as a smile broke out on his face. He screamed, "Yes!" and jumped out of his chair.

With Toronto's leads in hand, the FBI had headed straight to a Catholic school on the outskirts of the city. They had shown the picture to the principal, who immediately identified Jessica.

"We were ecstatic, all of us jumping up and down and high-fiving each other," McGarry says. They had done it—in thirty-three hours, they had found the little girl in the pictures. Now maybe they stood a chance of rescuing her.

When the FBI had arrived at the school, the administrators had informed them that Jessica had not come to school that day; she was sick, they said. Fortunately for the girl, the administrators said, her dad often worked at home as a computer programmer, so he could take care of her. That was enough for the FBI to dispatch agents right away to Jessica's house, fearing she could be in immediate danger. A surveillance team spotted her playing outside, on her bicycle; she was safe—for now. Back at the school, FBI agents had stayed behind to wait for Jessica's mother to show up to pick up her two sons. When they showed Mary Stevenson the photos, the shocked mother identified her daughter and confirmed that the man in the photo was her husband.

Now the FBI agents began to put together all the pieces they needed for a search warrant. Earlier that afternoon, they had given a heads-up call to the assistant U.S. attorney.[†] With close to two decades of previous prosecutorial experience, he was all too used to such calls: an astounding 60 percent of his caseload was now child porn. "The ones that I am most worried about are the guys that have good jobs, family, friends—and their computer," he said. "Those are the ones that I find to be dangerous."

It was dark outside by the time the prosecutor showed up at the judge's home with an FBI agent to get the search warrant duly authorized and signed. The FBI agent then sped off to the Stevenson home, where he had joined the rest of the surveillance team.

The FBI knocked on the door of Jessica's prison.

Burt Thomas Stevenson seemed nonchalant about the law enforcement visit. "I'm very impressed you got here," he told the FBI men. "So what do you want to know?"

With Stevenson arrested, the local FBI realized they would need the help of the bureau's computer forensics experts. Stevenson was quickly taken into custody, his family secured, but his heavily encrypted computers were going to be a challenge. "He was technically sophisticated at hiding and preventing us from getting to his stuff," says the FBI's state supervisor. "Usually encryption just gets in the way of what pedophiles are doing—they want their pictures or their videos and they want them now, so they seldom bother with it. But he had encrypted everything." He wrote his own encryption code instead of using an off-the-shelf program. Even his backup copies were encrypted.

She called up the Calverton headquarters and simply asked, "Can you send an analyst and perhaps an agent or two?"

HQ listened, immediately dispatching one of their best analysts— Emily Vacher—along with at least four other agents. The child abuse collection they found stunned even the veteran investigators. "I've seen a lot of child pornography in my time on the squad, but there are only a couple of images I feel I'll never be able to get rid of," said Vacher.

---

† The prosecutor cannot be named because that would help identify the victim and her father.

"Some of the images I saw in that case I can still see right now. They were that horrific."

She uncovered not just hundreds of thousands of pictures of abuse but leads on other victims and abusers. In computer crimes involving children, Vacher and her colleagues were learning that—unlike other types of cases—most of the work began after the arrest. A bank robbery, a kidnapping or a homicide investigation was essentially finished for the police when they had someone behind bars. With Internet child pornography, the arrest was just the start, because hidden on the suspect's computers there could be clues not just to his own history but also to other abusers and their crimes. And that could mean there were other real-life victims out there like Jessica.

Vacher also came across one special folder in Stevenson's computer that at first threw her. "What is this?" she said aloud, and the rest of the FBI analysts gathered around.

There were diagrams of the house and aerial photos of the neighborhood. "Then it just hit me: this is a murder for hire," she said. Vacher had discovered Stevenson's plot to have his wife killed.

As if she didn't have her hands full, the FBI supervisor got distressing news one day that school officials had barred Jessica and her brothers from returning to classes after the police had informed them about her father's murder plots.

"I went through the roof. That is the most absurd thing I ever heard," she said. Jessica was traumatized already by everything that had happened in the past few days: her father was behind bars, she was receiving counseling and her mother and brothers were trying to cope with the collapse of their world. The FBI agent quickly got on the phone to berate the school superintendent: "You have got to let these kids back in. You don't know what has happened to them. Their family's a mess, their mother is not working because she's trying to put her life together with the kids and protect them and you throw them out of school!"

The superintendent held firm: "I want something in writing that no one's going to come and shoot up the school," he said.

"Well, I can't give you that," the FBI woman retorted.

The school let the children in the next day, just in time for the holiday party. Jessica and her brothers told their friends they had missed a few days because they were moving. And eventually they did move away from the family home filled with such dark memories.

As most arrested pedophiles do, Stevenson confessed. He admitted to abusing Jessica. The police already knew that. But they were shocked to learn he also admitted to raping his three-month-old nephew. "He showed no remorse. None. He'd do it again," the FBI supervisor said, recalling that Stevenson told them that society just doesn't play by the right rules. "His rules are fine in his world."

The rescue of Jessica had been a thirty-three-hour frenzy of zeal, drive and just plain old luck—exceptional not only in its speed but in its triumphant result.

All too often, the cops knew, the children captured in those tens of thousands of abuse images remained untraced, unknown. "The only thing that mattered was that all our efforts and all the teamwork we had around the world made a difference in the life of this child," said Bill McGarry. "That child could be your child, my child. It could be a neighbor's child. The bottom line is, she is our child."

In the years leading up to Jessica's rescue and especially in the years after it, many of the players in her story—the Toronto cops, the FBI's Emily Vacher, Michelle Collins from NCMEC, the British investigator Paul Griffiths and others—were thrown together to solve a variety of baffling, at times discouraging, cases of child abuse online. Jessica's rescue was a snapshot of where the investigators stood in the ebb and flow of this global battle: it showed how far they had come but how much further they still had to go.

If they were ever going to stand a chance against this internet-fuelled crime wave, they were going to have to overcome several major challenges.

To begin with, they had to master the technology. For too long the porn practitioners had shown that they were much more technologically sophisticated than the keyboard cops who were just beginning to understand this new terrain of encryption, subterfuge and secret Web communities.

Next, they were going to have to get a handle on the flow of data or drown in it. In the Jessica case, they had had a tough enough time with hundreds of pictures; the police would soon have to find ways to manage the flood of data when they were processing tens of thousands of seized images.

Police would also need to break down their parochial barriers and cooperate better globally. Jessica was one girl in one city; the law enforcement agencies across the world would have to learn to share information more systematically if they were going to take on more complex, international porn rings. "The pedophiles don't respect borders, so why should we?" says Paul Gillespie. "There's no difference whether the child lives in Toronto or anywhere else. It's our job to rescue them."

Finally—and perhaps most disturbingly—police would have to probe the minds of the predators like Jessica's father. You cannot defeat an enemy you do not understand.

Two

THE "SPIRAL OF ABUSE"

*The simplicity of getting material . . . it's close to mind-boggling
. . . The more I saw it, the more I longed for it in my heart.*
—MICHAEL JOSEPH BRIERE, CONVICTED CHILD RAPIST
AND MURDERER, ON INTERNET CHILD PORN

It is common and understandable that many police officers—and
much of the public—see child predators like Jessica's father as
nothing more than monsters who should be locked up forever. "You
are looking into the face of pure evil," the prosecutor told the sentence
hearing for Burt Thomas Stevenson. "This man is evil and did evil
things. The government expects this man to never walk free again. He
should never see the light of day."

He won't. On October 20, 2005, Jessica's father was sentenced to
one hundred years behind bars—not the last sex offender in America
to be condemned to prison for a century or more. But not every
predator can be sent away for that long; and even if they can be, there
will always be new ones emerging.

"We don't have the luxury of allowing ourselves to see them as
monsters," said Joe Sullivan. "That may be a comfortable place to be,
but it's dangerous." A psychologist who helps treat offenders and a
forensic analyst who helps the U.K. police catch them, Sullivan has
probably interviewed more child molesters than most experts in the
world. He knows that many of the police officers he trains would just
as soon put a bullet in the head of the child molester if they could. But
he is convinced that unless police can unlock what makes each individual predator tick, they stand little chance of rescuing the children
being abused. "Seeing someone as a monster dehumanizes him, makes

him so different from us that we cannot really begin to understand him," he says. "We have to engage him, to humanize his behavior."

Sullivan's is not always a popular position. "No investigator should hope to fully understand why child molesters sexually assault children," warned a recent article in *Police Life,* an official law enforcement magazine in Australia. "Because to understand would require the investigator to accept the same distorted processes employed by offenders, something that is not advisable for the individual's own mental health."

But Sullivan feels that investigators must take that journey to the dark side if they ever hope to get a grasp on the crime and how to curb it. "You have to take the uncomfortable step of putting yourself in the room with the offender and his victim," he stressed. "You have to go places you wouldn't want to."

Sullivan's soft Irish lilt, his almost impish smile and quick wit make him a hit on the police lecture circuit, but these qualities have undoubtedly also served to disarm the hundreds of child sexual abusers he has had to grill—and tried to help.

He started treating and assessing offenders back in 1986, and by 1997 was consulting with the police; he began working with the National Criminal Intelligence Service full time in 2002, while continuing to treat offenders. Sullivan was part of the small but growing cadre of researchers looking into pedophilia. By scientific standards, the research into child sexual abuse and those who commit the abuse was a relatively new field, with only a few decades behind it. "It wasn't really a high priority," says Dr. Michael Seto, a clinical psychologist at Toronto's Centre for Addiction and Mental Health (CAMH). "We're slowly getting a handle on understanding them now."

The problem with understanding pedophiles begins even with the word itself. The dictionary definition of pedophilia is "a sexual perversion in which children are the preferred sexual object." According to the American Psychiatric Association, pedophilia is a mental disorder marked by "recurrent, intense sexually arousing fantasies, sexual urges, or behaviors involving sexual activity with a prepubescent child or children"

Unfortunately, in much of the media, in the public's mind and even among many police professionals, the word "pedophile" has become almost interchangeable with "child molester," but not all pedophiles are child molesters, and not all child molesters are pedophiles. In a fascinating study, Dr. Seto studied 685 men referred to CAMH between 1995 and 2004: some were convicted of molesting children, others of only possessing illicit pictures. To test their sexual arousal to children, his experiment monitored penile blood volume as the men watched certain slides. Amazingly, the offenders who had been convicted of possessing illicit pictures had three times the chances of exhibiting a pedophile attraction to children compared with the actual child molesters. "There are many reasons why men go out and attack children, but we can't find many reasons why men would collect child pornography," Seto concluded. "Pornography is a clearer indication of someone's sexual interests than their behavior has been."

A child rapist might have acted opportunistically, on the spur of the moment, in a drunken rage or out of pure cruelty—not because he exclusively prefers little children to adults. On the other hand, a pedophile—out of fear or shame or for any number of factors—may resist acting on his impulses and never sexually assault a minor. Many offenders—such as Burt Thomas Stevenson—straddle the borders: they are men in functioning heterosexual relationships with adult women, men who nevertheless have an insatiable desire to molest children.

"Label the behavior, not the offender," says Sullivan. "By putting people in boxes, we are limiting ourselves unhelpfully."

If the words to describe child sex offenders are imprecise, so are the numbers. A study done for NCMEC states that "one in five girls and one in ten boys are sexually exploited before they reach adulthood." The Sexual Abuse and Violence in Ireland (SAVI) Project conducted by the Royal College of Surgeons found even higher numbers: one in three women and one in four men experienced some form of contact sexual abuse or non-contact abuse—indecent exposure and the like—during childhood. Even taking the lower American estimate, that still means if you are in room with a hundred adults, between ten and twenty of them faced child sexual abuse. We cannot measure child sexual abuse more accurately than that because most victims do not disclose what happened: at least 88 percent of cases of sexual abuse go unreported according to the Crimes Against Children Research Center (CCRC) at the University of New Hampshire.

Within that wide range of sexual abuse, getting a fix on how many child sex offenders are out there is even harder. In an oft-cited study by the Department of Psychiatry at the University of Southern California School of Medicine, close to two hundred male undergraduate students were surveyed. One in five admitted to some kind of sexual attraction to small children; almost one in ten reported sexual fantasies involving children and 7 percent said they might even have sex with a child if they could avoid detection and punishment. In Canada, Dr. John Bradford of the Royal Ottawa Hospital's Sexual Behaviors Clinic, estimated anywhere from 2 percent and 7 percent of the population could have pedophilic tendencies. He compared that to a mental disease such as schizophrenia, which affects only about 1 percent of the population yet garners a lot more research funding and media focus. "It's of great concern to us that there is not enough attention paid to pedophilia," said Bradford. "A pedophile can victimize dozens of children. If you could understand this condition, find it early and treat it, you would be saving enormous health costs, traumatic injuries to children, court costs and incarceration costs. Why are we not doing more about it? Because people don't want to face up to it as a public health problem."

If we can only hazard a guess at how many pedophiles there are, we can pinpoint with much more accuracy who they are, thanks to arrest statistics, prison records and case files. The classic bogeyman image of the pedophile as a "dirty old strange man" lurking in a dark corner of an alley or on the Web is wrong on all counts.

For starters, child molesters are rarely strangers. "In the myth, we tell our children to watch out for the guy in a trench coat, the stranger," says Rachel Mitchell, chief of the sex crimes prosecutors' bureau in Phoenix. "We don't tell them to stay away from their baseball coach." The University of New Hampshire center estimates that "in 70 to 90 percent of child sexual abuse cases, the child knows the person who commits the abuse."

Most studies show that at least 90 percent of child sexual abuse is committed by men, but that still leaves perhaps one in ten children abused by a female, usually a mother. According to the Center for Sex Offender Management (CSOM) at the U.S. Department of Justice, in 1997 women accounted for approximately 8 percent of all rape and sexual assault arrests for that year.

Child sex abusers start young—or at least they know of their compulsions at a young age. In his extensive work with offenders, Joe Sullivan has found at least 80 percent knew by the time they were eighteen that they were sexually attracted to children.

"They know it doesn't go away," Sullivan said. "Once you've got it, you've got it."

Which of course raises the question, How do you get "it"?

Ask any psychologist, psychiatrist or clinician what causes pedophilia, and you get the same answer: "We don't know," said Dr. Peter Collins, who has seen his share of abusers as the manager of Ontario Provincial Police's Forensic Psychiatry Unit. "We don't know if it's a combination of hormonal, anatomical problems with the brain, whether there is a genetic component to it—we just don't know."

We know one thing that does not cause pedophilia: there is no causal relation between homosexuality and child molestation. When the scandal over Congressman Mark Foley broke in the fall of 2006, evangelical preachers and conservative commentators tried to make that connection. *The Wall Street Journal*'s editorial page asked, "Could a gay Congressman be quarantined?" and the Republican pundit Newt Gingrich suggested that Foley had not been reined in earlier because Republicans "would have been accused of gay bashing." The implication was that gays were a menace to children. But if anything, heterosexual men like Jessica's father are much more common among child molesters than homosexuals. The cold, hard statistics of the hundreds of thousands of child abuse images seized do not lie: the overwhelming majority of offenders are males attracted to young girls, not boys. According to NCMEC's exhaustive study, 62 percent of the men arrested for possession of child pornography had pictures of mostly girls. In the U.K., the Internet Watch Foundation, which monitors child abuse for the industry and police, concluded that 79 percent of all illicit images found in the past decade were of females.

A more complicated issue is whether being subjected to child sexual abuse can lead to a person's offending as an adult.

About one-third of pedophiles have been abused themselves as children—a proportion that remains remarkably consistent in many controlled studies. That indicates a much higher level of childhood abuse among child sex offenders than within the general population.

At the same time, it still leaves two-thirds of offenders who were not abused and must have other reasons for being sexually attracted to children. "That means there is some association, but it's not a cause," concluded Bradford.

In the end, when it comes to any sexual preference—heterosexuality, homosexuality, pedophilia—there is still much scientific debate about how much is nature versus nurture. Generally, the theories about what causes pedophilia can be divided into two: psychological and social factors versus the neuro-biological explanation.

Joe Sullivan, for his part, favours the psychological influences. "It's such a complex question: How does someone's sexuality evolve?" he asked. "I don't think people's sexual orientation is predetermined before they are born. People are not hardwired." While not ruling out that down the line medical science might discover some biological or mental factors that trigger pedophilia, Sullivan preferred to look at what he called "a collision of a number of factors" that early in their lives combine to drive certain people to become sexually interested in children.

"They learn through their experiences, through how they process, and how they learn to process is influenced by life events in their early years," the psychologist said.

Dr. John Bradford of Ottawa, on the other hand, sees it differently. "Hardwiring is probably the most likely cause and the other ones contribute and are secondary," he says.

"All of us around twelve or thirteen years of age go through puberty and it's like the computer program switches on: we become sexually interested. By far the majority of us are interested in people of roughly the same age and the opposite sex. Some of us are interested in people of the same sex and roughly the same age. But then you have some people where the age preference goes wrong. They are attracted to males or females but their computer, if you like, is programmed for pre-pubertal children and as they get older that gap widens. That is strongly indicative of hardwiring—a neuro-biological cause," he has concluded.

To find out what that hardwiring may be, Bradford and others have done some preliminary genetic studies that point towards "some kind of genetic vulnerability"—not a dominant or recessive gene passed on by one parent or both but perhaps something polygenic, that is, involving mulitiple genes. "Pedophilia is passed on between generations in families—that's how it looks, but it's done very weakly. It's not consistent. We don't know why," Bradford cautions.

Only additional research—for which, unfortunately, there is scant public interest or government funding—can unlock more of the mysteries. But all the experts agree that it is a combination of pressures that produce a pedophile. Clearly, social and psychological factors act on some people who, for various biological reasons, may be more susceptible than others to becoming sexually attracted to children.

"Everyone looks for the simple answer to why these guys do it and there isn't one," says Joe Sullivan. "I think we know how it works for some offenders that we worked with intensively for a long period of time, but I don't think there is any identifiable factor for everyone."

Take the story of Mark Langham,* a friendly, handsome man from Edmonton, Alberta, now in his early thirties. Currently serving fourteen years in a federal prison for abusing two of his stepchildren and two of their friends, Langham decided to cooperate with police to help them bring down a major international pedophile ring. He also agreed to sit down for a lengthy interview for this book.

As with about a third of child molesters, he says he was abused as a young child—in his case, by an older brother. His parents divorced when he was three; small for his age, he was constantly bullied in school. "I wanted to be a police officer," he says. "Didn't have the grades or the body for it. But the dream was still there. I didn't want to be pedophile."

But like most offenders, he knew at a very young age that indeed he was one. "As far as I can really remember I always had a preference for young children," Langham says. "I was always hanging around kids a lot younger than me."

"It is not about the sex itself, it's about the control," he explains. "It was just a revolving circle. I got bullied at school, I took my control somewhere else."

It started as voyeurism and fondling: the teenage Langham was hanging around swimming pools and school gyms, or visiting friends' houses where young children ran around in their underwear. By the time he was in high school, he was calculating enough to volunteer as a teacher's helper in an elementary school. "I was getting turned on."

At eighteen, Langham faced his first criminal charge for assaulting his four-year-old niece. He got ninety days' jail time. Within a year, while still on probation, he abused two boys under eight and was sentenced to twenty-one months behind bars.

"I felt embarrassed," Langham says softly. "I knew what I was doing was wrong. But this is the way I am. I was getting what I wanted."

That's the problem that intrigues psychological investigators like Joe Sullivan: how does a child molester or a pedophile ignore, turn off or get past the alarm bells that are ringing almost constantly in their heads as they prepare to do what they know to be wrong?

Because, make no mistake about it, Sullivan found that the vast majority of offenders with whom he worked "would have some level of sense that it's wrong, that they should not do it, or that there would be severe consequences if they were to do it." Randy Wickins, an Edmonton police officer who would later work with Mark Langham to catch other pedophiles, was struck by Langham's inner turmoil. "He has these thoughts, these fantasies, and he'd acknowledged that he'd hurt children," said Wickins. "And that it's like a huge conflict within him: he can't stop, but he knows he is hurting children."

To be sure, there are many brutes and sadists who show little initial remorse or qualms, but if they don't have any guilt to overcome they still have to get over the fear of getting caught.

In 2002, building on previous models by other child sex abuse specialists, Sullivan came up with the "spiral of sexual abuse," a clinical tool for analyzing offenders. Consumed by desire and arousal to abuse, a potential offender must break down a number of "brick walls" of both guilt and fear. To make those walls get progressively smaller, the offender uses increasingly powerful fantasies—coupled with masturbation and orgasm—to overcome any internal resistance. The next step down the spiral involves "grooming" the child or children in his sights, by breaking down their resistance through guile, gifts, friendliness or force—or a combination of all of these. Finally, he commits the abuse. The spiral can then start over, but each time the brick walls become easier to take down as he gets more and more consumed by his obsessions.

To overcome the guilt and fear, offenders have to go through a series of mental gymnastics that psychologists like to call "cognitive distortion." They might start with small steps, such as fantasizing about touching a child when she is asleep. "She didn't mind," one offender told Sullivan. "She hasn't told me no, so she must be enjoying it." Dr. Sharon Cooper, a renowned American psychologist who was called in by the authorities to examine the photos of Jessica and who has testified in dozens of child pornography trials, said that convicted sex offenders in prison often blame the victim: "'I didn't want to do it. The child seduced me,' they say. 'I would never hurt a child, but they were there and they made me do it.'"

As the brick walls collapse in the final preparations for his abuse, the offender must also carry out extensive grooming of his victim and the people around the child who might protect her. Often, they are exceptionally good at hitting all the right buttons. In England, a thirty-eight-year-old man from Wickford, Essex, pretended to be an online counselor for abused youngsters to earn the confidence of one his targets, a troubled thirteen-year-old girl. "Don't worry, there's a world of pervs and I'm a shining light," he wrote in one e-mail, according to testimony at his trial. "Something tells me you could do with a hug and someone to say 'I care.'"

A stepfather told Sullivan an easy trick he used: surrounded by three children, he suddenly asked which one of them had stolen $10 from him. All three denied any wrongdoing, but as he rifled through their schoolbags he would find the bill he had planted in his target's posession. She would tearfully deny the theft—becoming in the eyes of her friends both a thief and a liar—and be told she would be punished. The predator thus created both opportunity and suspicion about the victim's trustworthiness so he could later deny his crime.

The Internet has turned the spiral of abuse into a veritable vortex with limitless supply and support for pedophiles and child predators.

Each stage—the desire, the chipping-away of the brick wall of guilt and fear, the grooming of the victim, and even the abuse itself—has been magnified into unimaginable proportions by the most wide-reaching communication tool ever invented. Think of how the Internet has changed your life—finding pictures of that vacation hotel you booked, picking up some information for schoolwork or meeting new friends who share your passion for trading hockey cards. Now just imagine what the Web means for someone looking for pictures of girls being molested, or searching out expertise on encrypting illegal abuse images or meeting new acquaintances to swap child pornography images.

Child abusers and the images they produced were around long before the advent of the Internet. In 1874, the London Metropolitan police arrested a photographer who had 130,000 pedophilic images on glass plates. Predators would continue to flourish if the plug were pulled on the Internet tomorrow. But if the Internet has not created pedophiles, it has certainly created an environment in which they can be easily gratified. What was once a hidden scourge restricted to the dark corners of society is now widely available with any search engine.

"Unbelievable. I was just brought to a new world." Mark Langham remembers vividly the moment when he first clicked on a Web site promising illicit pictures of children. "I just couldn't believe my eyes. It was instant hard-on. That's when I started building my fantasies."

Langham was discovering that what the Internet provides the child sexual offender are the "three A's" he needs to thrive: Anonymity, Acceptance and easy Access.

"Before the Internet came along, it was actually quite difficult for sex offenders to find one another. Those that did seek others took quite considerable risks to do so," explained Sullivan.

"Years ago, someone who had an interest in this had to rely on magazines, films and videotapes and even Polaroids," said Ray Smith, one of the first U.S. postal inspectors to go after child exploitation material. It was hard to find and took a long time to obtain. "Now we've got the Internet and you can have video streaming into your living room anonymously," he said. Without leaving your home, or meeting anyone, or giving a real name or an address, the Internet will deliver to you a buffet of child abuse to feast upon. So the Web quickly and easily satisfies the first stage in the spiral of abuse: desire and arousal.

The Web then allows the offender's fantasies to blossom into the stage of acceptance—the sense of empowerment and even liberation that comes from discovering your urges to have sex with children are not unique. "No matter how isolated or lonely we feel in our convictions, we can be assured that there are others like us," says the U.K.-based Web site Inquisition21, which purports to fight police and state oppression of pedophiles. "If we have a worthwhile idea it can never be stopped, no matter how hard some try to suppress and censor it and to punish us for thinking and trying to promote it."

The final reward the Internet offers the budding molester is easy access—to each other, to the images of abuse they crave, and to mentoring and training. "Some people spent all their lives hiding their predilection and never spoke to anyone about the feelings they had," said Sullivan. "Now they were able to share ideas and get new ideas, develop their fantasies to another level."

The pictures, of course, are the most gratifying, immediate reward. Imagine if a Web site could offer cocaine or heroin samples for easy, instant download to addicts. That's what the Web offers the child sex abuser. "There's a blurring of fantasy and reality," said the Ontario Provincial Police (OPP) forensic psychiatrist Peter Collins. "In many of the pictures, the kids are smiling or don't appear to be harmed. The Internet can enhance cognitive distortions for pedophiles because they can say, 'How bad can it be for the children?'"

Better to collect all those pictures and look at them than act on those urges and have sex with real children—that's the argument offered by online traders, defendants in child pornography cases, their lawyers and pro-pedophile Web pages and organizations. By this logic, child abuse pictures act as a sort of safety valve—releasing passions and physical urges that could otherwise lead to dangerous assaults in the real world. "They're only pictures," runs that defense, and to criminalize online child porn criminalizes free thought.

"That's something that we often hear from offenders," said Joe Sullivan. "They say, 'Yes, I was downloading, but the reason I was doing that was to ensure that I wasn't going to progress to a real sexual offense with a child.'"

Pedophile Mark Langham at first rationalized that what he was doing was safe and not harmful: "I'm not doing nothing—I'm just looking at pictures on a screen. That was my mentality. I really didn't give a care.'"

"That's bullshit," he eventually realized. "All it does is make me want me to get more. And the further I go on and the more I see the pictures, the more I'm going to want to do something. It's just the next step before you start abusing."

There are several serious problems with the reasoning that viewing child sex images harms no one, not the least of which is that to create such pictures, real children somewhere have to be abused. What's more, the pictures are often manufactured explicitly for online trading on commercial child porn Web sites, so the downloader, in a sense, has helped make the assault possible.

But there is a more fundamental flaw with the "they're only pictures" argument, one that cuts to the heart of the dangers of online child exploitation material. Defenders in fact have it dangerously backward: evidence is overwhelming that, far from preventing physical abuse of children, viewing child abuse images on the Internet may encourage abuse in the real world. Sullivan called such Internet images "fuel for offending." The constant downloading and viewing of child abuse images to satisfy physical urges has two very significant effects on the brick wall that stands in the way of actually molesting a child. First, it's a form of self-brainwashing—as Sullivan said, "They confirm for themselves that children are sexual, or that children like this sort of thing or are not harmed by it."

Second, the images make a critical connection between pleasurable thoughts—which are generated by looking at pictures—and the pleasurable physical experience of orgasm. The offender may seek more thrills—more pictures that are more graphic, more violent—until pictures alone do not suffice, and the viewer needs the real thing. "Like the drug addict, they are upping their tolerance for the drug—always telling themselves that they will be able to control it, when it fact they are gradually eroding the brick wall," Sullivan concluded.

That process was tragically reflected in the downward spiral of abuse into which Michael Joseph Briere plunged in 2003. The thirty-six-year-old Toronto computer programmer had fantasized about molesting a young girl for "maybe a year or two" he later said in his confession. He fed what he called his "dark secret" on the Web—and he didn't need his programming skills to do it. "The simplicity of getting material . . . it's close to mind-boggling," he explained in his sixty-one-page confession document. "Viewing the material does motivate you to do other things. The more I saw it, the more I longed for it in my heart."

Finally, on a drizzly night, May 12, 2003, that longing pushed him over the brick wall of guilt and fear. "That night, I must have viewed some material beforehand. And I just got excited. I really wanted to do it," Briere said in his court confession. "I really wanted to have sex with a child. And that was all-consuming. I just came out of my place, and she was just there."

The girl was ten-year-old Holly Jones, walking home from a friend's house. Briere snatched her off the street, dragged her back to his apartment, where he assaulted and then strangled her to death—all in barely forty minutes. In a panic, he stuffed the girl's body in his fridge and later dismembered it. He then disposed of the parts in two locations—but it wasn't long before police made the gruesome discovery. Briere came under suspicion shortly afterward, when, in a neighborhood canvass by police, he refused to give a DNA sample. The cops instead got the DNA from a Pepsi can he had thrown away and matched it to blood underneath Holly's fingernails.

When the judge sentenced Briere to life in prison with no chance of parole for twenty-five years—the toughest sentence available in Canada—he decried the predator's "selfish sexual desires, fueled by pornographic images displayed on a computer screen."

Outside the courtroom, Toronto's chief Crown attorney, Paul Cutler, told reporters, "If this isn't a case that brings home to society, to government, to legislatures, and to those involved in the prosecution and resolution of child pornography cases that this cancer on society must be stopped, and stamped out, then I can't think of one."

Briere's story, sadly, is the rule, not the exception. Arrest statistics confirm that a sizable portion of so-called picture consumers have a documented criminal record of hands-on abuse. The numbers are surprisingly consistent from different law enforcement agencies and surveys: at least one-third of people caught with child pornography also assault children.

When NCMEC commissioned a study from the New Hampshire's CCRC, they surveyed 2,574 local, county and state law enforcement agencies as well as two federal agencies to come up with a list of 429 offenders arrested for possessing child pornography between 2000 and

2001. They found that 40 percent of those arrested were "dual offenders," who had sexually victimized children as well as downloaded images. The U.S. Postal Service inspectors came up with the same numbers: since 1996, 35 to 40 percent of the men they arrested for using the mail to transport abuse images were also child molesters.

Perhaps the most interesting research comes from Andres Hernandez, a psychologist who is the director of the Sex Offender Treatment Program at the federal prison in Butner, North Carolina. Working with convicted sex offenders for more than thirteen years, Hernandez was troubled by what he saw as a "great deal of misunderstanding" among law enforcement officials. "They fail to at least entertain the possibility that there may be hands-on activity—and that the person they have in front of them may be a child molester rather than a collector of images," Hernandez says. Judges in particular, he thinks, "feel very conflicted over sending defendants to prison for what they believe is 'just pictures.'"

His prison treatment program is voluntary: inmates do not receive any special privileges or the promise of a reduction in their sentences. In one study over many months, Hernandez did extensive interviews with ninety prisoners: sixty-two were Internet offenders—either image possessors or men who tried to use the Web to lure their victims; twenty-four were convicted of a contact sexual offense unrelated to the Web, such as abuse or assault; and four were serving time for nonsexual crimes, such as bank robbery or drug trafficking. Hernandez wanted to see if there was a difference between the number of known victims of these offenders and the real number of direct abuse crimes to which they were willing to confess once in prison. He compared the data in each prisoner's pre-sentence investigation report—a formal court document prepared by the probation service—with the number of self-reported sexual contact crimes divulged in the course of their prison treatment.

What he found was shocking. Overall, the men after sentencing confessed to a total of 1,622 victims—instead of the 106 officially on the record. But the biggest surprise was that the largest discrepancy—and the highest number of offenses not detected by the justice system—came not from the men jailed for actual sexual assaults but from the men jailed "only" for Internet crimes. More than three-quarters of the men arrested and convicted only for their crimes on the Internet later confessed to assaults or some other form of hands-on abuse. Indeed, Hernandez's interviews revealed that the "Child Pornographer" group averaged more than twenty victims per offender—more than double that of the "Contact Sex Offender" group.

"I knew the problem of underreporting was common with all sex offenders, but clearly what we're dealing with here is the tip of the iceberg," said Hernandez. "I would argue that far from being a safety valve, child pornography actually has the opposite effect."

It would be bad enough if the Internet supplied only the pictures and movies that helped push potential offenders over the edge. But much more than just a playground for predators, the Internet has become a school of abuse—a training ground where the new and the nervous can learn the tools of the trade from mentors and masters.

Mentors like Burt Thomas Stevenson. When the FBI agent Emily Vacher analyzed Jessica's father's computers, she discovered hundreds of chat logs of his conversations with fellow molesters. "These guys don't exist in a vacuum," she said. "The Internet really gave them a tool to find each other, to validate and normalize this behavior."

Stevenson's logs eventually led authorities to a bizarre triangle of abuse involving himself, a mother of three from Texas and a British loner. At thirty-seven, with a head of thick black hair and a pudgy face, Simon Grant was a reclusive piano tuner in Surrey, south of London. He lived in a small white trailer on his parents' farm and was a fanatic of sci-fi programs such as *Dr. Who* and *Star Trek*. "Quiet, lonely, immature with very few friends," said Rod Thompson, the Surrey police officer who ended up investigating Grant after the FBI tipped off British authorities. "He lived in this huge fantasy world that he had created."

Egged on by a constant barrage of e-mail chats with Stevenson, Grant progressed from a recluse in southern England with sexual fantasies to a transatlantic hands-on abuser. He followed so closely Joe Sullivan's "spiral of abuse" pattern that it almost seemed as if he had read the psychologist's work and was using it as a model. "We were able to chart his rise as a pedophile from a fumbling teenage boy to an international traveler who abused children," said Thompson.

In his teen years, Grant started with a huge collection of magazine ads of young female models. As an adult, he moved up to making audiotapes in which he invented stories of rape ("I ran up to her and grabbed her. I covered her mouth and told her not to make a sound."). Next, he progressed to phoning children anonymously, trying to engage them in obscene conversations. He snapped pictures of children at the schools he visited as a piano tuner, then cut out their faces and pasted them on pornographic pictures in his possession.

"It became quite clear that the spiral accelerated when he came into contact with Stevenson," said Thompson. Sometime in late 2002 and early 2003, Grant met Jessica's father and a woman from Dallas named Karen Harris* in an online chat group "set up for people who wanted to discuss fantasies involving incest," as she later told police. Harris had a more troubled background than either of the men: a twenty-seven-year-old self-confessed drug user whose husband was in jail for robbery and assault, she claimed she had been sexually abused repeatedly by her stepfather and her own mother.

Stevenson pushed both of these online acquaintances well beyond the realm of "fantasies." He openly boasted about molesting his daughter and sent them pictures of Jessica to prove it. He proposed doing the same to Harris's children: "He mentioned at one point that he was going to be in Houston for a work-related deal, and he could travel up on a certain day and rape the children and then go back," said Brooke Donahue, the FBI agent in Dallas who picked up Harris's trail after his colleagues working on the Stevenson case alerted him.

Harris spurned Stevenson's offer, but she did invite Simon Grant to visit her children—girls of four and seven and a nine-year-old boy. "Money—it was simply a question of money," said Rod Thompson. "As she said, she basically rented her children out to a pedophile."

Grant, now besotted with this woman he had met online, agreed to pay her credit card and phone bills, her rent and groceries. His first trip to Dallas lasted only a few days in late April 2003, a chance to meet the children and begin grooming them. Grant turned to Stevenson for advice and guidance. "Stevenson has been doing this for years, so you have a teacher-pupil relationship almost," said Thompson. "He's giving him tips on how to lure and abuse the children. And then [Grant] would come back and report to Stevenson."

What little remained of Grant's "brick wall" of guilt and fear had collapsed. When he returned to Dallas on June 16, he stayed several weeks and the abuse got under way, starting slowly with the fondling of genitals, sleeping naked with one of the girls and then sex games. In their constant chat logs, Stevenson urged him on. The two men talked about getting's Harris's older daughter to be "more obedient" by chatting online with Jessica. Stevenson also suggested to Grant a faster way to break her resistance: "I'll never forget seeing those chat logs on Stevenson's computer where he offers 'the advice of a fellow pedophile' to drug her to make her more compliant," said Emily Vacher. "That just blew my mind."

Grant, now more confident, stepped up the abuse on a third trip to Texas in November 2003—just weeks before his online mentor would be arrested. He groomed one daughter, showing her child abuse pictures on the Internet. Then Grant secluded himself in the bedroom with her and pinned her to the ground. "He panicked when she started screaming," according to Rod Thompson. "He put his hand over her mouth to stop her screams, and he thought at that point he had actually killed her."

Grant reported his failure at penetration to his teacher, and Stevenson appeared to be growing frustrated with his clumsy apprentice. "I'll come down and show you," Stevenson said in their chat logs, insisting that Grant had to be tougher: "You have to think of them as pieces of meat."

The two men made more ambitious plans: they talked about a joint trip somewhere—Eastern Europe, perhaps, or Latin America—to pick up a homeless girl and rape her. In one conversation, Grant recounted that, after finishing a piano tuning job, from his car he had spotted a little boy and contemplated kidnapping him—until the child's mother showed up. "Look how far he's come," said Thompson. "He starts with catalogs when he's a teenager, and now he's got to the stage where he's sitting on the side of the road deciding whether or not to abduct a five-year-old boy."

Grant was hoping to return to Texas, but on December 2, the FBI—acting on the tips from Paul Gillespie's squad in Toronto—arrested Stevenson. Ten days later, FBI agent Brooke Donahue knocked on the door of Karen Harris's apartment in a dreary working-class neighborhood in the northern stretches of Dallas. The police found plenty of child sex pictures on Harris's computer, and she admitted that she had effectively pimped her children to Grant. Family services took her children away, and Harris got a ten-year prison sentence.

Eleven days after that, it was Simon Grant's turn. On a cold December 23 morning, Rod Thompson and a phalanx of police officers raided his isolated farmhouse in Surrey. Alongside the *Dr. Who* memorabilia and the piles of rubbish strewn around his room, they found bags and bags of CDs filled with child exploitation material and even his scrapbooks of child advertisements from his teenage years.

He pleaded guilty to more than thirty-six charges and got a seven-year sentence.

Simon Grant, Karen Harris and Burt Thomas Stevenson were just three of the many offenders caught in the Web's cycle of abuse who played off each other's sicknesses and weaknesses. All three had exhibited criminal behaviour before they met online, but there can be little doubt the Internet fueled their obsessions and their actions.

"Everything that happens on the Internet is the 'x factor,' escalating in all ways and not just in numbers," said Drew Oosterbaan, the chief of the Child Exploitation and Obscenity Section for the Department of Justice in Washington, D.C. "The Internet didn't create pedophiles, but I fear that it is creating more aggressive pedophiles."

Law enforcement's understanding of the insights into the spiral of abuse by Joe Sullivan and other psychologists and psychiatrists did not come overnight. It would take several years for the experts and the authorities to get a handle on how the old crime of child abuse had taken on a new guise in the wired world. They eventually came to see that many offenders needed help as much as punishment, and that a surprising number were at least willing to try to change or to control their urges.

Like any new discovery, this one had a steep learning curve. And like any process of education, there would be some failures on the first tests.

Three

BURIED IN A LANDSLIDE

*The Internet provides a very short route indeed to some of the
most evil and shocking images of rape and abuse.*
—PETE TOWNSHEND OF THE WHO, AFTER HIS ARREST
ON CHILD PORNOGRAPHY CHARGES

One of the first American lawmen to aggressively target child
porn crimes, Ray Smith has a decidedly low-tech office in
Washington, D.C.

No calendar on his desktop computer insistently beeping to
announce his next meeting. No Palm Pilot in sync with his e-mail and
contacts file. As assistant inspector in charge of the Child Exploitation
Unit for the U.S. Postal Inspection Service, Smith still uses a pen to
scrawl his appointments on his paper calendar and fumbles for a name
in those ancient metal phone directories that flip open as you slide a
plastic button down to the appropriate letter of the alphabet.

On the wall above his cluttered desk hangs a painting of six well-
armed riders on horseback, and Smith is proud to tell you it was the
early postal inspectors who went after Butch Cassidy and the
Sundance Kid. Just as it was the postal police who first used
Thompson submachine guns to combat crime in the roaring twenties.
And it was the postal inspectors who first tackled child porn back in
the 1970s, when most of it still moved through the mail in plain brown
packages stuffed with magazines and Super-8 film.

Smith made his first child abuse arrest as a young inspector in New
Jersey in 1982, his only real clue a grainy film that showed a man's
thumb and index finger on a baby's genitals. Smith was able to match
the fingerprints barely visible on the film with the suspect—an elementary school principal—and helped secure a ten-year sentence.

To this day, a surprising amount of crime still relies on the regular
mail, one way or another. Smith worked on the Unabomber case, as well

as narcotics investigations and telemarketing frauds. Even online child abuse has a postal connection: people buy, sell and trade their images on the Web, but often they want a DVD or video shipped in the mail. In 1997, 33 percent of the child exploitation cases handled by Ray Smith's inspectors involved computers; by 1999 it had leaped to 81 percent.

As accustomed as he was to the degradation of child porn, Smith was somewhat startled—and more than a little nervous—when one of his postal inspectors called from the Jack D. Watson Post Office in Fort Worth, Texas.

"Ray, I'm not really quite sure," the man reported. "But I think I got a lion by the tail."

Thomas Reedy was a former nurse who had never earned enough to own a home. His wife, Janice, had spent most of her life in a trailer. Still, by the late 1990s, they were living in a luxury mansion and wiring cash to their local car dealership for a second $80,000 Mercedes.

The Reedys had tapped in to what one postal inspector later called "a gold mine in child pornography." The gold mine was called Landslide, a Web portal they created that—in exchange for a credit card payment—gave the eager customer access to over five thousand sites. More than a single Web page or series of pages run by one company, Landslide brought customers and porn providers together in a convenient one-stop shop. "The Reedys were like the gatekeepers," explained Ray Smith. "You paid your money to the Reedys and they opened the gate and allowed you access to everything."

"Everything" meant a vast online warehouse of both adult and child sex material, but Reedy—as he wrote in his own online diary—quickly discovered where the real money was to be made. He noted that after a few disappointing months of peddling only the adult fare in 1996, he started offering child abuse images—and revenues soared. One site available through Landslide, called Child Rape, garnered 1,277 registrations in a single month.

The Reedys never looked back. From September 1997 to August 1999, Landslide's total revenue was estimated at $9,275,900, according to later court documents. Reedy himself boasted that his business was "worth in excess of $20 million based on earnings." Their Web masters were offshore—in Europe, Indonesia and Russia—and their clientele was global: their business logged more than 300,000 credit card transactions from sixty countries. In a later interview with prosecutors, Reedy estimated that 30 to 40 percent of those revenues came from child exploitation images.

Tipped off by a citizen who complained about a Web site that appeared to be pushing illicit child sex pictures, Ray Smith's postal inspectors, along with the Dallas police department, began their probe of Reedy's empire in the spring of 1999. A police officer went undercover, using a fake name and credit card number, and signed on to the Landslide Web site on April 28. "What we found was no different from madams operating a whorehouse where children were offered for prostitution," said the Dallas police lieutenant Bill Walsh, who helped coordinate the investigation with Smith.

Once they had gathered enough evidence, the postal inspectors and the police needed solid intelligence about the layout of Reedy's operations to make their pending raid successful. What better spy than your friendly neighborhood postman? Ray Smith's team substituted one of their own inspectors for the Reedys' usual letter carrier. He chatted up the Reedys and the proud entrepreneurs offered him a tour of their facilities, filled with high-tech computer equipment. "They took us around, and we came out and made notes and diagrams," said Smith.

Armed with a search warrant and those diagrams, fifty agents raided Reedy's business, seizing computers, carting away company records and interviewing employees. By May 2000, Thomas and Janice Reedy—along with five international Web masters—were indicted by a federal grand jury for "interstate transportation of visual depictions of minors engaging in sexually explicit conduct." The Reedys tried to argue that the children being abused in the images and videos offered through their portal were not real but computer generated. So the prosecution brought in a top investigator from Britain's National Crime Squad to display slides from one of Landslide's most popular downloads. She showed the jurors pictures of two victims police had positively identified—an eight-year-old girl from Manchester and her six-year-old brother, forced to engage in sex acts with each other and with older men.

That helped settle matters quickly. The trial lasted only five days. The jurors found Thomas Reedy guilty of all eighty-nine counts and his wife guilty of all but two of them. He got 1,335 years in prison; Janice, apparently not seen as a principal mastermind behind the scheme, was sent away for only 14. Eventually Reedy got his sentence reduced to 180 years, but either way he was not going to drive his Mercedes for some time.

With the Reedys behind bars, the real investigation into Landslide was just about to begin. On the seized computers, the authorities found a massive database with 100,000 names, addresses, e-mail addresses and credit card numbers of their clients. At least 35,000 of the customers were in the United States. American authorities dispatched the names of the other suspects to their international partners—over 700 to Australia, 2,300 to Canada and more than 7,200 to the U.K. It was, as the prosecutor said, the "Holy Grail," because while "Reedy was just a greedy guy . . . the subscribers are people that actually could be pedophiles."

"Could be" being the operative term, since the authorities had to prove that any suspects did in fact access the child sections, not the adult Web sites, of Landslide. And they had to be sure the credit card owners were the ones actually doing the buying, and were not, for instance, the unlucky victims of fraud.

There was a third problem as well: by the time it was disseminated across the country and around the globe, the evidence from the database was old. "At the beginning it was already stale, and by the time they sent it overseas it was a year or so later," says Drew Oosterbann at the U.S. Department of Justice. "How long ago was that database operational? How long ago did the customers access it? When you act on stale leads, nothing happens."

Nothing except problems and mistakes.

Landslide was one of the first cases to test the mettle of the emerging army of global online child abuse investigators in the U.S., Canada, the U.K. and elsewhere. This was still, after all, four years away from the time when the police had become technologically sophisticated and organizationally collaborative enough in 2003 to rescue Jessica within thirty-three hours. Their journey to that level of expertise was an arduous one, full of setbacks and controversies. The Landslide case exposed for the first time just how widespread—and profitable—Internet child exploitation was. But it also buried police in the U.S., Canada and the U.K. with confusing evidence and false leads, exposing serious flaws in their ability to coordinate their efforts in each country, let alone globally.

The Americans used the Reedys' database as intelligence: pointers, not proof.

To freshen up the stale evidence from the database, they set up a sting named Operation Avalanche and created a fake child porn Web site to solicit business from the Landslide client list. Only about two hundred of the thirty-five thousand old customers took the new bait—enough for postal inspectors and other police forces to conduct 144 searches in thirty-seven states and arrest a hundred suspects for trafficking child pornography through the mail and via the Internet. When police moved quickly, it paid off in arrests.

Many other leads were sent out to police agencies around the country, but with little sustained coordination at a national level and uneven expertise on the ground most of the trails went cold. That didn't stop then U.S. Attorney General John Ashcroft from hailing the end of Operation Avalanche in August of 2001 as a victory of "unprecedented magnitude" in the dismantling of the world's largest commercial child pornography enterprise.

Before they had finished their own investigation, American officials had sent out lists of Landslide subscribers from other countries to police agencies abroad—and that's when things really got messy. For one thing, U.S. investigators did not always make it clear that many paying clients of Landslide could have been purchasing adult porn, which, while perhaps distasteful to some, was perfectly legal. To make matters worse, child Internet abuse was still a new enough crime that tested protocols for formal international police cooperation were not in place. In some countries like Canada, there was not yet a central law enforcement body with the responsibility for prosecuting child pornographers for the Americans to contact, so the transfer of information from the Americans happened in a haphazard way. In other countries, like the U.K., the designated national police body was so overwhelmed that it farmed out the information to local police departments, with little guidance or assistance.

It was in May 2000 that Dr. Peter Collins, the forensic psychiatrist with the Ontario Provincial Police, heard about the Landslide investigation almost by accident at a meeting in Dallas and passed the details on to the OPP. Collins even came up with name for the Canadian investigation: if the Americans had tens of thousands of potential suspects in Avalanche, it seemed appropriate that the smaller Canadian operation should be labeled Snowball. As Canada's national law enforcement agency, the RCMP should have taken the initiative on Snowball, but at the time they had yet to develop much expertise on Internet crimes against children. By January 2001, the RCMP cobbled together a National Strategy Briefing attended by investigators from across the country, but it fell to provincial or local forces to handle the flood of cases that they divided up among themselves. What followed were wildly varying levels of action among the diverse forces.

It was the OPP that showed the most initiative—and scored the most success—with Snowball. One of the first police forces in the country to set up a special investigative team, Project P, to go after child pornography, the OPP took the lead in getting the Landslide database from the Americans and dividing it up along provincial and police jurisdictional lines. Det. Insp. Angie Howe, who came to policing with a degree in psychology and a keen eye for balancing intiative with proper protocol, eventually took over the OPP's child porn section. She said that the OPP did not regard the Landslide database as a confirmed registry of pedophiles. "All we had was a list of suspects," she said. "So we did our background work." That meant finding out how often the suspects logged in to the Landslide site and checking to see if they had criminal records and children of their own or access to other minors. Like the Americans, the OPP also set up a fake undercover Web site to get fresh evidence, luring old Landslide customers into making new purchases. In the end, the OPP had enough to arrest about thirty suspects and secured more than a 90 percent conviction rate.

But in other provinces, the police did little or nothing. In Quebec, with 436 Landslide subscribers, there were zero arrests. It was the same story in British Columbia, with another four hundred Landslide suspects and no charges. Det. Noreen Waters, the sole Vancouver police officer at the time devoted to cracking down on child pornography, eventually resigned from the force, "frustrated by the lack of resources," as she put it.

In Toronto, Paul Gillespie's Child Exploitation team had more than a dozen officers, but between aging computers and overworked detectives, they could only do so much. When the Toronto cops got their list of more than 240 names from Landslide, all they could do was throw up their hands. Gillespie could hardly contain his frustration. "There are hundreds of suspects in Snowball we can never even get to," he complained privately.

Two years after Snowball had begun, by early 2003, the Toronto police knew that the information from the Reedys' massive credit card database was getting stale. They tried to make sure that anyone they arrested and charged had child abuse images still on their computer—not just old records suggesting they might have visited Landslide. By the spring of 2003, the Toronto team executed search warrants on ten residences, seized twenty-five computers and laid charges against six men.

"These Project Snowball arrests involve offenders from all walks of life, who live in every corner of the city," Julian Fantino, the city's police chief at the time, told a widely covered news conference. "They only have one thing in common, and that is the criminal approach to their relationship with children." It was not unusual for police to announce the arrest of suspects in high-profile cases with great flourish, leaving to the small print at the bottom of the press release any mention that those arrested are innocent until proven guilty. The police even had a slogan for it: they called it "naming and shaming."

This time it backfired. Badly.

One of six men named and shamed was James LeCraw, whose story first came to light in a CBC Radio investigation. A well-liked director of a not-for-profit organization that supplied refurbished computers to schools and libraries, he was immediately suspended from his job when the news of arrest broke. He was eventually dismissed. LeCraw did not deny that he had visited the Landslide site—after all, police did find his credit card number and used it to obtain a search warrant for his home—but he insisted he only paid for adult porn. He told one newspaper that when police searched his computer, they found four "pop-up" addresses of child porn sites and "a barely visible, tiny image" that the cops alleged to be of child abuse.

Five months after his arrest he made a brief court appearance, only to hear that all charges against him had been withdrawn. The Crown gave no reason except to say that the case was "discontinued on the basis of new evidentiary considerations." The dismissal of charges against LeCraw did not make the headlines that his arrest did. He was unable to find another job; friends drifted away, and LeCraw fell into depression. "I'm melting down with the inability to handle the anger, betrayal and frustration," he wrote in an e-mail. "So I guess there is no real innocence, just unproven guilt."

On July 19, 2004—a little over a year after he was publicly branded as a suspected child porn enthusiast—LeCraw parked his vehicle on a quiet country road outside Newmarket, north of Toronto, lit a small charcoal barbecue on the seat next to him and killed himself by inhaling the poisonous fumes. He was fifty-one.

Paul Gillespie never did meet LeCraw but said he deeply regretted his suicide. Gillespie insisted that he could not talk about specific cases but reiterated that in Project Snowball his team had arrested only suspects who had evidence of child abuse images on their computers. After that, he said, it was up to the prosecutors and the courts to decide whether to proceed with a trial. "Of course it's a sad state if someone is going to commit suicide," he said. "But we would never lay criminal charges unless we were absolutely satisfied we had enough evidence."

Of the twenty-two people arrested by the Toronto police, eighteen pleaded guilty. One was never charged, and another left the country, so the case against him was never pursued. And two of them—including the unfortunate James LeCraw—had the charges withdrawn by the Crown. Gillespie made no retreat on the police policy of naming and shaming. "If people are charged with horrific offenses involving children, then the public needs to know," he said.

If the Landslide investigation had produced mixed results in North America, the fallout was even bleaker—and more tragic—on the international front.

The Americans sent hundreds of names from the Landslide database to the Australian federal police. At the time, Australia had only a national sex crimes team that focused mainly on sex tourism; there was no dedicated federal force to coordinate complicated online child abuse investigations. The list "went into a drawer," said one disgruntled investigator.

In England, they called it Operation Ore. Different name, even worse problems.

"Operation Ore was difficult," admitted Jim Gamble, then deputy director-general of the U.K.'s National Crime Squad (NCS). "It was a new crime; we were taken by surprise. Ore came to us in massive numbers and we made mistakes."

A tall, imposing man with a booming voice and an easy smile, Gamble grew up as a Protestant in the streets of Belfast and proudly became a uniformed officer in his strife-torn city. His drive and intellect led him to become head of the Northern Ireland antiterrorist intelligence unit, where he earned a reputation for both toughness and creativity as a commander in the bloody war that police and soldiers fought in the streets of Northern Ireland. "More than any other person, he had this capacity to push the envelope to challenge existing ways of doing things," said Barry Fitzpatrick, who worked with Gamble in Belfast and is now a senior detective superintendent in the Northern Ireland police. "He was not afraid to go against the command structure or the status quo."

Now Gamble would have to learn to fight a different kind of guerrilla war, where the enemy often hid in the shadows and recesses of the Web. He would find, even without the bullets and bombs, that it could be just as challenging—and for some, just as deadly.

When Landslide hit the shores of England, Gamble and his U.K. colleagues were just beginning to get a grip on the scale of the problem of child exploitation material online. Their biggest operation to date had been Operation Cathedral, which took down the "w0nderland club," one of the first major international child abuse rings to be uncovered. It had 180 members in twenty-one countries. Coordinated arrests in September of 1998 by police in a dozen countries led to over a hundred search warrants and the eventual conviction in the U.K. of seven men. At the time, it all sounded like impressive numbers, but those statistics would be dwarfed by the Landslide assault.

"Great job—we did well; everybody congratulated us," said Gamble of the "w0nderland" takedown. "But the seeds [of the next crisis] were planted while we were quite complacent."

Gamble estimates that during the time of Operation Cathedral only about 9 to 12 percent of people in the U.K. had online access from home—at pitifully slow speeds. By the time Landslide hit, 55 percent of U.K households had direct online access at home, and fast Web availability neared 100 percent if you factored in schools, offices and Internet cafés. "So it was a different environment," Gamble said. "We were then shocked when Landslide came and the volumes were huge."

Huge, indeed. British police were hit with no fewer than 7,272 names from the Landslide list: that was triple the Canadian totals and more than ten times the Australian numbers. According to one leaked press account, the suspect list included at least twenty senior business executives, a senior teacher at an exclusive girls' public school, armed forces services personnel from at least five military bases and more than fifty police officers.

Initially, the British police let the American leads on Landslide languish. Prompted by pleas from Interpol to take action, the U.K police finally took a serious look at the Landslide list after several months— and then they scrambled. "There was shock, horror," Gamble recalled. "Panic set in."

In part to handle the Landslide onslaught, Gamble pushed for the creation of the Pedophile On Line Investigation Team (POLIT) in January 2003, a specialized team of investigators and analysts at the National Crime Squad to coordinate and assist national and international investigations of Web-based child abuse. The POLIT team pored through the lists and quickly divided the names up by geography—a daunting task, considering England alone has forty-three police forces, and there are also the agencies in Scotland and Ireland. Much of the information was dated—some of the suspects were dead; many had moved. London police got the names of men who didn't live there anymore, or who had only worked in London but lived elsewhere. There was a belated attempt by central police authorities to recentralize the investigation and prioritize the suspects by their frequency of visits to Landslide and their accessibility to children in their family or at work. That still left much of the fieldwork to local constabularies, where experience and expertise were uneven at best.

From the start, the lack of technical sophistication on the part of some police investigators was apparent. When a man in Ireland was arrested for having 189 child abuse images on his computer, he hired a computer consultant firm to show that he had eleven different Trojans—outside viruses that can take over functions of a computer—embedded in his hard drive. He was acquitted. A decent forensic analysis by the police before trial could have picked up the presence of the Trojans and easily determined whether they were in fact responsible for the illegal material.

The police also failed to account for the likelihood of credit card fraud on the Landslide site. One Yorkshire doctor who lost his job because of the allegations against him was able to show that while he was using his credit card to pay for a meal in a local restaurant, someone else had been making charges on it five thousand miles away in America. An angry judge dismissed some of the police evidence as "utter nonsense" and acquitted the man.

When cases did make it to court, the British police were at times hobbled by shaky evidence from American investigators, who had at first claimed that everyone who visited the Landslide Web site was greeted with a screen button on the front page screaming, "Click Here [for] Child Porn." In fact, the notice was found only in the less obvious pages of the Landslide Web site. One officer with the Merseyside police was so upset at what he saw as a "witch hunt" that he resigned from his job. "I began to doubt the validity of the evidence," he wrote in a letter to the *Sunday Times*. "I found it difficult to rationalize how offenders had been identified solely on a credit card number."

Then the bodies started piling up: Canada had seen one suicide, but in the U.K. the toll would mount to as many as thirty-five men who took their own lives, and twenty-one more who tried. The most prominent was the Royal Navy commodore David White, commander of British forces in Gibraltar who had once served aboard the Royal Yacht *Britannia*. The day after he had been recalled to England to face charges related to Operation Ore, his body was found in his swimming pool at the grand home he occupied as the senior British officer in Gibraltar.

Gamble, like his Canadian colleague Paul Gillespie, was unapologetic, insisting that the police took every possible precaution. "We are very conscious that if we make this kind of allegation against you today, we cannot simply wipe the slate tomorrow if we get it wrong," he said. He was equally adamant that the focus had to be on the children, not the suicides. He was quick to point out that Operation Ore had led to the rescue of 132 children in the U.K. from real hands-on abusers—including that brother and sister from Manchester whose images had helped convict the Reedys in the first place: "We're not about persecuting people. We're about identifying children at risk and rescuing them. What would people be saying if we hadn't investigated these cases?"

For all the understandable concern about some innocent people getting caught up in the Landslide, there was another part of the situation that was perhaps even more disturbing: there was little doubt that many more guilty clients got away—people who had willingly used their credit cards to see children abused and tortured and would doubtless do so again. Of the thirty-five thousand names located in the U.S., barely two hundred had been charged. In Canada, a list of more than two thousand suspects boiled down to under seventy arrests and even fewer convictions. The U.K. may have had the highest suicide rate among the accused but also had the highest number of successful prosecutions. By the time the legal dust settled, more than twenty-two hundred people were convicted, including about six hundred who received a "caution"—meaning that they accepted their guilt but avoided a court proceeding.

The best that could be said about Landslide is that it was a rude wake-up call—a brutal form of schooling in the modern complexity of Internet crime for predators, the public and police. That was well illustrated by the humiliation of the rock star Pete Townshend, the legendary guitarist of the Who. In January 2003, Townshend admitted that he had used his credit card to access child pornography via the Landslide site. Police seized fourteen computers from his house but found no offensive images on them. Five months later, Townshend was issued a caution and had to bear the shame of being placed on the Sex Offenders Register for five years. In a statement to the reporters and photographers who thronged outside his mansion in Richmond upon Thames, Townshend, fifty-seven, insisted that his dubious Web searches had been for research for an autobiography. "I accept that I was wrong to access this site and that by doing so I broke the law," he said.

Those familiar with Townshend's famous rock opera *Tommy* will recall its powerful echoes of child sexual abuse. In lengthy entries to "Pete's Diaries" on his Web site, the musician claimed he had memories of being abused when he was five and six years old, but "cannot remember clearly what happened.

"I was arrested, suspected of wallowing in the very shit that most upset me. It sent me a clear and loud message," he wrote. "As I have demonstrated, the Internet provides a very short route indeed to some of the most evil and shocking images of rape and abuse. I can assure everyone reading this that if they go off in pursuit of images of pedophilic rape they will find them. I urge them not to try."

Townshend appeared to have learned his lesson: muck around in the illegal waters of child abuse images, regardless of your excuse, and you get dirty.

The question was, Were police willing to learn theirs?

Four

DEAR MR. GATES . . .

We're taking back the Internet. The bad guys have long used it as their communication tool. Well, it's our turn. And we'll see who is left standing.
    —Det. Sgt. Paul Gillespie, Toronto Police

A good cop learns as much—if not more—from his or her mistakes as from the successes.

Landslide had its share of victories, but there were plenty of lessons to be drawn from the setbacks and failures. Internationally, the police had done a poor job of mastering the technology and sharing information, much less understanding the offenders. In Canada, the U.K. and the U.S., different agencies had begun rethinking and restructuring even while Landslide was still winding down.

The changes they set in motion would have a profound impact on the global fight to rescue the child victims of Web exploitation.

In the wake of the turmoil from Landslide, Jim Gamble wanted nothing less than a revolution in how police in the U.K.—and around the world—tackled this new crime. For the deputy director general of Britain's National Crime Squad, that meant changing three things: how police look at pedophiles; how police are organized in the U.K.; and how they cooperate internationally.

No police officer in the world has embraced the insights of the psychologist Joe Sullivan about the workings of the predator's mind more than Jim Gamble. If Gamble's experience with "the Troubles" in Northern Ireland taught him anything, it was that a police force could not go up against an underground, sophisticated, opponent without knowing who they are and how they think. "Let's better understand the nature of this crime, let's better understand the nature of the person who commits the crime, and then let's see if we can police this environment in a wholly different way," said Gamble.

The U.K. police made good use of Sullivan's skills. He trained officers to look for the various stages of the spiral of abuse. He helped investigators understand the kind of offender they were dealing with during undercover work, and he helped debrief and interview suspects. Gamble was realizing that police had to stop seeing the suspects as "the enemy" in traditional police terms. "If we're going to divert people from this, we're not going to do it by continually arresting people," Gamble said. "We recognize that some offenders are more dangerous than others, but for many of the others we need to have a crime reduction strategy, a diversion strategy." It was a bold initiative: the top cop in England in charge of protecting children from pedophiles was saying that jailing the bad guys was only part of the solution.

"A lot of police officers wouldn't see that as being their job," said Sullivan, "but I think Jim, being in the position he is, goes beyond where a lot of police officers are at." Even as Operation Ore was progressing, Gamble began changing the language he used at news conferences. It was less punitive and more prescriptive: "If you're sitting at home tonight, listening to the radio or watching TV, or reading this article, and you have inappropriate feelings toward children, for goodness' sake go and seek help now," he would say. "Go to your doctor, go to someone you can trust . . . divert yourself from this path. Otherwise, in this day and age, more than likely you're going to destroy your life and that of your family. Because we will catch you."

Clearly the rash of suicides in the wake of Operation Ore had shaken Gamble, but not his resolve: he saw the outcome as a sign that he was on the right track. "People began to think about consequences. Thirty-five of the suspects killed themselves. Why? Because nobody wants to be the individual with the blue blanket on their head being led from the back of a police car into the court. There's a real issue here about consequences. I genuinely believe that you cannot rehabilitate pedophiles, but you can influence and moderate their behavior by the fear of capture."

If Gamble was going to capture more predators, he realized he had also to reorganize his troops. Operation Ore showed the need for better centralization, coordination and training: simply sending out the names of suspected pedophiles to local police forces was not going to work. Just a few floors below Gamble's office at NCS headquarters was a small room that housed the Pedophile On Line Investigations Team that he had set up in early 2003 in the midst of the Operation Ore upheaval. POLIT was designed to be a single point of contact in the U.K. for international police agencies reporting Internet child abuse. POLIT would assess and disseminate the information, as well as conduct the more complicated investigations.

Gamble wanted more. He set about creating a national center in the U.K. that could not only coordinate the massive amount of information and allegations flooding in to the police but also train and educate investigators. It was to be a center that would incorporate POLIT and a beefed-up team of analysts, plus civilian agencies and charities devoted to protecting children, in addition to academics and representatives from the Internet industry. It would take time, money and three years of intense lobbying to turn Gamble's idea into a reality.

In the meantime, Gamble had wider ambitions than simply reorganizing the British police approach to child abuse images: he wanted to set up a new global policing approach too. Like terrorism, which Gamble had been officially tasked to fight for much of his police career, here was a crime that knew no borders or boundaries. Gamble realized that police in different countries could not simply dump thousands of files from their investigations into the laps of their foreign partners. "We were creating problems for each other. We're continually dealing with the symptoms, whereas we need to be talking to each other, saying, 'What are you doing, where are you doing it and what will that mean for me? How can I help you?' That sounds sensible and easy, but in international law enforcement, it's a nightmare. If we want to get everyone around the table, how do we do it?"

Interpol, the international police agency based in Lyons, France, was already trying to coordinate global police efforts on this front, but it had to deal with dozens of countries and grapple with the protocols of international treaties and jurisdictions. Gamble wanted something simpler, more supple, more proactive. With top police officers from Australia, Europe, Canada and the U.S., Gamble began to put together a sort of virtual global police presence that could patrol the Web and rescue children, 24/7, across all time zones and in every corner of the globe where the Internet had penetrated. He called it, aptly, the Virtual Global Taskforce (VGT). Four national agencies immediately signed up—the Australian High Tech Crime Centre, the National Crime Squad for England and Wales, the Royal Canadian Mounted Police and the U.S. Department of Homeland Security—along with Interpol.

Taking a page out of Joe Sullivan's program of understanding the predators and not just demonizing them as monsters, Gamble came up with an idea for a sort of radar speed trap on the information super-highway—something that could be both punitive and preventative. The VGT created a fake Web site with the look and feel of a child abuse page, though without any pictures. The banner on top of the Web page announced in no uncertain terms what was on offer: "Red hot hard-core child sex pics." Colorful boxes on the side gave the visitor a tantalizing array of choices, depending on his perversion. Under Pre-teen Girls and Boys, the discerning shopper can opt for Child Rape, Russian Lolitas, Asian Dolls or S&M.

The Exit sign is decidedly larger than the Enter button, but if you opt to pursue your tastes, a second Web page again offers more menus. There is Incest Central, Pretty Boys, Cute and, for the more daring, Extreme Action.

One more click and you're through—or at least you expect to be.

Then, to your shock, the next page that appears has no illicit images. Just a menacing message, bordered by the black-and-white-checkerboard design of police roadblocks:

POLICE
You've just attempted to view indecent images of children. This is an offence for which you could be sentenced to 10 years in prison in the UK.

A further warning tells the Web surfer who clicked all the way into the site, "Periodically, visitors to this site will be traced and their details passed on to the local police." In light of Gamble's new approach of trying as much to deter as to detain the potential offender, the Web site also tried to frighten visitors into seeking help. Immediately after the police notice popped up was a direction to a self-help page, with a Search button to find confidential therapy and psychological counseling. Not quite the heavy hand that came down against the Landslide clients in Operation Ore.

"By this time, you're in a pretty bad way if you're a pedophile and you think you've been caught," said Gamble. "We recognized that you needed to have some form of strategy for those people who suddenly think, My world has ended."

"The message is, Get help or get caught," said Gamble.

Even more important, Gamble wanted to get help to children no matter where they were on the World Wide Web. In the eyes of Gamble, for too long the Internet had been an untamed frontier for child predators and porn merchants. It was time for the sheriffs of the wild, wild Web to take back the information superhighway. "The Internet is just another public place, just another public park or public building. It's as good or as bad as the people who congregate there," he said. "We as the police can no longer abdicate our responsibility by saying, 'Well, whose area is it?' We have to be there."

If there was going to be a team of coordinated international sheriffs keeping the Web safe for children, they were going to need more than rusty old six-shooters. And Paul Gillespie was tired of going after the bad guys with aging weapons.

It was the end of a miserable day in Toronto in January 2003, and the detective sergeant who ran the country's largest child exploitation unit was growing increasingly frustrated. At the height of the Landslide battle, Gillespie realized that the police were hopelessly underequipped. The offenders—often young adult males with advanced computer skills—were using the latest gadgetry and swapping intelligence in covert exchanges over the Web. The cops, many of whom had grown up tapping out police reports with two fingers on old typewriters, often didn't even have decent computers, much less the skills and the network to exchange information.

"The reality is that if you are just a little bit sophisticated, it's almost impossible to be detected. You can act in anonymity," said Gillespie. "When you combine that with the fact that the people being tasked with this challenge are basically street cops who are basically being told, 'Oh, by the way, tomorrow you're a computer cop,' and they're not given any equipment or training and then they're expected to catch up with these people who stay on the cutting edge. It makes you wonder how there have been any successes at all."

There was another problem facing the child abuse cops, the opposite from the kind most police officers face. At a murder scene or a robbery, investigators are always hungry for any evidence, any clue they can grab—a blood sample, a fingerprint—but the porn investigators had *too much* evidence from seized computers and e-mails. In the previous year, Gillespie's unit alone had seized three million graphic images of young children. "It's just so overwhelming. We were being swamped, and we didn't seem to be making any headway," he said. "The bad guys are winning. The damned computers, which are the cause of this massive distribution, had to be turned around to help us. I'd had enough."

Gillespie stared at his keyboard. If the system is broken, he thought, why not blame the man at the top? And then he did what many computer users only fantasize about: he fired off an angry e-mail to none other than Bill Gates of Microsoft basically saying: Your technology helped me create this mess; help us clean it up. "I never expected to get a reply—I didn't even keep a copy," he said. "I went home and forgot all about it."

But Gates did not. The richest man in the world and the most powerful computer executive read Gillespie's e-mail and immediately reached out to Frank Clegg, then the chairman of Microsoft Canada. "Frank, this one looks interesting," Gates told his Canadian director. "Can you see if there's anything we can do? See if you can help."

Clegg, a father of two teenagers, liked to recount that one of his daughters once asked him to help her with a problem she was having with Hotmail and he couldn't fix it; Clegg used that anecdote at board of trade lunches as a springboard to explaining that most adults are spooked about talking to their kids about the Internet. That's dangerous, he said, because children who have been taught from day one not to talk to strangers in the park might think nothing of chatting with an unknown person online. He pointed to a federal government survey that showed that about a quarter of kids have been approached to meet somebody face-to-face that they have only met online. And the scary part, according to that same survey, is that 15 percent actually agree to meet the stranger.

There was also, Clegg admitted, a pragmatic business reason for Microsoft to get involved. "If people are not safe and they are not secure, they are not going to use technology. If they are not going to use technology, then we won't continue to grow."

Within a matter of weeks, some of Frank Clegg's top computer experts were meeting with Paul Gillespie's cops. It became clear rather quickly to the police that however well intentioned, the Microsoft people, like most civilians, didn't really get it about child exploitation online. So Gillespie did something deliberately provocative. He showed them just a handful of the abuse images his officers have to deal with every day.

"He warns us there are five pictures; turn your heads if you want," recalled Frank Battiston, the senior team leader for the project. "It was horrific. Absolutely horrific. I saw one, looked at number two. And I just turned away. Didn't want to see anything else. And to this day I still have those two burned in my head. I want to get rid of them, and I don't know how. But it certainly inspires you to do what you can to eradicate these problems."

If he was shocked by the brutality of the images, Battiston was just as stunned when he first walked into the police Sex Crimes Unit. If he was expecting something as high-tech as *CSI,* he found instead a low-tech version of *Kojak*—phones ringing, people clamoring and officers huddled at cramped desks. For a nine-year veteran of the high-tech mecca that was Microsoft, it was like a time warp. "The police were being asked to catch pedophiles, and the task would be equivalent to sending somebody out in a rowboat in the middle of an ocean and saying, 'Catch some fish.' And the only fish that they're really able to catch are the ones that jump in the boat!"

So for several months in 2003, Battiston and the Microsoft geeks questioned the police on what worked and what didn't. Microsoft and the cops soon agreed that the best tool would be something to help police make sense of the millions and millions of pieces of information they were being inundated with—e-mail addresses, aliases, credit card numbers. They wanted to build a kind of internal search engine for cops: a database that could compile and connect police data to draw links based on "social networking," as Battiston called it. "Don't assume that any piece is unimportant. Look at all the information available to you and make the connections."

They brought in investigators from about twenty police agencies in Canada, along with Scotland Yard and Interpol, and made some changes to the test versions. By the spring, investigators from the FBI and the Department of Homeland Security came to Toronto to tinker and suggest more changes. "Our overarching vision here was a system designed by investigators for investigators," said Battiston. "We wanted their input from beginning to end. Our motto was, "If it sucks, it's your fault!""

They called it the Child Exploitation Tracking System (CETS—pronounced *kets*), and its future as a worldwide platform for police was secured when Gillespie, along with Clegg, made a fateful trip to Microsoft's famed international headquarters in Redmond, Washington. Gillespie had persuaded the Canadian contingent from the company of the urgency; now he had to face senior executives in charge of some of the software giant's major divisions from across the United States who had flown in for the presentation. It was not the kind of PowerPoint slideshow they were accustomed to seeing, as Gillespie took them on a frightening journey to the dark underbelly of the Internet they had helped to build.

"If you didn't know about the worst horrors of the Second World War, could you imagine them?" his first slide asked. Gillespie then flashed a grainy photograph of bodies from a concentration camp piled in a mass grave. The image lingered for just a few moments, then dissolved to another question on a blue slide: "What do you imagine child pornography to be?"

Up came a sunny picture of a smiling blond girl, not yet in her teens, standing naked by a lake. This is what child porn used to be, Gillespie told the Microsoft crowd. Then—as he had done with the executives from Microsoft Canada a few months earlier—he hit them with the stark horrors of what child exploitation online has become in recent years: images once rarely seen and now widely available on the Web showing infants and toddlers, some barely six months old, forced to endure unspeakable sexual violation.

"Oh, my God!" was all the Microsoft managers could mutter.

Gillespie had flashed only a handful of images for under ten seconds, but it was enough that the audience needed a break to compose themselves. "I think they got it—perhaps never having realized the full extent to which Microsoft software was being used to disadvantage children," Gillespie said. "I think this opened their eyes."

And their pocketbooks.

Microsoft committed to spending several million dollars not just to test CETS in Canada but to push its spread around the world. "What's your home run? What's your dream?" they asked him in Redmond.

Gillespie thought for a moment, and then, hoping he wasn't being too bold, he answered: "Ultimately, we could be a global database for child abuse that every law enforcement agency had access to."

CETS was still in its infancy when the software helped police rescue a four-year-old Ontario girl, isolating a sliver of a clue and putting together two seemingly disparate cases on two continents.

It began in New Jersey when the U.S. Immigration and Customs Enforcement (ICE) busted an international child pornography credit card enterprise with more than twelve hundred paying clients in the United States and around the globe, including France, Australia and Canada. One of their customers was a thirty-seven-year-old shutterbug from Toronto named Robert Noel Clemens— though the police didn't know his name yet. All ICE had passed on was more than seventy credit card numbers to the Toronto police, where the information was dutifully tabulated into their new experimental database from Microsoft.

Meanwhile, police in Staffordshire, England, using information from a recent unrelated FBI bust of an online trading newsgroup, arrested a man who was swapping images with a Web correspondent in Toronto. The Canadian was peddling pictures of a young girl, claiming she was his child. Police had only his online alias, but they passed on the clues to Toronto. The man had used a false name in his electronic dealings with the U.K., but oddly enough he supplied part of his real postal code—the same postal code connected to the credit card that turned up in the separate American probe. It was the kind of obscure detail that humans would miss but CETS could catch.

When the data from the British and American operations were loaded into the Microsoft test program, they set off alarm bells. "CETS found one very small consistency in the two bits of information that not only linked the two cases but pinpointed enough information so we could make the determination who the person actually was," Gillespie said.

Robert Clemens, it turned out, was a very active member of a family nudist club called Ontario Roaming Bares. Armed with a warrant, police went looking in Clemens's home and found thirty-five hundred indecent images, plus 150 videos, DVDs and CD-ROMs—and camera equipment. While examining one camera, they found close-up explicit pictures he had taken of one girl. The cops had a face but no name. For the next two months, Gillespie's officers interviewed children who would have known Clemens throughout southern Ontario and as far away as Ohio—until at last one fifteen-year-old girl identified the youngster in a photo as Sarah,* the daughter of one of the couples from the nudist club.

What she told them—along with the pictures police had found on Clemens's camera and on the Web—was enough to charge him with several counts of distributing child pornography and sexually assaulting the little girl. He was eventually sentenced to four and a half years in prison.

If his punishment was brief, Sarah's, in many ways, is eternal. The pictures of Sarah he had uploaded to the Internet can never be taken back. "It's heartbreaking," says Lori Haggett, one of the officers who found Sarah. "Those pictures of her have gone international, and that's what she's going to have to live with for the rest of her life."

Back at Microsoft's Canadian headquarters in Mississauga, Ontario, the news that CETS had helped save a real girl spread like a computer virus. "That went through the building in about two minutes—faster than e-mail," said Frank Clegg. "The passion was just electric." That passion would help inspire Microsoft to invest millions more in the coming months and years, as CETS began to take on a global scope wider than Gillespie or Clegg could ever have imagined.

"We're taking back the Internet," Gillespie said. "The bad guys have long used it as their communication tool. Well, it's our turn.

"And we'll see who's left standing."

* * *

The tough talk was understandable, given the horrors of abuse that the police were seeing and their frustration at not being able to stop it or even make a serious dent in the trafficking of the images.

They were scrambling to get a grip on the technology, the flood of data and evidence and the obstacles to international cooperation. But even as the police were learning new skills from Landslide, there were other investigations that also began to force the police to change their priorities in more dramatic ways.

From the start, the police were consumed with tracking down the perpetrators. It's what police do naturally: catch bad guys. Some of the cops who worked the first cases came from vice squads and had done this kind of cleanup for years. They had carried out the obscenity raids on the porn shops, seizing the dirty "kiddie magazines" and grainy videos. Find the lawbreakers, make the bust and move onto the next case.

But it was slowly dawning on investigators that this emerging Internet-fueled crime against children was much more like a kidnapping—only rather than a one-time snatch-and-grab for ransom, this was an ongoing assault where the victim's plight was being displayed over and over and over again.

In other words, unlike most policing, finding the culprit with the contraband was not the end of the investigation in this crime. It was just the beginning.

They had to rescue the victims.

And the best clues were in the pictures.

Five

A NEW FOCUS

There were a lot of real perpetrators and a lot of victims that could be directly related to those perpetrators, so we were focused on finding the victims.
—LARS UNDERBJERG, DANISH NATIONAL HIGH-TECH
COMPUTER CRIME UNIT

Paul Griffiths remembers when it first hit him that maybe he was doing things backward.

As an officer in Manchester, England, tackling sex crimes, he had seen how the Internet had radically redrawn the landscape in just a few short years. In 1990, 84 percent of his unit's cases dealt with adult obscenity issues and only 3 percent of them involved child abuse. By 2000, some 87 percent of their cases involved children. Griffiths would eventually move to London, working with Jim Gamble's team of investigators. When not consumed by massive investigations like Landslide, he found he was spending most of his time doing what most officers in the early days of this crime wave did: scouring the Internet, looking for names and clues in the newsgroups and chat rooms, finding perpetrators willing to send abuse images by e-mail to someone they did not know was a cop, and sending them to jail.

Then one incident jarred him into taking a more proactive approach: as a result of a victim's complaint, a man who had been abusing a local Manchester girl about eight or nine years old was arrested. For some time, Griffiths and his colleagues had seen a series of her photographs among the well-traded collections on the Web; but they were shocked to discover that the girl lived only a few miles away from the police station. "Was there not something else that we could have done that would have brought this abuse to an end sooner?" Griffiths said. "We thought, Well, wait a minute. Are there other series of images out there? Instead of waiting until these people are arrested, could we actually go search for them?'"

It was a revolutionary thought: the pictures of the victims of online child abuse were not only evidence of a crime that could be used against a suspect *after* you arrested him, but they could actually be used *at the start* to find and arrest the suspect and rescue the child.

Like all revolutionary ideas, it came without a rulebook. There was no manual on how to decipher the clues in a picture, no guide on how to enhance or manipulate the images to discover an important lead. Griffiths—and the growing number of investigators in Europe and North America who soon followed him—learned by doing.

They began with the basics, like trying to figure out place and time from a two-dimensional photograph. In one picture, behind an abused boy were some computer boxes in the bottom left corner on gray steel shelves. Griffiths was able to zoom in and read the barcode on the boxes; he then contacted the company to figure out where the shipment had been sent. In another photo, a commercial for Milky Way could be seen on the TV in the image. The company informed the police that that particular ad had run for only a specific three-month period on a cartoon network in the U.K.

As the Internet grew in scope and sophistication, Griffiths also discovered there were legions of experts on obscure but sometimes crucial tidbits. In one instance, he contacted a local manufacturer because he guessed that a bed in one abuse image was made by them. The businessman came up with evidence as solid as fingerprints: "It's definitely ours," the manufacturer said. "If you look at the knots in the wood, it's Brazilian pine. Others use African pine, but we don't."

"There are people out there who know these amazing things," Griffiths concluded. "You just need to find out who they are."

His first big success in using pictures to find a victim came as early as October 1999, when he found a video on the Web showing a man raping a girl who looked to be about six. Back then, with Internet speeds and computer capacities just beginning to grow, video—

compared with photographs—was still relatively rare, and it offered an unexpected bounty of clues. Griffiths played the audio track to a linguist who described the abuser's speech as a "modified southeast regional accent," which included about half of the population of the U.K. Griffiths and his colleagues narrowed it down to somewhere south of Birmingham. The man had distinctive tattoos that showed in a few snapshots. Griffiths could also build a composite mugshot from two separate quick camera movements that caught only parts of his face. It was enough to consider going public on the BBC's *CrimeWatch* program, hoping someone could identify the man.

Then, just days before going to air, Griffiths had an unexpected breakthrough from America. The first place he had spotted the abuse video was on Internet sites in the U.S., so he had contacted the staff at the U.S. embassy in London. They transmitted the video to law enforcement agencies, and a sharp-eyed Customs investigator from New York reported that one of the pedophiles he was tracking had been in touch with the man in the video. Even better, the suspect's computer logs had an IP (Internet protocol) address that the British man had used when he logged on. An IP address is a unique string of four sets of numbers separated by periods that every computer or network is assigned on the Internet, a sort of digital signature. With that lead, Griffiths was able to get an exact name and address from the Internet service provider and did not even have to bother with broadcasting a Wanted picture on a TV show. The abuser eventually pleaded guilty and got twelve years behind bars; the victim was his own daughter.

It was not the first time British police had rescued a victim in an online child abuse image. "But this was the first time we had actually set out to do it," said Griffiths. The British cop learned two things from that first picture case: "You can't do it on your own," he notes— in this case, the American customs cops were crucial. "And you can't do without a bit of luck."

If an individual picture had the potential to be a kind of treasure map pointing to the location of a child victim, it stood to reason that authorities needed to put together the best collection of maps possible. One of the first steps in that direction came from Ireland, where two academics at the Department of Applied Psychology at the University College Cork had been actively researching child abuse on the Web since 1997. Known as Combatting Pedophile Information Networks in Europe (COPINE), it developed into a vast archive of Internet child pornography—one of the world's first and most comprehensive databases, eventually comprising more than seventy thousand items. The academics cataloged the images and compared them, always on the lookout for previously unseen pictures that appeared to represent new victims of abuse. Their database helped police across Europe in several cases and led Irish police to arrest many suspects during Operation Ore.

COPINE's archive was eventually transferred to Interpol. For several years, the international police agency had been building its own massive database of images, thanks in large part to the work of Anders Persson, a crime intelligence officer with the Trafficking in Human Beings Sub-Directorate. Persson, who now travels around the world to train police officers in identifying children abused online, had been a chief inspector with the Swedish national police in the late 1990s. "Not a lot of people knew how to operate a computer at the time," he said only half jokingly. "I could start a computer, insert a diskette, print a document out, so I became the computer expert."

He expanded on that expertise by building an image database for the Swedish police with 150,000 child abuse pictures by 2001. Unlike other early databases that required human memory to retrieve similar photos of the same child, the Swedish model was searchable, albeit at a basic level. "We had software that recognized images, which was a big breakthrough," he said.

As a result, Interpol brought Persson and his database to Lyons to serve as the basis for the world's first coordinated international police database of abused children. Persson and Interpol did not stop at simply amassing photos. They began to use pioneers like Paul Griffiths to teach officers in other countries how to analyze the photos. Interpol also sponsored an annual international conference that enabled investigators from different countries to bring unsolved cases and promising leads to the table, share expertise and swap pictures, hoping someone else might spot a clue they had themselves missed.

Indeed, it was just after one such gathering in June 2003 at Interpol that Paul Griffiths came upon the first disturbing pictures of Jessica and began circulating them to his colleagues in North America. Paul Gillespie had been to the same Lyons meeting and had stopped in England on his way home to meet with Griffiths. That trip inspired him to re-energize and reorganize his team in Canada by following the Europeans down this new and exciting path of image analysis and victim rescue. The hunt for the girl in the dog cage became their first test case, and Jessica's dramatic rescue—in the end a European-Canadian-American success story—gave an early boost to Interpol's new push for international cooperation. "It was a good-news story," says Griffiths. "There was a lot of momentum from those meetings, and the fact that we got a series identified so soon after really kept everybody on board."

"Very rarely, one investigator or even one country has all of the pictures," explained Interpol's Anders Persson. "That's why it's so important that we all share this evidence material. The ones who have all of the puzzle pieces have the biggest chance of putting the puzzle together."

If that was true, it was also true that most of the pieces of the puzzles were likely to be found in the U.S.

For all the talk of a worldwide Web, the United States—home to about 21 percent of the world's estimated 713 million Internet users in 2006—accounts for the single biggest chunk of traffic and number of Web pages. As Landslide had shown, the U.S. was also home to much of the child abuse images that were flooding the Internet. The U.K.-based Internet Watch Foundation estimated that half of the child exploitation Web sites were based in the U.S.

American law enforcement officials faced the same obstacles as their Canadian or British counterparts—only more so: they were burdened with too much evidence, most of it dispersed and unsorted. On top of that, there were too many cops wearing different badges, working for different jurisdictions, chasing after a myriad of underground porn producers and purchasers. The crime of child porn is intimately local, yet ultimately national and international. It starts with the abuse of a young child like Jessica in a small town somewhere, in a quiet city neighborhood or at a local school; then her pictures are uploaded onto a single computer, and from there they spread across the country and worldwide. How could the estimated eighteen thousand separate police agencies scattered across the U.S. expect to cope with such a networked crime?

The only hope of a centralized assault plan lay in Washington, but there were four competent and sometimes competing federal departments that had a hand in the child porn battle: the U.S. Postal Service, the Department of Homeland Security (DHS), the FBI and even the Secret Service. "Four federal agencies have some jurisdiction and they don't by nature work with each other," said Drew Oosterbaan of the Department of Justice. "It's all about turf and territory. And no one takes the lead."

Historically, the postal inspectors had the most experience, but less and less of the child sex material was actually moving through the mail anymore. Customs agents traditionally handled international contraband traffic—including pornography—and thus had some of the best international links. But in the aftermath of 9/11 they were folded into the bureaucratic nightmare that was the DHS; it took some time for the newly christened Immigration and Customs Enforcement branch within the DHS to find its legs. ICE eventually set up a Cyber Crimes Unit at a discreet headquarters in Vienna, Virginia, slowly building a massive database of more than 100,000 seized pictures of abused children and adding new pictures and clues every day.

Meanwhile, on the other side of Washington, D.C., in Calverton, Maryland, the FBI had its own huge image database that had started from the hunt for a single boy almost a decade earlier.

Back in May 1993, an FBI team from the Baltimore-Washington area was investigating the kidnapping of a ten-year-old named George Stanley "Junior" Burdynski, who had disappeared while riding his bicycle. In the course of their probe, police discovered that Junior and his friends had spent a lot of time at the home of a sixty-four-year-old man named James Kowalski, playing computer games and sending e-mail. The Bureau called in a relatively new agent, who held degrees in both mathematical and computer sciences, to inspect the computers. What she found was something that the FBI had never seen until then: pedophiles trading pictures of child abuse online. The missing boy was never found, nor was Kowalski ever charged with his disappearance. But he and a friend were arrested and jailed on multiple counts of child abuse and pornography.

The investigation soon went nationwide, as the FBI discovered a large ring of men using AOL to swap pictures and information. The

FBI was able to trace about two hundred accounts and four hundred screen names, garnering enough evidence to raid more than 125 homes nationwide and arrest more than a dozen people.

By 1995, the FBI gave the project an official name—the Innocent Images National Initiative, still headquartered in Maryland. Over the years, the number of cases ballooned into the thousands, with dozens of agents and specialists spread across the country.

So while ICE had the foreign connections, it was the FBI that had the most domestic troops on the ground: it had dozens of agents assigned to more than forty regional task forces scattered across the country, bringing together local police agencies and federal agents.

This was the confusing array that Drew Oosterbaan found when he arrived in Washington after a long stint as a federal prosecutor in Miami, specializing in major drug cases. "Sure, it's great to take down a big drug lord, a big drug conspiracy," he said. "But you know if you put him away, the drug lords are still going to be there. When you rescue a kid, there's a sense that you're actually making a difference."

Oosterbaan, who soon took over the Child Exploitation and Obscenity Section (CEOS—pronounced *see-os*) in Washington and became in effect the Justice Department's top prosecutor in charge of coordinating child abuse cases, knew that the various police agencies didn't necessarily always trust one another, much less the lawyers from his department. There were competing egos, competing budgets and the constant need to keep many investigations and leads confidential. In Canada, at least, the RCMP was the only police force with a national mandate; in the U.K., it was the National Crime Squad; in Australia, the Federal Police. In the United States, there was never going to be a single, top-down police entity that would run America's war on child porn. But perhaps there could be a non-police entity that could at least coordinate it.

Oosterbaan found a natural ally in Ernie Allen, the tireless executive director of the National Center for Missing and Exploited Children (NCMEC), once a small private, non-profit organization that, since its creation in 1984, was evolving into a child-rescue behemoth. Oosterbaan began working behind the scenes—cajoling, coaxing and corraling the investigators from the FBI, ICE and the U.S.

Postal Service to put aside their differences and work through the one place everyone trusted and no one could control: NCMEC.

"NCMEC can be the uniting force," said Oosterbaan. "It's neutral territory."

To the Canadian, British and other Euorpean police forces, it seemed somewhat jarring that a civilian agency should wield so much clout in law enforcement circles. NCMEC was a strange beast—an officially government-sanctioned institution blessed with millions from Congress and private industry and bolstered by powerful allies in Washington. President Ronald Reagan inaugurated NCMEC in 1984, thanks in part to the lobbying of John Walsh, who would soon go on to TV fame as the host of the popular *America's Most Wanted* program. Walsh became an outspoken advocate of children's rights after his son Adam was abducted and killed in 1981. Walsh pushed for the Missing Children Act of 1982 and became a co-founder of NCMEC, still serving to this day on its advisory board. NCMEC became best known for its work in finding abducted children—pioneering the widespread publicity of Missing posters. By 1990 Congress assigned NCMEC to be the official liaison for law enforcement agencies tracking missing children.

Then in 1997 a new electronic frontier was opened when Congress established the Exploited Child Unit at NCMEC to tackle online child pornography and sex tourism. NCMEC had been handling a few such cases since its founding. "But it was a very contained underground phenomenon," said Ernie Allen. "Then the Internet came, and it exploded. The problem was who do you call if you think your child is being targeted online? Most law enforcement was not online at the time. So we came up with the idea of having a central place to deal with this."

Ironically, what gave NCMEC its first major boost in the fight against child abuse images was a Supreme Court ruling that many feared would set back the cause of rescuing children. Congress passed the Child Pornography Prevention Act in the fall of 1996, making illegal the visual depiction of a minor in sexually explicit conduct—or what "appears to be" a minor or "convey(s) the impression" that the victim is a minor.

Those extra few words turned out to be the law's Achilles' heel.

Challenged by the adult porn industry and civil liberties advocates, the law took a beating first at the federal court level because, the judges ruled, it "trampled on the First Amendment and amounted to illegal government censorship." In June 1997, the Supreme Court upheld the lower court ruling, declaring key parts of the law unconstitutional—notably because it proscribed computer images that may not involve "the use of real children."

For police officers already losing the tech wars to increasingly sophisticated child pornography users and producers, the ruling added an additional burden. In effect, the courts were saying that abusing minors was wrong, but first you had to show they were minors: if they were either adults over age eighteen "pretending" to be children or, conceivably, computer-generated pictures, the government was engaging in censorship.

Suddenly, finding thousands of images of children being tortured on someone's computer was not enough to lay a charge: the authorities had to prove that at least some of the children portrayed were real. Real names. Real ages. The problem, of course, was that so many of the tens of thousands of child porn images circulated on the Web were anonymous. The suffering of a girl like Jessica was all too real, but until police rescued her, nobody knew her identity. The Supreme Court ruling meant that in every case prosecutors had to bring in either the child—an unlikely and unnecessarily cruel scenario—or the cop who had found the victim.

Fortunately, the following year, in March 1998, NCMEC set up a CyberTipline to allow the public, police and Internet companies to report images of child abuse. That was also the year a young college graduate named Michelle Collins joined what was then a small team. While earning a BA in psychology and an MA in criminology, Collins had spent time mentoring at a local jail and interning at the FBI. "I wasn't the Harlequin Romance type of girl," she said with a laugh. Her contacts at the FBI told her about an emerging agency that was starting to hunt online predators. She went for an interview at NCMEC on Christmas Eve and kept calling back for the next six months until she landed the job.

That year, NCMEC was averaging fewer than two hundred reports a week to its CyberTipline. Within two years, by 2000, the total quadrupled to more than twenty thousand a year, and it kept on growing. "There was a lot of scrambling," Collins said.

The Supreme Court's ruling simply accelerated what the NCMEC team had been edging toward, in any case: a full-blown child victim identification system. NCMEC's analysts would spend hours each day looking at the faces of the unknown children who had been reported to the center. "Some of them you see in only ten pictures, and then you never see them again, but there are those you always see," Collins explained. "Looking at the same children many times over, you kind of wonder, What happened? I wonder if the abuse stopped." When Collins heard from a police officer that one child frequently seen on the Web had been identified and rescued, she put together the details into a story that NCMEC could hand out to new employees as a morale booster. Informally, more names of rescued children were added to NCMEC's list until they had close to three dozen "known" children.

Collins's team quickly set to work formalizing what had been informal. They began to put together a more detailed database, with the photograph of any identified child porn victim: his or her real name, age, location and the name of the police officer who could testify about the case. Prosecutors and police across the country got used to the idea that every time they made a porn bust they shipped the photos to Alexandria for immediate analysis. This created a self-feeding cycle: the more pictures sent in for analysis to comply with the Supreme Court ruling to prove some of the images matched a "real" child that had been rescued, the more NCMEC's database of potentially identifiable children grew. In a few short years, NCMEC's list of identified and rescued children would blossom into the hundreds.

Slowly, police officers across the country were learning that NCMEC, as a central depository for seized child abuse images, was an important place to turn not just to report pictures after a bust but for help at the beginning of an investigation. Early in 2002, Collins got a call from a sergeant in the San Diego police department.

"Hey, Michelle, there's something happening that we think is going to be pretty big," he said. "We're going to need your help."

Collins readily agreed. "When you start one of these," she warned, "you never actually know how big it's going to get."

They had no idea.

* * *

It was called Operation Hamlet, and it became the first major test of the ability of the Americans and Europeans to grapple with the new focus of not just stopping the predators but finding their child victims.

As luck would have it, it was Anders Persson who first got the piece of the puzzle that uncovered a pedophile network stretching from Denmark to California. He had taken a brief leave from Interpol to finish some work in Sweden when a local children's rights group, Save the Children, contacted him in November 2001: they had discovered troubling new pictures on the Web of a young girl, at most eleven years old, bound and gagged.

Behind her towered a man in a blue short-sleeved shirt; it appeared to be some kind of uniform, with the company name visible over the left pocket. A check through the Web search engines came up with the business's full name and location—a small IT firm in East Jylland, Denmark. Persson got on the phone immediately with a colleague he knew well from Denmark, Lars Underbjerg. The call reflected another lesson the child abuse cops were learning: they needed a network of trusted colleagues they knew personally. Despite all the convenience of instant e-mail communication, nothing replaced face-to-face friendship. "You can always get help or operational support from someone, especially if you know them and trust them," said Persson. "What if I didn't know someone in Denmark? Then I would have to write a report, send it the official way and it would have taken a week."

Instead, it took only minutes for Underbjerg to move into action. Burly, six feet two inches tall and 253 pounds, he looks like the tough drug cop he once was. Underbjerg today is the group leader of an overworked team of six investigators in the National High-Tech Computer Crime Unit who have to cover all of Denmark. Back in late 2001, Underbjerg was half of an even more overworked team of just two officers, but he jumped on the case right away.

"The urgency was that it was a very new picture, very recently posted," he said. "And there was no doubt that there was sexual abuse going on."

It was 2 P.M. on a Thursday. Underbjerg called the police in East Jylland to get them to show a cropped picture, with just the blue shirt and the logo, to company officials. The local officers wanted to hold off until Monday; Underbjerg made it clear that they did not have the luxury of waiting. The next morning, company managers confirmed that the logo was theirs; they also provided a description of their current and recent employees. One description was a close match to a former worker named Eggert Jensen, whose pale skin, blondish hair and thick mustache made him easy to recognize. By that afternoon—under twenty-four hours after the tip had come in from Sweden—the police were barging through his door with a warrant for his arrest. In his home, police retrieved cameras and ropes that matched those seen in the bondage photos.

From the angle at which many of the images were shot, Underbjerg was certain about one thing: "There must have been someone else taking the pictures." That someone else turned out to Jensen's wife. The day police arrested the Danish couple, their daughter was immediately taken into safe custody.

"Normally, I don't think about my cases too personally," said Underbjerg. "But when I got home on Friday, I knew that if we hadn't made the arrest, that little girl was going to be abused again, so finding her was quite satisfying."

Underbjerg needed all the rest he could get that night; there would be little in the weeks to come. His voyage into the heart of darkness was just about to begin.

His interrogation of Jensen revealed the typical pattern of the offender who overcame his brick walls of guilt and fear in his "spiral of abuse," thanks to the encouragement of his Internet buddies. He professed to having low self-esteem and a history of sadomasochistic sex. "He was not able to have a normal social connection," said Underbjerg. He had begun his online porn career peddling pictures of children wrestling in bathing suits but soon found himself filling requests for children with less and less clothing. "This world was his virtual identification where he could build himself up," his interrogator concluded.

Jensen willingly gave up his password for the encryption key to his hard drive, and in so doing, unlocked the secrets of a vast network of abuse. For the next two months, Underbjerg's team pieced together the evidence through a careful forensic analysis of Jensen's chat logs and image database. The Danish man was neither a founder of the group nor its ringleader, but he was one of its many hubs. The group didn't have a name, although in some e-mails they referred to themselves as "the Club." In fact, Underbjerg began to realize, there really wasn't a single group but overlapping circles of abuse. The members of the club came from all over Europe—France, Italy, Germany, the Netherlands and the U.K.—but especially from the U.S.

The international scope of "the Club" in itself was impressive but not unusual. What was unusual was the level of direct physical abuse of their children that so many of its members carried out. Underbjerg had come across plenty of child porn rings that traded horrific pictures. In many such groups, status was often accorded to anyone who was not just trading but producing his own material—even more so if the child was his own and if he could customize the abuse to the demands of his fellow predators. You could move up in the ranks depending on what you could deliver.

"But here there was nothing about 'moving up' because almost all of them abused children directly," said Underbjerg. "That's what's different from a lot of the other groups. We could see from their pictures that they were really abusing their own children and their friends' children. They were all really bad guys."

Well aware that this case would be huge internationally, Underbjerg wanted a name that would instantly remind people that it had all begun in Denmark. So he settled on Operation Hamlet. Never one for diplomatic niceties, Lars Underbjerg wasn't going to wait around and contact various embassies and consular officials, imploring them to pass on information to their respective police agencies. "My experience is that when you have a case when you're sitting on actual abusers, there is no time to do it the official way," he said. "You have to act very quickly." Just as Persson had reached out to him, Underbjerg reached out to the informal network of child porn investigators that was beginning to form among police officers around the world. In February 2002, after he had completed his two-month analysis of Jensen's computer, he called for an international powwow in Copenhagen to jump-start Operation Hamlet. From the United States, there were senior officials from ICE; also on hand were representatives from England, Switzerland, Germany and Interpol.

Underbjerg handed out six CDs filled with information on each of the forty suspects he had identified by then. Every target got his own folder: name, occupation, IP address, e-mail address, screen name and photos of the children he was abusing. The Danish investigator also imposed what he called the Denmark way of doing things: less talk, more action. "Let's sit down, let's look at things, take a decision and then we do this," he said. "It was great. I still hear remarks that it was one of the best days—and the quickest meetings—they had."

It soon became apparent that although the ring was global much of the activity was concentrated in the United States, particularly the West Coast. Two follow-up meetings were held in San Diego and Washington State. The pictures were everywhere, on the tables and plastered on the walls. The American investigators had never seen so many easily identifiable—if not immediately traceable—children associated in one case

"It was off the charts," said Betsy Perino, a young agent from Immigration and Customs Enforcement from the Washington, D.C., headquarters who was thrust into her first major child exploitation assignment. "The photographs filled up the entire conference room, going all the way around the room."

"It was an eye-opener. In some pictures, you could just see the terror and the distress in the children's eyes," she said. For Perino, then only thirty years old, it was a rude introduction to high-tech crime. With two older brothers in the FBI, Perino was determined to work in law enforcement but wanted to strike her own path. She applied to the Customs service while still in law school and found herself with a gut-wrenching case as her first big assignment. The children ranged from older teens to infants three or four months old and barely able to move. The brutality, too, ran the entire scale from leashes to bondage to instruments of torture. In one series, a blindfolded girl had a pink ball gag in her mouth; in another, a child's hair was being pulled roughly from behind; in a third series, she was tied down. The most gruesome depicted machines "built for the purpose of torturing and extending limbs in ways they shouldn't be extended," as Perino put it.

The pictures were organized into series—often with hundreds of photos to a set—named for a child; or "pink ball" for the images of the gagged girl; or KG, presumably for victims of kindergarten age. The members would actively trade in chat rooms and e-mail for missing photos to complete their sets. Such behavior was typical of all

Internet child sex collectors, but the Hamlet group took it a couple of steps further.

First, they would make specific requests for pictures tailored to their fantasies. One man wanted to see another man's daughter assaulted while she wore her school uniform; another wanted to see violent spanking. To prove the abuse was live and on-demand, they asked for special messages to be written on cards or paper that the girls would hold. To make sure the messages could not be faked and superimposed with a digital imaging program, the men asked for the message cards to be crumpled, since it was much harder to recreate that kind of texture. Indeed, the girls would be forced to communicate with each other with these signs, as if they were enjoying the abuse. One sign read, "Hi Valeria,* my name is Linda.* I am 8 years old. Want you to be my girlfriend."

Another photograph showed a blond girl, perhaps twelve, asleep with most of her face buried in a pillow. Piled high behind her on the bed was a green turtle and other stuffed animals. Her abuser wrote in magic marker on a cardboard sign:

> Don—
> Thanks for letting me stay with her while you were away.
> She's real sweet
> S.B.

That last message indicated that some members of the ring made special trips to meet other "club" members, swapping their children. "They would travel and trade their children, and often they would ask a violator to violate their child in a very specific manner. They would then make a real-time video feed from the abuse," said Perino. One image in particular haunted the ICE agent: a seven-year-old girl with platinum blond hair. She wasn't the most violently abused, or the prettiest. "It wasn't because she was beautiful—all these children are beautiful, you know," Perino said. "It was the way she stood out because of her bright hair. I just kept seeing her picture again and again and again."

Lars Underbjerg, the veteran Danish police officer who had started the ball rolling, understood. "This case had a big impact on how investigators worked," he said. "There were a lot of real perpetrators and a lot of victims that could be directly related to those perpetrators—so we were focused on finding the victims."

The first arrests in the United States came quickly and easily. In their raid on Jensen's home, Danish police retrieved an envelope with a San Diego return address and the name of the sender: Paul Whitmore. Underbjerg also found plenty of chat logs on Jensen's computer that convinced him that Whitmore was as close as the group had to a leader. "He had very technical skills. He was the IT administrator for the group," said Underbjerg.

Whitmore also had other skills. He worked with children with developmental disabilities such as autism and cerebral palsy at a private education center in Grantville, a neighbourhood of four thousand just north of San Diego. Though none of his victims came from the school, as a child and family therapist with a degree in education Whitmore had access to children and groomed them for their roles in what Jeff Dort, the district attorney who later prosecuted him, called "a circle of hell."

"He was using mind games against the children," said Dort. "He understood the power that he had."

Over seven years, he assaulted eight girls and boys. In one series of photos, he humiliated a nine-year-old by parading her around a house in a pet collar, forcing her to drink water out of a cat bowl. Whitmore also arranged trips with a fellow club member who lived just twenty miles away in Poway. Brooke Lockwood Rowland, forty-four, a former advertising salesman, would swap victims with Whitmore and film their assaults for the rest of the group. Rowland was arrested shortly after Whitmore.

Still, police were in a bind. Whitmore, who had schooled the group in high-tech protection techniques, had encrypted his own files so well that the authorities could get at only about 10 percent of the material on his hard drive. And Rowland had had enough time to wipe out most of the incriminating evidence on his computer. It was a third man in the California triangle who provided the cops with the break they needed.

Lloyd Alan Emmerson was a well-liked, busy chiropractor and father of four in the Fresno suburb of Clovis. As historian of the Parent

Teacher Club at the Tarpey Elementary School, Emmerson had an excuse to shoot hundreds of photos of children at various school events. Police were later able to use those photos to identify many of the twenty-six children Emmerson had assaulted. More than ten of his victims were current or former students at the school, from kindergarten to fourth graders. "His computer literally puked porn," John Weaver, the Clovis police detective who helped lead the local investigation, told the media when they arrested Emmerson. "We seized forty CDs containing over a million images."

For all their international sweep and high-tech arsenals, massive police operations like Hamlet often turn on luck, and with Emmerson the police were doubly fortunate: first that he was such a prolific collector who discarded little. Second, Emmerson's crimes fell within the jurisdiction of a small, local police department that had the vision and talent to grab Operation Hamlet and run with it. Talent like Mike Casida, a Clovis police detective who used to take apart computers as a teenager and then rebuild them. He had long been pushing his police department to take computer crime seriously, so when the international tentacles of Hamlet penetrated the suburb of Clovis, it was only natural that Casida, along with two colleagues, got the assignment.

Their first obstacle was cracking Emmerson's encryption code. The Hamlet enthusiast had used BestCrypt, one of the toughest security software programs with a virtually unbreakable barrier. Whitmore had successfully blocked police from seeing most of his hard drive; Rowland had erased most of his; and for a while it looked as though Emmerson's stash would be equally impenetrable. BestCrypt allowed the chiropractor to double or triple encrypt his files. He would store them in "containers," or virtual drives, of 650 megabytes, then transfer them to CDs that held the same encryption.

Matt McFadden, one of Casida's fellow officers, kept looking for a weakness in Emmerson's defenses, and he finally found one. He knew he couldn't break the encryption, but he found a flaw in the program—a spot where BestCrypt wasn't cleaning up after itself. When incorrect pass phrases were entered, bits and pieces of the code were left behind. McFadden pieced together snippets of files and text, and then, after three days of nonstop work, he came up with the twenty-four-character password: "I sang a song called it aint so."

Until that moment, Lloyd Emmerson had been confident. When police came to visit him in jail that morning, he was almost blasé.

"He kind of looked at them like 'Yeah, yeah,'" said Casida.

Then the police said his pass code to him.

Emmerson was so rattled that he soiled himself. "He had a little accident," Casida said. "Basically at that point he knew he was done for."

And not just him, but much of the Hamlet network. Emmerson was, as Casida put it, "the ultimate pack rat. He saved everything." Not just haphazardly, but in a systematic, organized fashion, making it easy for the cops to see who was trading what. He would take bits and pieces out of his chat logs, strip them into a text document and save it. He created a folder for each of his Hamlet correspondents: some names—such as P. J. Crew—were unclear and would only make sense later in the investigation. Others were obviously first names, like Paul. In that folder, for example, were copies of the pictures Paul Whitmore sent and records of their conversations. "You got videos, audio, and still pictures with Whitmore doing some horrific things," Casida said. "Everything you needed to put him away forever was right there." It was the ultimate nightmare for the avid child porn producer: you could hide or destroy your own files, but you could not control what happened to them once you'd sent them over the Internet to your buddies in cyberspace.

In all, the police found about 1.3 million files on Emmerson's computer, of which Casida estimated about 450,000 were child abuse photos. "We started realizing that Lloyd Emmerson was one of the major keys to this whole mess," Casida said. "We were sitting on something big, and we needed to pull out all the stops. We had kids being abused right now that we could do something about."

Casida got his marching orders from a boss who didn't mind that most of the children saved would be far beyond Clovis's borders. "Do whatever it takes," Police Chief Jim Zulim told them. One officer was assigned full time just to deal with tracking down and helping Emmerson's twenty-six local victims. The chief also let Casida and two other officers spend more than six thousand hours over the next eleven months working on a national level with ICE and NCMEC to identify other victims and predators across the country, thanks to clues hidden in the friendly chiropractor's computer.

It was a high-tech hunt that would eventually track down two dozen abusers of more than one hundred children.

Their first rescue came within two weeks of Emmerson's arrest, in a small Mormon community in Idaho.

Mike Casida and his partner, James Gentry, were working side by side on two computers, analyzing the photos and data. They kept coming across arty, well-staged pictures of the same young girls modeling dresses and bathing suits produced by someone called Paul Jones. Not porn, not even erotica, but certainly suggestive. As Casida put it, "All tasteful stuff—except who wants to look at an eleven-year-old girl in a bathing suit?" Then they found the child abuse content—different girls, but the background was often similar: the same carpet or wallpaper. "These little girls being abused are in the same house as some of these pictures of these clothed girls," said Casida. "So we realized this guy is also an abuser."

As they began to piece together more pictures from the same collection, they came across photos of a girl posing in front of a small windmill in a park. In the distance, they could make out a Mexican restaurant. Another picture of a little girl in a hallway had a newspaper article pinned to the back wall; they could zoom in enough to partially read the headline and make out a reference to the town of Burley. A shot of a young model showed her next to a fire truck adorned with the banner "Burley Kiwanis."

There were only two towns in the United States named Burley, one in Washington, the other in Idaho. It was 3 A.M. when Casida picked up the phone to call a police dispatch officer in the Washington town to ask if they had a park with a windmill. The man thought he was crazy.

The next call, to a woman in Idaho, was more productive.

"Well, not in Burley, but in a little town right near here there's a park just like you're describing, and the restaurant is the restaurant my husband and I eat at," she said.

Casida was excited. He was fairly confident he had a location for Paul Jones, but he was far from certain he had his real name. Casida and Gentry were both exhausted after staying up most of the night, but they were not alone at the police station. Matt McFadden, who had broken the code on Emmerson's computer, happened to be walking by their desks when he overheard Casida and Gentry talking about Jones's identity.

"Hey, you're not going to believe this," he told them.

He had stumbled on a text file in Emmerson's computer labeled, conveniently enough, "PJ Crew real name." It identified the photographer of the young female models as Pete Bowcut. With a few clicks on the Web, the cops had the address of a Leslie "Pete" Bowcut in the Burley area and pulled down a satellite image of his neighborhood. They called a local police officer, who agreed to drive out to the residence to take a discreet look. Casida had some pictures of the front yard, so he was able to forward a detailed description. Within half an hour, the officer called back.

"It's just like you explained."

They had him. Now they had to make sure they got him the right way. From the start of his investigation a few weeks earlier, Casida had been in touch with Michelle Collins at NCMEC. He knew the national center had not only a growing database of victims but also a team of investigators with an almost uncanny memory for the individual faces of children. He urged the local police in Burley to get in touch with NCMEC before they made any moves.

As it happened, Collins had been following the twisted career of a mysterious Web poster named Paul Jones since 1999, shortly after she had started at NCMEC.

"We knew he was running a photography company," she said. "We just didn't know where he was."

Collins had first seen him post his suggestive pictures of young models in newsgroups dedicated to "child love"—edging up to the borders of pornography. She grew alarmed when his pictures of the girl went from erotic posing to sexual abuse. She tried to run a trace on Paul Jones but could get little more than possible hints that his e-mails originated somewhere in the Midwest. "He was always good at hiding himself," she said. "We just kept tracking him, hoping one day someone would end up finding him."

Then suddenly she got a call from the Burley police officer.

"I heard I should give you a call to see if you can help," he said.

"Who do you have?" she asked.

"Some guy calling himself Paul Jones," came the reply.

Collins nearly fell off her chair. "Are you kidding me? Oh my God!" she exclaimed. "I know this guy. Let me pull his stuff together."

She was able to send the police a detailed file, with pictures of two little girls the photographer was abusing and even a shot of the tie he once wore when assaulting them. "When you go in with your search warrant, look for this tie, look for this blanket, look for this carpet," Collins told them. "This is what you're going to find."

And they did. When the police raided Leslie Bowcut's home on February 15, they discovered thousands of pornographic pictures of children on his computer. Bowcut later admitted taking about five hundred of them himself—including many they had found on Emmerson's computer. One folder, labeled "Bondage," depicted a bound and abused female toddler. The layout of the house matched the description in the abuse images that Michelle Collins had been trying to trace. They even found the tie.

Leslie Bowcut confirmed the rule that the only stereotype for the online child molester was that there was no stereotype. To all appearances, he was a paragon of virtue. The eleventh of thirteen children, he had been an Eagle Scout and an active member of the Church of Jesus Christ of Latter-day Saints, where he had met his wife. He dabbled in various businesses but seemed to hit his stride with his photography of child models, all the while doing some Web design work and fixing computers. The town of Burley had a darker past, renowned in years gone by for its seedy bars and prostitutes, but it had cleaned up its reputation, in part because more than half its residents were Mormons. Local parents had no qualms about the amiable Bowcut taking pictures of their girls wearing dresses and bathing suits, for "print advertisements," he claimed. "If you're a good, active Latter-day Saint person in this community, they trust you," a Bowcut family member told the media later.

What Bowcut did not tell the girls or their parents was that he was posting their pictures on a commercial Web site called P.J. Crew (the name of one of the folders police found on Emmerson's hard drive). He set up an online "fan club" for the models; according to prosecutors he pulled in between $7,000 and $10,000 a month selling subscriptions to eager customers who sent in special requests for the models to don certain clothes that turned them on.

With Emmerson and other members of the club he had also traded child abuse images. Five months after Mike Casida started tracking down "Paul Jones," Bowcut pleaded guilty to fourteen counts of sexually exploiting a child. A few months later, when the judge sentenced him to thirty years to life in prison, he sobbed, collapsed and had to be helped out of the courtroom.

Mike Casida had little time to ponder whether Leslie Bowcut got what he deserved; he was too busy chasing down other Hamlet leads. "The hard part is when you sit and stare at these kids over and over again," he said. "I've seen these kids so many times that I recognize them just as much as I recognize my own kids."

"If it was not for the Clovis police department, this would have stopped at four or five offenders caught, four or five children saved," said NCMEC's Michelle Collins. "They would not let this go." By the time they were done, Casida and his colleagues had pictures of more than five hundred abused children that they had isolated from Emmerson's computer. By May 2002, Hamlet investigators had gathered enough evidence to arrest seven suspects in California, Nevada, Texas and Washington. Eventually that number would almost triple.

The Clovis cops stayed in constant touch with ICE and NCMEC managers, back in the Washington, D.C., area. One was a law enforcement entity created out of the old Customs branch, now under the sprawling Department of Homeland Security; the other had become the largest civilian agency dedicated to protecting children. Both were still feeling their way as national organizations, and Hamlet gave them the testing ground they needed. "Hamlet was much more successful because of the networking," said NCMEC's Collins. "It was the first time the hubs began to work."

While ICE focused on coordinating the investigations of dozens of local and federal agents in the field, NCMEC concentrated on burrowing deep into its database records for clues. For Michelle Collins, the Hamlet case had started as a regular Technical Assistance report when the California cops had first phoned in a request for some help. By the time Michelle Collins had finished with it almost two years later, she had sixty-nine entries and 136 pages in her Cybertip report on the case. Each of those entries would be another piece of a suspect's or a victim's puzzle—an e-mail trace, a posting in a chat room, a driver's license.

"NCMEC was as cutting edge as you can get," said Casida. "They were the ones looking at it all the time, piecing it together." He never failed to be amazed by Collins's almost encyclopedic capacity to connect pictures and children.

"Hey, I got a little blond girl sitting on a couch," Casida recalls once describing a picture he found to Collins. "Looks like a European country—"

"Uh-huh," Collins cut in. "Is there a red towel lying over the edge of it?"

"Yeah, yeah," said Casida, shaking his head in disbelief.

Over at ICE, Betsy Perino was tracking the activities of dozens of such investigations across the country. From Clovis and other centers, ICE would gather the local leads and tips on potential suspects, everything from chat screen names to more pictures for forensic examination. At ICE headquarters, they dug further to identify the targets, locate their city and then send the information back out into the field. "It leaves here with enough probable cause to go ahead and be ready to kick in a door," said Perino.

Through it all, the investigators had to balance the urgency of rescuing the victims with the risk of tripping the wire and alerting other offenders with a premature arrest of one suspect. What worked to their advantage was the loose, informal structure of this pedophile network: while Paul Whitmore in San Diego played the most dominant role in the global club, he did not control all the lines of communication. "It was more like a series of spiderwebs out there," said Perino. "There was no one person who's the core, so if he goes down, then all the dominoes fall."

Still, the investigators were careful. Where possible, they persuaded newly arrested members of the club to cooperate in return for slightly reduced sentences and to allow police to take over their online identities and activities. Their sudden disappearances from the Web while they were in custody were explained away with the acceptable excuses of everyday life: "I was in a car wreck" or simply "I haven't been online." As Perino explained, "Our goal was to make sure that the investigation as a whole wasn't compromised by any single takedown."

And it worked.

By August 9, 2002, the U.S. attorney's office in Fresno released a sixteen-page indictment against fifteen suspects for the "sexual exploitation of children," including Paul Whitmore, Lloyd Emmerson, Leslie Bowcut and several others from Florida, South Carolina, Kansas and—because they had committed offenses by distributing their child abuse images in the U.S.—against several foreigners, including Eggert Jensen and his wife, along with citizens of Switzerland and the Netherlands. By then, the Hamlet team had rescued forty-five children, thirty-seven in the U.S. alone. The youngest was only two; the oldest was fourteen. Within five more months, the arrest numbers had climbed to twenty-four people, and Mike Casida calculated that their work had helped track down the abusers of more than one hundred children, ninety of them in the U.S.

Lloyd Alan Emmerson, the Clovis chiropractor whose hoarding habits helped unlock most of Hamlet's secrets, eventually pleaded guilty to sexually exploiting children and distributing child pornography. Standing in front of the judge in a red prison jumpsuit, he stared right at the magistrate and answered, "Guilty," as each charge was read out. He got thirty years behind bars.

But Paul Whitmore, who led eight children into degrading acts of molestation, opted for a trial, forcing the prosecutor, Jeff Dort, to ponder the unthinkable but also the unavoidable: "I would have to call each child to the stand, forcing them to relive the experience and look at the photographs," he said. "And juries do random things every time you walk into a courtroom."

It would be four years after the raids in Denmark before Paul Whitmore would face justice.

The number of children rescued in Operation Hamlet was about the same as the number of victims found in the Landslide investigations.

The difference was that in Hamlet the rescue of the children was the main goal and not just the consequence of busting online offenders. In Landslide, untold numbers of clients—and their child victims—got away as the evidence trails went stale; in Hamlet almost all the suspects were found.

Where Landslide saw international police cooperation that was at times haphazard and accidental, in Hamlet the process was planned and centralized. The flow of data and intelligence was efficient, and the police grasp of technology was better as they succeeded in cracking encryption codes and tracing e-mail and computer log-in addresses.

Hamlet would inspire investigators on both sides of the Atlantic to do more of the same, but even better. From now on—as happened with the rescue of Jessica several months after Hamlet wrapped up— the identification and rescue of child victims of Internet porn would be the priority, not just the aftereffect of an arrest. As Lars Underbjerg, the Danish National Police investigator who started Hamlet, put it simply, "Our goal is to stop the actual abuse. If there is no abuse, there aren't any child abuse images."

It was not going to be easy, because the victims were hiding in plain sight. "The kids that we're looking at are not missing kids," said Michelle Collins of NCMEC. "The kids are going to church, they are on soccer teams—these are kids that are going to school with your kids." Their abusers were inevitably in their immediate circle: family members, neighbors, schoolteachers or coaches.

And the abusers did not leave much of a trail, because of the speed and vastness of the Internet and proliferation of online trading of child abuse pictures. "If I were to take a photograph and put it online, by the end of tonight, let's say five hundred people have it. By the end of the weekend, five thousand people have it," said Collins. "You're law enforcement. Tomorrow morning how are you ever going to track it back to me?"

It was, Collins admitted, a seemingly impossible challenge: "All we know is that these pictures were taken on planet Earth," she would tell her staff. "It's your job to figure out where on earth they were taken."

PART TWO **A PICTURE IS WORTH A THOUSAND CLUES**

Six

ONLINE UNDERCOVER

*—Are you a police officer, or do you work for any law
enforcement agency?*
—No, I'm in the ninth grade.
—Good, thank you . . . lots of cops online pretending to be girls.
—They don't let ninth graders in the CIA!!!!
— ONLINE CHAT BETWEEN A FORTY-FOUR-YEAR-OLD
MAN AND AN UNDERCOVER FBI AGENT

The fifty-six-year-old man from Liverpool, England, sends money to a
twelve-year-old girl for bus fare so she can travel two hundred miles
to see him on Valentine's Day. An employee in his fifties at a Michelin
tire factory in Nova Scotia, Canada, pretends to be a seventeen-year-old
lesbian in order to seduce at teenage girl from Toronto. The forty-four-
year-old weapons designer for the U.S. Department of the Navy can't
wait to meet his thirteen-year-old date at a mall in Maryland.

Three men. Three countries. All three assumed false personae on
the Web—pretending to be much younger than they were. What
they never suspected was that the joke was on them: the "girls" at
the other end of their steamy e-mail courtship were police, often
male police officers at that. Sometimes the police take over the identity of a real child who has been ensnared by an older man; other
times the agents have built entirely fictitious online characters to
lure the predators.

In the shadowy world of Internet intrigue, the predator and the
police play what seems to be a dangerous game of cat and mouse.
Except that it's not a game, and the fates of real children are at stake.
In the U.S., the police call these types of predators "travelers"; in the

U.K., the offense is called "enticing"; in Canada it goes by the name "luring." But it amounts to the same thing: grown men prowling the Web looking for lonely children, the underage victims. According to a study published in the *Journal of Adolescent Health,* 76 percent of the victims of online abuse met the offenders in a chat room; another 10 percent hooked up via e-mail.

To catch these men, police have to get inside the minds of the predators, figure out how they think, what turns them on and what risks tipping them off.

These are not men who sit at home content to trade illicit pictures of children or even to take pictures of their own children being abused; instead, they actively seek out complete strangers to assault. These online lurkers are the Web's equivalent of the proverbial "dirty old men" in the park, turning the Internet into their playground. To stop them, police have had to come up with equally devious undercover techniques that sometimes push the envelope—going too far, their critics say, into the morally dubious and legally tricky terrain of entrapment.

"Are you a cheerleader?" the man asked the thirteen-year-old girl in the online AOL chat room called "I love older men." It was one of many anonymous meeting places on the Web filled with lonely children in America. They come to play, to pretend—and sometimes to meet up with men who are deadly serious about their intent.

"Must be hot if you're a cheerleader," George Paul Chambers wrote. The girl dutifully sent him her photo, and over the next four months he courted her until she agreed to meet him at a bakery shop in a mall. Chambers must have thought it was his lucky day when he made that date at the mall, but he had the misfortune of crossing paths with one of the FBI's keenest undercover operatives. Emily Vacher, the investigator who worked closely with the Toronto police and helped the FBI dig up the forensic filth on Burt Thomas Stevenson's computer after Jessica's rescue. Vacher had a fervor for her job made all the more intense by the long road she had taken to get there.

"I'm a Jewish kid from outside Manhattan," she said with a laugh. "I didn't know any police officers, much less any FBI agents."

She got a bachelor's degree at an upstate New York college, then enrolled in pre-med studies at Cornell. She did volunteer work as a paramedic, but at the last moment switched from medicine to get a master's in counseling and education. She ended up working with children with disabilities—until she decided she wanted to be a lawyer.

"At twenty-four, I had four degrees, and my mother said that I had to go work," Vacher joked. Her first job at a law firm allowed her to concentrate again on children, through education law. When she asked a colleague who had been an FBI agent what it was like to be part of the famed bureau, "he just lit up. The way he talked about it—I wanted to feel like that at work."

The next day she went down to talk to the FBI and within a few weeks found herself at the training center in Quantico, Virginia. There she heard about the FBI's Innocent Images Program, and her mind—finally—was made up. "I knew I wanted to do something where I either got to work with or help kids," she said. In the spring of 2001, she was lucky enough to get her first posting in Baltimore, not far from the Calverton headquarters. When the 9/11 attacks hit, like almost everyone else at the FBI she was consumed by antiterrorist work in the subsequent months. In December 2001, she finally began training to become the FBI's latest undercover Internet agent.

The FBI had to make sure that its agents talked and looked like teenagers. Early on, the bureau brought in a couple of real teenage girls—one was the daughter of an agent—to school the adult agents in the lifestyle and lingo of the wired generation. Online predators often ask for pictures from the children they are in contact with, but FBI agents—and other police officers from around the country who began to emulate the bureau's undercover work—could hardly use pictures of real children. So they called on the image specialists at NCMEC, who usually spent most of their time employing the latest photo-manipulation software to "age" children who had gone missing for many years. For the adult undercover agents, it was the reverse: NCMEC's experts were tasked with mastering the art of "age regression."

"It snowballed," said Steve Loftin, one of NCMEC's image specialists, who was getting a half dozen requests a week from agencies across the country.

Sometimes Loftin uses an officer's childhood photos and only has to alter the clothing or hairstyle to match the right decade. Other times he asks them to have a picture taken of themselves in a childlike setting—

on a swing or clutching a teddy bear—and wearing age-appropriate clothing. Then Loftin goes to work, changing bone density, altering muscle definition, smoothing out skin and adding some baby fat.

A few hours' work and decades have been wiped out.

Changing appearances was the easy part for Emily Vacher. She decided she didn't need any technical wizardry. She dug up a snapshot of herself at thirteen in a summer camp performance of *Grease*—decked out in white T-shirt and a brown leather jacket. She might have looked thirteen in a photograph, but how could Vacher, at the time thirty-two, think and sound like a teenager? "I don't have children, I haven't been thirteen in a while, and when I was thirteen the world was a different place," she said.

To pick up teen habits, Vacher spent a lot of time on the phone with a thirteen-year-old niece, listening to her voice, expressions and grammar (or lack thereof). When she visited her niece's home, she checked out the latest posters on her bedroom wall; Vacher became a regular reader of *Teen People* and *Teen Vogue,* an avid MTV fan and an aficionado of boy bands. Her homework paid off. One adult correspondent, who happened to have a real teenage daughter enthralled with heartthrobs like the Backstreet Boys and N'Sync, once asked her if she favored lead singer Lance or Justin. Vacher, immersed in teen culture, could easily come up with the convincing answer of a connoisseur.

For her first undercover role, Emily Vacher took the name EmmaMDGurl—the MD standing for Maryland. With as many as ten or twelve men pursuing her online at a time, Vacher had a notebook in front of her when she went online to keep her stories straight and make sure she was telling the right lies to the right people. "These predators use the same system," she said. In one raid, she discovered a man had a bulletin board filled with index cards for all the girls he had been pursuing—their names, their ages, siblings, bra sizes and even whether they had pubic hair. "So they would check on us just as much as we would check on them," the FBI agent said. "It's important as an investigator to be consistent."

To maintain that consistency, she modeled as much of her online persona as possible after herself. EmmaMDGurl had an eight-year-old sister, just as Emily Vacher did when she was thirteen; both the online fictitious girl and the real-life FBI agent enjoyed playing lacrosse.

Other parts of her story were concocted to help her undercover work: for example, she pretended that she split her time between the homes of her divorced parents so that she could explain away long absences from her computer, claiming she didn't have Internet access at her father's house.

Vacher liked to joke that catching online predators was not rocket science—until the day she caught a rocket scientist.

George Paul Chambers, a forty-four-year-old father of two young daughters, worked at the Naval Surface Weapon Center in Indian Head, Maryland, developing weapons and building systems to disarm explosives and land mines. "His brilliance is outstanding," his defense lawyer later said.

When Vacher signed on to the AOL chat room called "I love older men" just after 4 P.M. on February 1, 2002, she had been an FBI agent for less than a year and assigned to the Innocent Images project for only three months. Suddenly she found herself immersed in the murky universe of cyber-stalking, where adult males shed a few years and most of their inhibitions as they go hunting for vulnerable girls online.

To avoid any suggestion of of entrapment, the FBI's undercover cops are trained not to initiate contact, not to be forward, not to make any suggestions for meetings but only to respond. So Vacher was as passive as could be. "I went into that room and I didn't say a word," she said. "I was just sitting there and he contacted me."

"Do you like older guys?" came the query from laxfan314, the AOL screen name that Chambers used (short for "lacrosse fan").

Over the next four months the Navy weapons designer doggedly pursued what he thought was a precocious cheerleader. He didn't waste time. On that first day, he sent EmmaMDGurl a picture of his penis. He eventually sent a picture of his face as well, albeit one that showed him ten years younger. Vacher sent him the photograph of herself at thirteen. They would talk several times a week. She had to put in long hours because she could only go online in the afternoon after "school" was out; she came in on the weekend to work from the FBI's secure computers (which could not be traced) because she could not sign on undercover from home. Chambers often asked if her parents or any adults were home as they chatted online. He pushed to talk to her on the phone, but she refused. He soon wrote about getting together to meet his young cheerleading fan in person.

Chambers must have had some fears as well. On March 24, he asked EmmaMDGurl if she worked for the FBI.

"Since when does the FBI hire teenagers?" she replied.

Later that same day he again asked if she worked for any law enforcement agency.

"Uummmmm no," she replied.

Two months later, on May 21, Chambers raised his worries one more time. "Are you a police officer or do you work for any law enforcement agency?" he asked.

"No, I'm in the ninth grade."

"Good, thank you . . . lots of cops online pretending to be girls."

"They don't let ninth graders in the CIA!!!!"

The FBI agent playing a ninth grader was busy doing her homework on her online chat partner, running background checks to ascertain his real identity. A subpoena to AOL revealed basic information about Chambers; the picture he sent Vacher matched a driver's license photograph of George Paul Chambers that the FBI obtained.

All that was left was the face-to-face meeting. Vacher had repeatedly delayed and canceled, in part to give Chambers every opportunity to bail out. He kept insisting, until finally the date was set for Saturday, June 6. There was no mystery about what would transpire once the navy scientist met the thirteen-year-old schoolgirl.

"He wanted to have sex with me," said Vacher. "When I had mentioned the issue of condoms during our chat, he specifically told me that he was not going to bring condoms because he wanted to get me pregnant." As hard as it was to fathom, Chambers had good reason to believe a girl in a chat room would want such a meeting; as Vacher and other investigators were later to discover, there would be plenty of real girls who would find themselves ensnared in an Internet-initiated relationship with an older man.

EmmaMDGurl suggested they meet at a bakery on the second floor of the Howard County mall in Columbia, Maryland, where her "mother" could drop her off. Chambers got into his car that day and drove the fifty miles from the Naval Surface Warfare Center in Indian Head, never spotting the FBI cars that were following him.

When he got to the rendezvous site, Chambers stood about twenty-five feet from the bakery, waiting for the teenage date who never showed. FBI agents moved in to arrest him.

"I can't believe I came out here today," he said, according to later testimony by one of the agents. "My life is over."

In his car, the FBI found a computer Zip disk containing child pornography; more pictures turned up on his home computer. Back at the FBI office, Emily Vacher walked into the interrogation room where Chambers was seated. "He was one of my first cases, so I was still a little nervous," said Vacher. "As a new agent, you don't want to make mistakes. But I was also excited: what I'd just done potentially was save a real child from harm."

For all his brilliance, the Navy scientist still had no idea that the young field agent sitting across the table from him was the thirteen-year-old cheerleader he had been plotting to assault. Chambers declined to speak without his lawyer present, so Vacher sent him off to jail. The next morning, she picked him up and took him to his first appearance in front of the judge. Only later, through court papers and as the trial unfolded did Chambers discover who EmmaMDGurl really was.

In fact, it was surprising that Chambers opted for a trial. In these kinds of cases, the defendant often goes for a guilty plea and a lesser sentence, because the details of his attempted online seduction of a child are so explicit—and downright embarrassing—that few want a jury or the public to hear them.

"It was my first trial as an agent and I had obviously put a lot of time into the case. I was the undercover, I was there at the arrest, I did all the investigations," said Vacher. "I was scared to death."

Given the amount of evidence against him—Vacher naturally had saved every scrap of conversation, every image he had sent—Chambers had only one viable defense strategy, a tactic almost all Internet predators use because it offers their sole chance with jurors: it was all a fantasy.

"It's a way of stepping out of your real life; you could be somebody else for a while," Chambers testified, insisting that he went to the mall out of curiosity, with no plans of sex. His attorney told the jurors that his client was "a nice guy with a crazy twist. But he's not a sexy guy," the lawyer said. "On the Internet, though, he can be Don Juan."

The real culprit, he argued, was the FBI and its special agent Vacher, who tried to lure and entrap Chambers. At one point in his cross-examination, the defense attorney asked Vacher if she thought her picture as a thirteen-year-old was "sexy." The judge berated him for "inappropriate" questions. Vacher took it all in stride. After all, she had been an attorney herself. Still, she was upset by the defense's insinuation that she took pleasure from her online encounters. "He was trying to make it seem that I got any kind of amusement out of this, that I enjoyed the sexual chat with his client. And I'm thinking, Ugh. The last man on earth. This behavior is revolting.

"You just hope that a jury of twelve people will listen to our side, listen to their side and decide who is telling the truth."

But they couldn't decide.

After eleven hours of deliberation over two days, the jurors failed to reach a unanimous verdict. Most were certain he was guilty, but there were at least three holdouts, including the jury forewoman. "People do misrepresent themselves [on the Internet], and it's not a gross misrepresentation for him to engage in something like that and not know," she said. With a hung jury, the prosecution could have dropped the case or opted for a plea bargain, but they choose instead to go after Chambers again.

Vacher wanted to be sure she won the next time. When Chambers' second trial began in March of 2004, she was ready to attack the weapons designer for what he said under oath the first time. "I got a transcript for the entire trial, and I went through it with a fine-tooth comb," explained Vacher.

The Navy scientist had testified that child pornography was "repulsive" to him. Vacher pored through the logs of thousands of chats on Chambers's computer. "I found conversations that he was having not only with other children but also with other pedophiles, looking at images of children being sexually abused."

Chambers also insisted he never had sex with anyone he had met online, because after all that was just his fantasy world. From his computer logs, Vacher tracked down a young woman—legally an adult at eighteen—whom Chambers had met in an AOL chat room; he had ended up with her in a hotel room. Finding the woman was one thing, persuading her to testify quite another. "She was completely scared, and you could feel empathy for her," said Vacher, "but I told that her testimony was important to make sure that somebody who had a sexual interest in children was not on the street."

The woman had lost a lot of weight since she had met Chambers, so he did not recognize her at first when she showed up at trial. When she walked to the stand, however, it sank in; he stood up and ran out of the courtroom. Running from the evidence, though, was not as easy. In his summation, the prosecutor attacked head-on Chambers's claims that his online actions had all been make-believe.

"The question in this case is, Where does the fantasy end and the reality begin?" said the prosecutor. "If you fantasize about going to Ocean City, Maryland, it's a fantasy. When you get in your car and drive there, it's reality."

The reality began for George Paul Chambers when the jurors came back, united this time, with a guilty verdict. Reality sank in deeper in June 2004, when the judge sentenced him to six years in prison.

Chambers's only comment was, "Obviously, I think six years in prison is ridiculous."

Vacher, for her part, just wanted to move on. "There are no winners here. Not only did he commit the crimes but he has a wife and children, so the damage is done. Besides, I had other bad guys to catch."

Oddly enough, Chambers was not the last military man Vacher had a hand in arresting. Six months after the first Chambers trial, the Maryland police asked the FBI for assistance in an undercover sting they were running. Wayne David Sharer was a decorated navy commander and pilot who used his computer at the Pentagon to solicit sex on the Internet from what he thought was a twelve-year-old girl. Like Chambers, he traveled to meet her—in his case, to another mall in Columbia—where he was arrested. He got three years in prison.

Vacher also caught flak for her undercover work. As one of the rare luring cases to go to trial, the Chambers case garnered much media attention, including some sniping from commentators like Joe Bob Briggs, whose shoot-from-the-hip columns were syndicated by UPI. He took Vacher to task because she "flat-out lied" to Chambers when he asked if she was a cop (as if an undercover cop buying drugs from a dealer would flash his badge before making the buy). His main beef was that "there's no victim" in this crime; instead of going after "hard-core child molesters," the FBI was chasing "some lonely guy [who] . . . is crossing imaginary lines with the equivalent of a blow-up party doll."

Such arguments infuriated Vacher, who pointed out that far from entrapping people, she always gave them an escape hatch. "I never raised the issue of having sex, never raised the issue of meeting in real life, never," she said. "I don't sit in a chat room and say I'm thirteen and I want to have sex with an adult. They don't have to hit on me. If you're not interested in having sex with a child, then don't write to me."

And far from fantasies about a "blow-up party doll" the online predators are after real flesh-and-blood targets. Indeed, at times Vacher was required to take over the identity of an actual child who had already fallen into a risky Internet lure. A Virginia girl had begun an intense online relationship with an older man from Colorado; her parents, when they discovered the predicament, alerted the police, and the file landed on Vacher's computer.

"He wasn't hiding his intentions: he was looking for a teen sex toy," said Vacher. He mailed her cash for a bus ticket, confident enough that his teen target would travel by bus from Virginia to Colorado. FBI agents arrested him as he waited for the bus to arrive, expecting a teenage girl to step out and greet him.

"What would have happened to her?" Vacher asked. "If anyone wants to make the argument that what I do is wrong or pushing the bounds of the law, look at that child. Had it not been me at the end of the computer, it's going to be a real child they're going to assault."

Between 1996 and 2004, there was a 2,241 percent increase in the number of Innocent Images cases opened—from 113 to 2,645—and an equally impressive 1,195 percent increase in convictions or pleas. "Like shooting fish in a barrel," said Arnold Bell, the unit chief of the Innocent Images project since 2002. Bell did six years in the army, followed by years of police work on homicide cases and Los Angeles gang wars. This was just another battlefront for him, albeit ever shifting and evolving.

At his headquarters in Calverton, Bell has more than twenty people at work on various undercover stings. By 2005, the task force boasted that it had generated more than three thousand leads in the United States and two thousand abroad. Every agent who does similar work in the field—and there are more than forty of them in twenty-eight FBI bureaus scattered across the country—goes through an intensive undercover boot camp. The FBI has also hosted investigators from a dozen countries at its Calverton training center—including a steady stream of Canadians.

Paul Gillespie of the Toronto police was one of the first to make sure his squad took advantage of the FBI's expertise. In late November 2002, a team of investigators from the child exploitation section of the city's Sex Crimes Unit went down to Calverton, including a young detective named Paul Krawcyzk, who had just joined the squad five months earlier. "It was amazing," he recalled. "They seemed so ahead of their time. It was a real eye-opener."

The four-day course—including sessions with Emily Vacher—had an immediate impact. Within a week of returning to Toronto, Krawcyzk got his first undercover assignment. A woman had contacted the police with concerns that her fifteen-year-old younger sister, Rebecca,* was getting too close to a stranger she had met in an MSN chat group called "Girls4Girls." Rebecca had a learning disability, and her mental age was closer to ten. Her new friend called herself Karla Conrod; she claimed to be a seventeen-year-old student at Clayton Park High School outside of Halifax. Her online profile sounded wholesome and cheery:

Nickname:	Goldilocks1121
Name:	Karla
Age:	17
Gender:	Female
Favorite Things:	read mystery novels
Favorite Quote:	only 2 things in life are free, fresh air and happiness

Karla sent Rebecca two photographs of herself: they showed a young blonde. In one shot she had pulled down her bra to expose a breast but kept on her underpants and shoes; in the second photo she was lying on a blanket, nude, with her legs spread. Rebecca and her Nova Scotian friend talked about the possibility that Rebecca could go to visit over Christmas. She had supplied her real name, her home address and phone number, the address of her school and a photograph of herself.

Krawcyzk had doubts that Karla was who she claimed to be, but he also knew that even if he could prove Karla—whoever she or he was—was trying to lure Rebecca for the purposes of sex, he could not make an arrest because the age of consent in Canada was fourteen. But the Toronto cop also figured that anyone who was trying to lure a teen into sex was also likely a trader of child porn online. He could at least try to nab the suspect for that.

With the permission of a reluctant Rebecca—who was still convinced that her online friend was genuine—and her mother, Krawcyzk took over the girl's account and immediately changed the password to make sure he alone had access to it. He discovered that Karla had sent sixty-one messages to Rebecca in the previous eight days. Krawcyzk was certain that Karla was an older man. Now he had to convince the suspect that he was fifteen-year-old Rebecca. It was not easy. Rebecca had not kept any copies of her outgoing e-mails; thankfully, in many of Karla's replies the original message was included, so the Toronto cop could get a sense of how Rebecca talked. "Basically, no grammar, no upper cases, just one big run-on paragraph," Krawcyzk said.

He pulled it off, and Karla kept the chat coming. By early December, Karla felt comfortable enough to send her young friend some child pornography. In one e-mail with the subject header "u and me with her" she attached a jpg file showing a young girl lifting up her skirt and exposing her genitals. The message read:

> Rebecca, I wish u and me can please her.
> What do u think? Love Karla

Krawcyzk had enough to lay a charge for the possession and distribution of child pornography. Now he just had to find out who Karla really was. He ran an IP trace and found that most of the communication came from the large Michelin Tire plant in Pictou, Nova Scotia. Krawcyzk passed the file on to the RCMP; they did more digging and were able to trace the messages to a single desk computer. It belonged to Ronald Stuart Laing, a supervisor at the company for twenty-three years. Married, with no children, the fifty-six-year-old apparently was so new to computers that he did not even own one at home and learned all of his skills at work.

When police arrested him, they found eighty more images on his office computer. He pleaded not guilty, but on the morning of his court appearance he switched his plea. In theory, he faced a maximum penalty of five years for possession and ten years for distribution, but he needn't have worried. The judge called the images shocking, but he accepted a joint recommendation from both the prosecution and defense that Laing could serve just one year under house arrest. The Toronto cops were going to find that no matter how hard they worked to gather the evidence, many judges were reluctant to sentence the defendants to any real jail time.

Still, Krawcyzk and his fellow team members kept luring predators in the months and years that followed. Det. John Menard never ceased to be amazed at how desperate the online predators were. In one case run by the Toronto team, he recalled, an officer working undercover as a thirteen-year-old girl had no fewer than fifteen males clamoring for sex with her within twenty seconds of going online.

In another investigation, the Toronto team trapped the pastor of an evangelical church. Kenneth Synes spent four months trying to groom what he thought was a twelve-year-old girl. "The chat became more sexually explicit, to the point that he was prepared to drive across the city and meet in a public place," said Det. Const. Scott Purches, who did the undercover work. U.S. authorities eventually contacted the Toronto cops with evidence that the pastor had tried looking south of the border as well for victims, with no apparent success.

Synes, discharged from his church, pleaded guilty and got a year in jail for his sins.

In the United Kingdom, they take undercover Internet work so seriously that police officers have to get special accreditation before they can become keyboard criminal catchers. About ninety-five "covert Internet investigators" have been trained at a national course run by the Association of Chiefs of Police Officers.

At New Scotland Yard, one of those qualified undercover agents was Jim Pearce, a chain-smoking detective constable who shared his cramped quarters with five other investigators of the High-Tech Crime Unit at the Yard's headquarters near St. James's Square. The modern banks of computer hard drives, image scanners and hacker software seemed out of place in the old-fashioned office filled with battered desks, with its fading paint and scuffed floors. Pearce had a bone-weariness etched on his face and a darkness in his eyes that only a veteran cop who has seen it all can carry off with grace. His Liverpudlian-accented speech, like his detective work, is slow and methodical. He had walked the beat of London's Battersea district for seven years as a uniformed bobby, then put in eight more years in the Clubs and Vice squad, patroling the seamier side of London. Now he was patroling the underbelly of the Web and finding the technology had changed but not the crime.

His first undercover case began when the local Cambridgeshire police were contacted by a panicked mother on Christmas Eve 2004. She had discovered that her twelve-year-old daughter, Alison,* had been flirting online with an older man who said he was eighteen. The family had reason to be nervous. The Cambridgeshire county, after all, had been the site of the notorious murders in the town of Soham just two years earlier, when the entire country was gripped by the disappearance of two ten-year-old girls; they were later found dead, after having been lured into the home of a school caretaker. Alison had gone to the same school as the two victims.

Alison's older brother had discovered her online communications with the man, dating back to the previous July. They had met on a children's site known as Pogo.com, which allowed users to chat while they played games; the man and his young target soon migrated to more intimate talk through instant messaging. When police came to the family home that Christmas, they found a heart-shaped piece of paper inscribed with what appeared to be the man's initials in the girl's room, along with a Christmas card and several letters, all proclaiming his love for her. The stranger had convinced Alison to let him use one of her friends' addresses for the packages and gifts he sent to her.

In one letter, he gave Alison his address on Longreach Road in Liverpool. A discreet police check there turned up a fifty-seven-year-old resident named Oliver Jordan. The man did have an estranged teenage son who lived with his mother. The police were fairly confident that the predator was the father and not the teen, but they could not be certain. Worse still, there was not enough evidence yet to lay a charge: the man's courtship of the girl had been inappropriate but to date not explicitly sexual. And while he had spoken to Alison about meeting, he had not yet made any specific arrangements.

They decided to call in Scotland Yard to ask Jim Pearce to take over the girl's online identity. Pearce was keen, but he realized he faced numerous challenges. By this time it was already January 18, and there had been an unexplained gap of two weeks of silence from Alison. Moreover, Jordan had an intimate knowledge of his prey, having corresponded with her since July; Pearce, on the other hand, knew little about teenage girls, much less about this particular child from Cambridgeshire.

"Basically, you've got this lonely twelve-year-old who's probably got her first ever boyfriend, even though he's a virtual one," said Pearce. "It's her little secret."

With the family's permission, the police made a mirror-image copy of her hard drive. Pearce wanted not just her chat logs but all her directories—to get a sense of what she was doing in school, what her musical tastes were (a boy band named Busted seemed high on her list) and how she organized her life and her thoughts. He also had to learn how she spoke, or at least typed. He noticed, for example, that she always signed on with Jordan—who used the screen name jameso0231—by saying, "Hi James, Wot u up 2?"

Pearce wrote out pages and fifty-two code words, translating letters and words into Alison's versions:, such as BF for "boyfriend," G2G for "got to go" and OIC for "oh I see." Four days later, Pearce was ready to flip the switch and go online as Alison. By now, it was Saturday, January 22, 2005. Jordan had not heard from her since January 3, when he had sent her a New Year's card. Pearce sent a simple instant message: "Hi James, please talk to me."

All he got back was an automated response from Jordan: "I'm away from my computer."

On Sunday night, Pearce typed in another short missive as Alison saying she would be home after school the next day.

The response he got back on Monday was cold and harsh: "Look, I don't know who you are, so please don't send me any more stupid IMs [instant messages]," Jordan wrote. "I'm sick of your little games. If you persist you'll leave me no alternative but to inform AOL about you invading my privacy."

"This is blowing up the first day," a worried Pearce told his police mates. The police knew that Alison had told Jordan that her brother was on to them and reported something to her mother; they hoped Jordan was just worried about that but did not yet suspect the authorities were already involved. Still, it was obvious that their suspect was on edge. "What can we do to try to get him back on our side?" they asked themselves.

Pearce went back into the logs and found a reference to a conversation in which Alison asked Jordan about a girl he met at a pool. Taking a chance, Pearce wrote a new message: "Look, if you don't want me as your girlfriend because of the girl at the pool, please tell me. I love you."

"Why have you not been talking to me online or by letter?" Jordan shot back. "Answer me: why not?"

Pearce, as Alison, played the soft touch: "Doing school stuff. I just wanna know, do you still love me?" He added an explanation for her erratic behavior, telling Jordan that Jimmy, Alison's brother, "said something to Mom, that's why I'm not being allowed online."

"I missed you, Alison," Jordan replied, apparently consoled. "Yes, I still love you."

It was early February at this point; Pearce had been running the sting for almost two weeks. Time to pull in the line. By this time, the police had confirmed beyond a doubt Oliver Jordan's real identity. They got hold of the photos he had supplied for a passport application, and these matched the pictures he had sent Alison. His handwriting on the passport application was the same as on the note he had written on the New Year's card to Alison. Now that they had the proof that they were speaking to a fifty-seven-year-old man, the police had to see if he would follow through on his promise to meet a twelve-year-old.

"I want you here, I don't care how I do it, I just want you here with me," Jordan wrote.

"I want to be with you, but how?" Pearce asked.

Jordan came up with a scheme. Alison had her half-term school break starting the next Monday, February 14—Valentine's Day. He would send her £30 in cash—through her friend—and a bus schedule for her trip to Liverpool from Cambridgeshire.

"Don't tell your mom about this," he cautioned. "Delete my details off your computer. Let me know what coach you're getting and I'll come meet you."

Pearce played the innocent: "I'm only twelve. How am I going to get on the coach?"

"Look, just tell them that you're being met at the other end; it won't be a problem," Jordan assured her. Then he detailed what he had planned for their first face-to-face meeting. "Do you still go to bed naked? I'll undress you slowly until you're naked and kiss you all over."

Now at last the police had everything they needed to lay a grooming charge: Jordan had sent his victim travel money and made clear his sexual intentions. All that remained was to spring the final trap.

Jordan had told Alison that he was having problems with his computer and that she should send confirmation of her trip by mail since he would not be online. The police figured he was being cautious, trying to ensure that there was no electronic trace of his rendezvous with the girl. Scotland Yard got a handwriting specialist to pen a Valentine card in Alison's style, telling Jordan she would be on the afternoon bus to Liverpool. Pearce had hoped to arrest Jordan as he waited with his Valentine flowers for his young date to arrive at the bus terminal. But they made one mistake: the card was delayed in the mail.

As the Liverpool police ran their surveillance on Jordan's home, they noticed he had gone out to buy new bedding; he had also visited the bus station to get information on the schedules. But by late afternoon on Valentine's Day he had not left his house. They made the decision to move in for the arrest all the same.

The late card arrived the next day, but by then Jordan was already in custody—and in deep trouble. He had the misfortune of trying to seduce Alison just after a new law came into force making "grooming" a crime even if the person never touched or even saw the victim. Jordan faced a maximum of fourteen years, but a guilty plea served him well: he got three years in jail, a permanent spot on the Sex Offenders Registry and a lifetime ban on working with children.

Pearce never spoke to the real Alison either before or after the case; that was standard dispassionate police procedure. But he did find out from her family that they had told her what the police had done to save her.

Barely four months after the arrest of Jordan, Pearce and his colleagues at the Yard found themselves in an even more bizarre online chase, trying to track a predator claiming to be a female nurse in her late thirties.

She said her name was Holly Chadwick. Like "Karla" from Nova Scotia, who struck up a friendship with the young Toronto girl, Holly too claimed to be a lesbian. Her photo in her Hotmail profile and in an online dating club known as Hi5.com showed a simple woman in her thirties; she said she was a nurse who had been hurt by a man in a previous relationship, which seemed to make her sympathetic in the minds of impressionable teens. "These young girls feel they have a trusting older woman as a friend," Pearce explained. Holly persuaded vulnerable girls she met online to perform sex games for her with their Webcams.

Pearce had the suspect's Hotmail address, though he had his doubts that Holly was, indeed, female. In her Hotmail profile, Holly cited Oscar Wilde's famous line, "We're all in the gutter, but some of us are looking at stars." By coincidence, Pearce had seen that quotation inscribed on the statue to the well-known playwright near the Charing Cross tube station when he used to work at the local police station close by. There was also a hospital nearby, so another Scotland Yard detective spent hours going through their employee photos to see if a female nurse matched Holly Chadwick's online photo.

No luck. The only way to catch Holly was through what Pearce called "good old-fashioned police work." He went undercover, assuming the role of a fictional twenty-two-year-old lesbian named Samantha, who had a fifteen-year-old sister. He set up an account in the same chat rooms where Holly hung out, and the two of them easily struck up a friendship. Holly explained that she went online at an Internet café because she did not have a Net connection at home. Scotland Yard ran an IP trace on Holly's chats and determined that the suspect was frequenting a large Internet café near Trafalgar Square— not far from Oscar Wilde's statue.

They were closing in but not there yet. Every computer in the café would have the same IP address, and there were five hundred machines spread over four floors. The police had to come up with a better way to narrow down the target. Pearce by now could predict when Holly would come online and for how long. A fellow detective, Sean Robbie, and another officer went to the café, posing as employees, while Pearce kept chatting with Holly. The two cops went around with clipboards, asking customers if they needed any help—and looking over shoulders to see what people were doing online. Within minutes, Robbie spotted the person chatting with Pearce (they could even see the photo Pearce was using in his fake profile as Samantha on the suspect's computer) and, as police had suspected, Holly was a he, not a she. With the camera in his mobile phone, Robbie snapped a picture of the man.

When the suspect left the café, the police followed him home. That gave them an address and quickly his full name—and his criminal record. Alan Pemberton was on the Sex Offenders Registry. Before the days of widespread Internet use, he used to phone young children, pretending to be a doctor, and persuade them to perform "medical exams" on their private parts. Pemberton's photo in police files matched the grainy shot Robbie had taken inside the café.

All that remained was the final sting. Holly arranged to meet Samantha at Victoria Station; she even asked Samantha to bring her fifteen-year-old younger sister to make it a threesome. As Pemberton was typing out the arrangements for the rendezvous on the computer in the café, the police were discreetly standing not far away, this time with a video camera filming his keyboard crimes. They moved in to make the arrest; with Pemberton in custody, one of the officers typed the last message that would ever come from Holly Chadwick, the nurse who liked quoting Oscar Wilde.

Back at the Yard, Pearce smiled as he saw the words appear on his computer screen: "All secure."

Pemberton was convicted of sending child abuse images to Pearce and—more seriously—of inciting someone to rape a child. "It was very satisfying," said Pearce, "paying him back for deceiving others."

Deceptions within deceptions. A male child abuser pretending to be a female nurse chatting with a twenty-two-year-old lesbian who was in fact a middle-aged Scotland Yard male detective. Pearce closed the file, but he could not help wondering how many other predators were out there, pretending to befriend a lonely child.

Seven

CSI: PORN

I have to be strong. Why? Because I know there are wicked, evil people like you who like to hurt kids.
—ANN,* TESTIFYING AGAINST THE TEACHER WHO
ABUSED HER

Back in the United States, NCMEC was well on its way to becoming the central clearinghouse and coordination center for the exploding number of child porn investigations. By 2003, its CyberTipline was getting more than eighty thousand reports a year; within three years, they were receiving almost that many reports in a single week.

When Michelle Collins joined NCMEC in 1998, she was one of only four people working directly on child pornography. By the time she became director of the Exploited Child Unit, in 2004, she was supervising a staff of over thirty. On the fifth floor of NCMEC's headquarters, alongside an army of civilian analysts, there were designated officers from each of the major American law enforcement agencies charged with tackling child abuse: the FBI, ICE and the U.S. Postal Service. It was this combination of civilian and police resources that made NCMEC unique, allowing it to draw in leads and intelligence from three major sources: the public, the police and the private Internet companies.

Parents, children or concerned citizens phoned a toll-free number or filed an online report with the CyberTipline at www.thecybertipline.com if they came across a Web page or e-mail that contained what they thought was illicit child exploitation material. "We process the leads and figure out where the crime has been committed," said Christina Fernandez, who directs more than a dozen analysts who field the three thousand tips that come from the public every week. "We're basically giving law enforcement a wrapped package. Here's this guy, here's where he lived, here's what he's doing: go get him."

The simplest tip can have enormous consequences. Fernandez recalled an anonymous lead from a citizen that led NCMEC to a Yahoo group advertising "free little boy pics." An e-mail posting of some pictures from one participant came with the message, "I have child bestiality, enjoy." As Fernandez noted, "He was not the sharpest tool in the shed"—the man used his real name in the e-mail. When police visited his home in the Cincinnati area November 2002, they were expecting a routine arrest for possession of indecent images of children. What they found was a run-down house in a shambles—though the man clearly could afford a computer and Internet access. On the wall in one room were scrawled the words "Daddy's sorry." Once questioned, the man's daughter revealed that she had been abused. Her father got twenty years in prison for rape and the production of child pornography.

"This girl has since been adopted, and she is doing great," said Fernandez. "What started off as an investigation into a posting in an online group led to the uncovering of a real-life molestation. And without that anonymous tip, that child would still be a victim."

Police agencies around the country were also shipping images they seized from suspects' computers to NCMEC in compliance with the Supreme Court's ruling to prove the pictures represented "real" children. Just as the Toronto police, north of the border, were working with Microsoft to develop the Child Exploitation Tracking System (CETS) in 2003, NCMEC was going to have to come up with a sophisticated system that could process pictures quickly. The difference was that CETS was designed to manage mainly text files—names of suspects, e-mail addresses and other identifiers. NCMEC needed something that could make sense of tens of thousands of pictures.

NCMEC developed its own robust software nicknamed CRIS (Child Recognition Identification System) based on what is called a "hash value" of a picture. The hash value is a sort of digital fingerprint of a photo. An algorithm "chops and mixes" all the data in an image (hence the term "hash") and reduces it to a unique string of random-looking numbers and letters. Law enforcement around the world use what is known as MD-5 (Message-Digest algorithm 5) to categorize child porn images. That way, every copy of the same photograph gets tagged with the same hash value.

CRIS matches the hash value of any pictures found on a suspect's computer with identical pictures of victims who have been identified in previous cases. For example, several pictures of Jessica or one of the California children rescued in Operation Hamlet might turn up in a hard drive seized in Nebraska. But the police or prosecutors in Nebraska might not know that. They forward the material to NCMEC. CRIS displays the results in an easy-to-read screen for the NCMEC analyst, putting a red frame around every picture that matches the hash value of an identified child's image. A simple click on the head shot of the child gives NCMEC the contact information for the investigating officer or prosecutor in that solved case, which can be fired off in an e-mail report to the people in charge of the new case in Nebraska.

It's a brutally efficient system: CRIS can process a thousand images in twenty minutes. NCMEC can assure prosecutors that no matter how many images they send in, the central computers can spit out the results for "real children" within four days at most.

That's only the first step. NCMEC analysts also need to make sure human eyes review all the seized material. The visual check is needed because computers relying on hash values can be too precise: if an offender downloads a picture, then slightly crops or alters it in any way and reposts it, the "new" picture will have a different hash value, even though it is really the same photo. Similarly, the hash system will not recognize common traits in different pictures; for example, CRIS cannot tell that a well-traded picture of Jessica inside her bedroom and another picture of her standing outside her home are of one and the same girl. Originally, the Jessica series had 450 distinct images, but the NCMEC team found at least three thousand different versions of those pictures and had to manually add all the hash values to the Jessica category. Once the new hash values for Jessica were added to the system, any future matches may also be spotted by CRIS as a match.

When the CRIS software has finished scanning and matching the pictures, the real hard work for the humans begins: finding the children. The NCMEC investigators are always on the lookout for "new" pictures seized in the field that CRIS cannot match to any previously stored image, because there is a good chance that the abuse is recent and may be ongoing. The child's life could be in danger.

That's why NCMEC set up a special unit—separate from the growing team of analysts taking in the thousands of cybertips from the public, companies and police—devoted entirely to the hunt for clues in the pictures.

The seven people who make up the Child Victim Identification Program (CVIP) are about as far from geeks as one could imagine. Indeed, only two have advanced computer skills: a digital imaging specialist and a graphics expert who help enhance backgrounds or sharpen pictures. The others come from such diverse backgrounds as the Marines and library science studies. "We look for people with drive," said Jennifer Lee, the supervisor of CVIP. Lee herself came from the National Wildlife Federation. "People who are out there, trying new experiences and not afraid to test the boundaries or challenge themselves."

People like Christine Feller. At twenty-seven, she had a university degree in economics that had led to several years as a research assistant at the Federal Reserve Board and litigation work for the accounting firm of Arthur Andersen before she tired of "helping the rich get richer," as she puts it. She went back to school to get a master's in criminal justice and landed an intern spot at NCMEC in 2002. She's never left.

Feller laughs at the make-believe technology displayed in TV high-tech crime dramas. When her fictional counterparts on popular TV programs like *CSI* zoom in on a minuscule detail in a blurry photograph, it magically seems to get clearer—usually revealing a telltale license plate number or a phone number on a discarded piece of paper. In reality, of course, pictures get fuzzier, not sharper, the more you blow them up.

Feller and the other CVIP analysts were crime scene investigators, except that they were turning traditional detective work on its head. In most instances, police always know *where* the crime has been committed because they are called to the scene. They then try to gather evidence to find out *who* did it. With online child pornography, the steps are reversed. Police have all the evidence in the photos themselves that a crime has been committed; they almost always have a face, if not a name, of the victim and occasionally even the face of the culprit. But they do not know *where* the crime was taking place.

Think of it as *CSI: Porn.* "We just have to figure out the clues and find out where the crime and that child are," said Feller.

Feller's attention to detail has served her well. In early November 2002, Interpol contacted NCMEC to share information about a series of forty photographs featuring a young girl with blond ringlets. None of the pictures was sexually graphic, but because they were heavily traded in child porn Internet newsgroups and found on the computers of convicted pedophiles in Europe, police were concerned. Feller, along with Collins and Lee, began scrutinizing the series for clues. On the TV screen in the background of one photo Feller saw the logo "GPTV"—Georgia Public Television. In another shot, the little girl was holding a high school yearbook; by magnifying the text in the book, Feller was able to identify a school in that state. Now she had to try to narrow down the girl's location even further. With the help of COPINE—the database maintained by academics in Ireland—Feller obtained over nine hundred additional pictures of the girl. More pictures, more clues.

In the hunt to rescue a child, investigators never know which small clue will be the casebreaker. The list was growing: there was a red Toyota Supra GT with no license plates; a white house with burgundy shutters; shell casings from Remington ammunition on the floor; pictures of two other girls, including one with her name on a necklace. In one photo taken on a summer day, the girl was wearing a cast to protect a broken left wrist—leaving open the possibility that police could check hospital records. In another picture, she was wearing a tiara in her hair and there were balloons in the background—suggesting it was her birthday. By matching the date imprinted by the camera in the coding of the photograph, the CVIP team could pinpoint her approximate date of birth.

As it turned out, none of those clues was decisive. The big break, instead, came from a simple photo of the girl sitting on the floor of a wood-paneled den. On the shelves behind her were various sports trophies and photographs of award winners. Feller blew up the clearest one, showing a man smiling. Local police in Bibb County, Georgia, took the picture to the high school Feller had already singled out thanks to the yearbook. The school was able to identify the award winner: he turned out not to be the offender but he was able to identify a neighbour, Troy Ray Bennett, who had access to the girl in the photo as well as two other children. In early March 2003, when the police went looking for Bennett, they found him living in a shed behind his mother's house. Amid the barren setting, multiple computers were hooked up. It was Bennett who was behind the seemingly innocent pictures of the blond girl widely distributed online. But investigators were certain there was child abuse as well. Sure enough, under a mattress, police found many 8 1/2 x 11 glossy photographs of the little girl—this time, in clearly exploitative poses. Police linked Bennett to several rapes in the area and he eventually received two hundred years in prison on various accounts of child molestation.

Videos of child abuse were growing increasingly popular on the Web because they provided offenders with more details—but for the NCMEC sleuths that also meant more visual and audio clues to uncover. In May 2003, NCMEC received a twenty-one-minute pornographic video from the Naval Criminal Investigative Service that had surfaced on the Web in Japan. It showed a man engaged in sexual acts with two prepubescent girls. The movie was labeled "Gordo"—"fat" in Spanish—perhaps a reference to the porky physique of the abuser.

"Red flags went up immediately," said Michelle Collins. Her staff was used to seeing the most popular videos and stills over and over again, but these were new. "We had never seen these children before."

Videos—with rapid camera movements, pans across a room and sounds of people talking—are usually much richer in evidence than tightly controlled photographs. Feller and her colleagues isolated three distinctive tattoos on the man—the name Ismael on his left hand; a heart, pierced with an arrow and the Marine Corps initials U.S.M.C. on his right hand; and a knife with an anchor on his left arm. The man and his victims spoke Spanish; there was a snippet of one of the girls' names. Perhaps the best clue was a brief shot of a campaign poster on the wall in the room with the slogan "Working with Mayor Mike." Feller began to compile American cities whose mayors had that first name.

NCMEC also put out the word to Interpol and European law enforcement agencies that they were working on this video. Within days, Swedish authorities contacted the Americans with a new, apparently more recent video. The CVIP analysts immediately noticed that the girls had aged a couple of years and—perhaps most worrisome—they had become more accustomed to Gordo's abuse.

At one point in the second video, Feller could hear a radio jingle from "Big D 103," a station Feller was able to track down to Hartford. That city was also where a mayor named Mike Peters dominated the political scene for much of the 1990s. The radio station was promoting a contest for a free lunch at a local restaurant; when Feller contacted the station, she was able to pinpoint the time of the contest—and therefore the most recent video—to about five years earlier.

Now Feller had the place and time; she needed the IDs. She isolated the best head shots of Gordo, as well as various close-ups of his tattoos and other bodily features. Then she took the clearest pictures of the girls' faces to NCMEC's Forensic Imaging Unit, which helps to locate missing children by creating computer-projected images of how they would look several years after their disappearance. In this case, Feller asked them to age the girls about five years. With these pictures in hand, the Connecticut State Police and the U.S. Postal Inspection Service began an exhaustive search, combing through motor vehicle, military and police records as well as canvassing local schools. It took six months, but eventually they located both girls—by then ages fifteen and sixteen—at a school. "They were stunned," said the police officer who showed the girls excerpts from the movie. "[They were] emotionally angry and upset that the video had made it so far away."

One of the victims identified Gordo as the ex-boyfriend of a relative. The girls said he had given them money and first approached them to "model" bathing suits and lingerie. Through another informant, police learned his address—and the fact that he was about to flee. On October 10, 2003, they burst into the apartment of Ismael Cohen, a native of Peru who had lived in the Hartford area for nearly thirty years. Police found two airplane tickets to Peru and eight packed duffel bags in the apartment, which matched the room shown in the video NCMEC had analyzed.

The farthest Cohen got to travel was to a jail cell in Hartford.

*   *   *

Sometimes the saving of a child starts simply by believing her. The sleuthing talents of Feller and the CVIP team, along with database of cybertips that NCMEC was amassing, were put to the test when an Indiana investigator had an unshakable conviction that a little girl was telling the truth.

She was a bright if sometimes difficult student. The fourth-grade teachers at the Walt Disney Elementary School saw Ann* as a "kind of a troublemaker," as one of them put it. She told lies, they said. A shame, they all agreed, because Ann was lucky to have one of the most popular teachers, Timothy J. Wyllie. "He gets along fantastic with the kids," said one of his co-workers.

Even Ann's parents were fans. "My parents told me how lucky I was to have you—to have a teacher like you," Ann later said. "I listened to you. I trusted you."

Ann lived in the small town of Mishiwaka, a middle-class community just outside South Bend, Indiana. The kind of pleasant town parents flock to because it feels so much safer than the big cities. But Ann had a secret too terrible to share. During lunch or recess, Mr. Wyllie would summon the nine-year-old girl for "tutoring sessions." What he taught her was to submit to him while he forced her to undress as he took pictures of her—and then did much worse.

"Every single day I was scared to go to school," Ann said. "I hated going to school."

"If you tell anyone, I'll post your picture on the Internet," Mr. Wyllie had warned his pupil. "And I will flunk you."

So the frightened pupil stayed silent. Besides, who would believe the stories a troublemaker told about one of the favorite teachers in school?

The hardest predator to catch was the one who hid in the open.

Ann's burden was all too typical of the dilemma faced by countless other child victims of abuse: whom do I tell? And if I tell, will they blame me? "Most children are too frightened to come forward," said Chris Feller of NCMEC. "And so we're only hearing about a small fraction of the abuse that is taking place."

In Ann's case, it took her two years to muster the courage to open up, but when she did, there was no stopping her. It began on a Thursday, February 6, 2003. Ann was now almost twelve. Her mother had confided to her that she had not yet quit smoking, something she had promised to do. Then she added: "I want you to know that you can come to me and talk about anything."

That was all Ann needed.

"I've got a big secret to tell you," she told her mother, spilling out her grief.

Ann's mother had the presence of mind to immediately call the police; an officer arrived by 8:30 P.M. and took a report. He told Ann's mother to take her daughter to the Child Abuse Services, Investigation and Education Center (CASIE), where a trained child interviewer would meet with Ann. Police officers can be very good at interrogating suspects, but it takes a special skill to get a young victim of abuse to open up. The CASIE professionals were trained to ask simple, open-ended questions without leading or manipulating the child in a certain direction.

At 11:20 the next morning, the forensic interviewer began speaking with Ann. Authorities videotaped her allegations while a police officer and a deputy prosecutor watched. It was an unsettling day for the girl, but Ann got lucky: her case was turned over to a newly hired computer investigator for the prosecutor's office, a dedicated cop named Mitch Kajzer whose high-tech expertise was matched only by his zeal to save children. "If she had reported three months earlier, it's possible it would have been buried, nothing would have happened," says Chief Deputy Prosecutor Ken Cotter, who headed the Family Violence/Special Victims Unit. "But Mitch was Mr. Bulldog. He wasn't going to let this go."

As a long-serving police officer, Kajzer was shot four times in line of duty in 1992 at a routine traffic stop. The permanent nerve damage numbed the entire back of his left leg; he forced himself to return to work for five more years, but found the constant pain in his leg after riding around in a patrol car all day too much to bear. He left the force, took certification courses to enhance the computer forensic skills he already had and landed a high-paying job as a computer programmer and network engineer in the private sector. But as his wife told him one month into his new career, "There's no sparkle in your eye."

Kajzer agreed: "I missed doing some kind of meaningful work. I missed that personal satisfaction of actually helping people."

So he seized the chance to come back to policing—even if it meant a steep cut in salary—when the St. Joseph County prosecutor's office asked him to join their team as a computer analyst. Initially they wanted him to focus on drugs, helping with seizures of dealers' electronic files and tracking police statistics of gang activity. Two weeks into the job, at 10 a.m, Kajzer walked into Cotter's office.

"I'm bored. I'm done for the day," he told the prosecutor. "I'm running out of things to do. Here's a thought."

Kajzer's thought—he had already typed up a proposal and checked out all the legalities—was to do locally what Emily Vacher and other FBI agents were doing across the country: undercover, online. He got the go-ahead and began to track down local men, who were distributing and trading images, posing as a thirteen-year-old girl. But after weeks into that job, Kajzer suddenly found he had a very real girl on his hands.

At 3:30 in the afternoon of Friday, February 7, he sat down to watch the videotape of Ann's allegations and began taking notes. "One thing that really struck me as I was watching Ann is that she was actually on the floor doing the various poses she said Wyllie forced her into. A child that age shouldn't know how to pose like that. I was thinking, There's no way this child is lying. There's no way this child can be making this stuff up."

Kajzer dashed off a search warrant and rushed to the judge's home that evening. The magistrate read the warrant but then looked up with a frown on his face.

"You've got the allegation, but has anything more recently come up?" he asked.

"What do you mean?" Kajzer responded, fighting a sinking feeling in his stomach.

"Anything happen today or yesterday?" the judge continued, referring to the fact that search warrants generally have to relate to a current or ongoing criminal offense.

"No, there's not. This is what we've got," the investigator said. Kajzer felt the "staleness" of evidence wasn't an issue. Kajzer knew that unlike fingerprints on a weapon, for example, traces of online child porn activity can leave a digital trace for years on a computer or a backup CD disk.

The judge wasn't buying it: here was a child's allegation against a respected teacher about something that happened two years ago, with nothing to substantiate it other than the child's word. Kajzer tried to convey how truthfully he felt Ann came across in her interview, but to no avail. In the end, the judge denied the search warrant.

Strike one.

That same evening, two officers dropped by Wyllie's home for what police euphemistically call "a knock and talk." Wyllie, then thirty-seven, was a handsome man, his neatly combed brown hair barely touching his ears, and his soft eyes highlighted by stylish rimless glasses. A single man, never married, he had been an attorney before turning to teaching. A local paper ran a laudatory story back in 1992 about how a well-paid lawyer was leaving his practice to become a teacher because he wanted to work with children. No doubt in part because of his legal background, Wyllie showed poise and confidence when he greeted the officers—so much so that he agreed to accompany them back to the police station for a chat. Once there, the police kept their remarks about their investigation to generalities.

"Do you know of any student who would make that kind of allegation?" they asked.

"Yes. Ann," came the teacher's immediate reply.

"Why is that?"

"Because she likes to tell stories, and she makes up lies a lot," Wyllie said, and he left the police station a free man.

Kajzer, meanwhile, had returned home later that evening, discouraged. He called a good friend who was a teacher at Walt Disney Elementary and who also happened to be assigned to the classroom right next to Wyllie's.

"Tell me about him," he began.

"One of the best teachers there," she said, without missing a beat. "Well respected by the staff. He frequently fills in as principal and is in line to become a principal."

"Tell me about Ann."

"She gets in trouble at school a lot," his teacher friend said. "She tells a lot of lies."

Just what Kajzer needed. Strike two.

The teacher's characterization of Wyllie didn't bother him—some offenders do get along well with kids—but Kajzer was concerned about

Ann. Not that he didn't believe her story for a minute. "If she had a reputation of telling lies—even if she is truthful about these assaults—then she is opening herself for some tough cross-examination if she does have a history of fabricating," Kajzer explained. He needed incontrovertible proof that Ann was telling the truth.

Kajzer wasn't giving up. On Saturday morning, he typed up a prosecutor's subpoena—which required a lesser burden of proof than a search warrant—for Wyllie's computer at school and went back to the same judge.

"Well, I guess there's more than one way to skin a cat," the magistrate said with a smile.

That same day, police went to the school and seized the computer and some disks right next to it. By midweek, Kajzer had finished his forensic examination and came up empty. Not that he had really expected Wyllie to have been so reckless as to leave compromising material on a public computer. There was some fragmented text evidence that adult porn sites had been visited, but that was it—no images, no cached Web pages and nothing related to child abuse.

Strike three.

School authorities, of course, quickly learned that something was up, and with a police report on file, they had little choice but to suspend Wyllie. He would eventually resign by the end of school year and leave town to pursue a law career in the Chicago area. No one knew that Ann was behind the allegations, but many of the staff and students were sad to lose such a popular teacher. Ann, meanwhile, was finding that speaking out was just the beginning, not the end, of a grueling ordeal. She was frustrated and bewildered.

"I told the truth, but he hasn't been arrested," she complained.

"We do believe you," her mom said, trying to comfort her. "The police are working on it."

In truth, there was not much more Kajzer could do. He sent some head shots of Ann to ICE, which, along with NCMEC, kept a database of child victim images to see if they could find a match, but they came up blank. He tried to keep in touch with the family to assure them he had not forgotten them.

"I do believe your child," was all he could say. "I know this guy did it."

Over his many years of policing, Kajzer had learned one important lesson: "Never take cases personally, because you'll end up going
nuts." To that end, he had even avoided meeting Ann face-to-face
because he didn't want any sympathetic feelings for her to color his
investigation. Every time he went over to her house to talk to her
parents, they arranged for Ann not to be there or to stay in another
room. But it didn't matter—her story got to him: "I broke my own
rule. This is one of the few cases that I took personally. I was going
to prove it."

But how?

For Kajzer and the prosecutor, Ken Cotter, the challenge was twofold:
they had to be able to prove Ann's allegations of abuse, and they had
to find some trace of the photos she claimed her teacher took. She was
very specific that Wyllie used a digital camera, because she remembered being shown some of the photos in the screen on the back of the
small camera. Cotter knew that if they ever went to trial, the first thing
the jury was going to ask was, Where are the photos?

It took more than fifteen months after Ann filed her complaint for
the first break to come—and it was not quite what Kajzer and Cotter
had expected. It happened thanks to the key role that NCMEC was
beginning to play as a national hub of information and coordination.
One of the national center's steady stream of tips came from the
Internet service providers who by law had to forward reports of any
illegal images they find on their servers. The ISPs generally kept cached
copies of the offending Web pages or chat postings for several weeks,
if not months. It was this rich database of massive files that allowed
NCMEC to help investigators in Operation Hamlet track down some
of the Web histories of the offenders. Now it was going to prove instrumental in helping a girl from Indiana.

As part of its regular filings of child abuse found on its servers, on
May 25, 2004, Yahoo had sent NCMEC a CyberTipline report on a
user named kluvsitruff@yahoo.com—an abbreviation for "kid loves it
rough"—who had uploaded child abuse images to a chat group. Yahoo
had also provided the IP address of the user. Initial analysis indicated
that the IP address was related to a dial-up account using an ATT
account out of New York, but a subsequent subpoena to ATT revealed

that the account was held by one Timothy Wyllie of Indiana. By law, these subpoenas can be kept confidential from the suspect until charges are laid.

NCMEC passed on the information to Indiana authorities, and by mid-June it came to the attention of a very excited Mitch Kajzer. "I saw who it came back to—and I was very pleased," he said. Just as he had hoped, the man's digital footprints had turned up sooner or later in the muck of online child porn. Kajzer immediately went over to the apartment complex listed on the account, only to discover that Wyllie had moved to Wheaton, Illinois, a suburb of Chicago. But the trail was hot now, and Kajzer stepped up his pursuit. On June 16, he fired off an e-mail to Chris Feller at NCMEC, giving her Timothy J. Wyllie's full name and his Yahoo username.

Back in Alexandria, Feller tapped in to NCMEC's vast database of child abuse reports, suspects and chat room logs that had been filed over the years by Internet providers, police or concerned citizens to look for any scrap of information on Wyllie.

Nothing came back on his online name. But when Feller ran Wyllie's surname, she found a technical assistance report that NCMEC had provided to the Dallas police when, in an operation called Sitekey, they took down a Web site called daily-lolita.com and obtained a database of its subscribers. In that database was a credit card number for a Timothy Wyllie and an e-mail address with the name luv2teach10yos— the last three letters shorthand for "ten-year-olds." Next, Feller traced that name through NCMEC's computers and came up with two older CyberTipline reports that Wyllie had made to a Yahoo group.

Like many in the Yahoo community, "luv2teach10yos" had filled out a detailed profile. He was pretending he had a ten-year-old daughter:

Name:	TJ
Marital Status:	Divorced
Occupation:	Teacher
Hobbies:	Loving my 10 yo [year-old] daughter. Looking for like-minded traders with real pics.
Latest News:	having lots of family fun.
Favorite Quote:	"Who has a daughter out there?

By the next day, June 17, Feller filed her detailed report with Kajzer, and he kept digging. In his Yahoo profile, "TJ" had also provided his ICQ account number. Short for "I Seek You," ICQ is one of the oldest and most popular forms of instant messaging on the Internet, with about 150 million registered users—ideal for a quick chat but also a perfect place for pedophiles to meet. Kajzer accessed the man's public ICQ profile. There too he had listed his first name as TJ and this time used "teacher" as his nickname. "Love preteen and young teen girls with tight little bodies," he wrote in his profile. "Nothing taboo for me."

TJ said he was interested in trading pictures of real daughters and boasted he "had a special ten-year-old angel who will do anything that Daddy says." Right there on his ICQ Web page, TJ had posted a picture of his "angel." It showed a fully clothed girl standing in front of a kitchen table.

And Mitch Kajzer froze.

Because he recognized the furniture. And the girl. She looked about four or five years younger, but in his gut Kajzer knew the girl in the photograph was Ann.

Yes, I've got you now! the investigator thought.

The photo was not proof—yet—that Wyllie had abused Ann. But it was evidence of his sexual obsession with young girls, and it tied that obsession directly to the pupil who claimed he had molested her. "It corroborated her story," said prosecutor Ken Cotter. "Now at least we had a fighting chance if we went to court."

Kajzer had to make sure the photograph was indeed of Ann. At 3 P.M. that day, he went over to her house and showed it to both her parents—independently—and they confirmed that it was indeed their daughter. Her mother recalled that Wyllie had asked Ann and her fellow students to bring in family photos for a class project, and Ann had selected that one.

Later that evening, Kajzer went back online—this time assuming one of his undercover disguises as Justine, a twelve-year-old girl living in Indiana who liked "chatting and shopping." He added luv2teach10yos to his ICQ buddy list to see if Wyllie's account was still active—and sure enough the next day Kajzer got a message back that TJ had added Justine to his buddy list. Kajzer then got subpoenas to get Yahoo and ICQ to confirm that Wyllie was the owner of those accounts. Finally, he sat down to draw up the arrest warrant, charging Wyllie with one count of molesting Ann.

This time, Kajzer had no trouble persuading a judge to sign the warrant. He was closing in on Wyllie. "But we were a long way from being able to prove it beyond a reasonable doubt in court," he said.

Kajzer's case got an unexpected boost when he discovered that the FBI also had Wyllie in their sights—although that discovery came about only through a remarkable coincidence of timing. Kajzer had reached out to an officer in the police department in Wheaton, Illinois, to execute his arrest warrant for Wyllie. On the afternoon of Friday, June 25, as the officer was at the state attorney general's office getting the paperwork in order, the FBI also happened to be there, asking for the name of a trustworthy police officer who could help them serve a warrant without the chance of any leaks. They were referred to the officer helping Kajzer, and they immediately realized they were after the same man.

Six months earlier, the FBI's Innocent Images Task Force had taken over the online identity of a Miami resident after he had been arrested for possession of child pornography. They infiltrated a Yahoo chat group called "running and giggling," and one active participant who went by the name of "dynamictwist" had posted at least five still photographs and one video of child pornography. A subpoena to Yahoo helped the FBI trace dynamictwist back to Wyllie's Wheaton apartment. Another search warrant on Yahoo accounts found 370 additional pornographic images that Wyllie had stored on Yahoo servers.

Kajzer and the FBI agreed to coordinate their actions: he had an arrest warrant for Wyllie's arrest for hands-on abuse; they had a search warrant for his apartment and computer. Kajzer drove up to the Chicago area on Sunday to meet with the FBI agents. The next morning at five o'clock, sixteen police officers raided the suspect's small one-bedroom apartment.

Kajzer got his first look at the man he had been trying to nail for the past year and a half as the FBI led him out to a police car. Wyllie looked self-possessed—and for good reason. Inside his apartment, the FBI's quick search had found nothing on his computer. (When Kajzer was able later to do a more careful forensic study he found indications that Wyllie had used an external Zip drive.) Wyllie asked for a lawyer.

"Are you through?" he asked the FBI agents as he sat in their vehicle, confident that he'd avoided any legal problems.

Then Kajzer approached the car and politely asked the former teacher to step outside.

"I work for the state prosecutor's office in St. Joseph County in Indiana, and I have a warrant for your arrest for child molestation," Kajzer said.

Wyllie rolled his eyes, as if to say, What, this again?

Kajzer simply handcuffed him, then read him his rights. The investigator looked stoic, but inside he was beaming.

"Cuffing him felt fantastic," he recalled.

At 8:30 A.M., Kajzer called Ann's parents. Her father picked up the phone, and Kajzer told him the welcome news. There was a long period of silence and then heartfelt words of thanks. Wyllie was finally behind bars.

Kajzer was determined to keep him there. The suspect was in jail, and there was plenty of evidence showing his online habits. The photo of a fully-clothed Ann as his "ten-year-old angel" posted on his Web page would help support—though not prove—any claims she made of sexual abuse. For Kajzer, Ann's case had become a passion, if not an obsession. He didn't want the case, if it ever went to court, to degenerate into a "he said, she said" debate, especially between a frightened child and a savvy teacher. He wanted direct proof that would make Ann's allegations unassailable.

Once more, NCMEC's database would hold the key. The FBI had gone over Wyllie's computer carefully, but Kajzer was convinced that there was more. The feds had found a few hundred pictures that Wyllie had taken of children inside the school—nothing illegal, but Kajzer found several of Ann. Wyllie had used some of those ordinary pictures in his various Yahoo profiles, spicing them up with lewd captions. He listed Ann's Occupation as "Play toy for Daddy and friends." Under her Hobbies, he wrote, "Playing naughty naked games with whoever makes me." Most important, while the FBI came up with only six screen names that Wyllie had used while on his home computer, Kajzer found twenty-nine Yahoo names and fourteen ICQ accounts.

He reached out again to Chris Feller at NCMEC and asked her to run the screen names. This time she hit the jackpot. There were dozens of reports connected to these newly discovered names that Yahoo had filed with NCMEC. Because the ISPs connect to NCMEC through a secure server, the companies can forward not just information but the images themselves. NCMEC, in turn, can then make the images available to law enforcement through a safe internal network known as VPN—Virtual Private Network. In effect, the pictures are not being distributed—they are sitting on a server until designated police officers need to access them. That way, neither the ISPs nor NCMEC's civilian staff are directly possessing or distributing the material, which in strict legal terms can only be handled by law enforcement.

Using the VPN, the Indiana State Police burned a CD with the photos for Kajzer to examine. It was late on a Friday after Kajzer got back from a training conference before he got a chance to look at the CD from NCMEC. He started going through the hundreds of graphic pictures of child abuse one by one. It was going to be a long night.

When he stumbled across one image, he suddenly stopped.

A young girl sat completely nude, her legs spread. Behind her was a kiln. Exactly the way Ann had described the arts room where Wyllie had assaulted her. And the frightened ten-year-old captured in that picture was Ann.

"This is it!" he remembered thinking. "I got goose bumps."

He cropped the photo to show only Ann's face and the background of the room, drove to her home and showed the picture to her mother.

"That is Ann," she said. "And I know that room."

"That felt very good," Kajzer recalled. "That was the first rock-solid piece of evidence we had."

He walked into the office of Ken Cotter, holding the photo in his hand. "I don't know if you want to see this," he said, warning the prosecutor about the distasteful and graphic picture of abuse. "But it came off Wyllie's computer."

Cotter knew he had Wyllie nailed. "It was a huge sense of relief. Now there didn't seem any question that a jury could find him other than guilty."

He picked up the phone to call Wyllie's attorney. "Just so you know, we have a nude photo of the girl—in the school," he said. "You're welcome to come take a look at it."

"That won't be necessary," was the quick reply.

The prosecutor offered Wyllie a thirty-year sentence if he agreed to plead guilty to one count of child molestation. No room for any bargaining. Take it or leave it.

Wyllie took the deal.

Cotter was always pleased when he secured a plea in a child abuse case, because even if he won a guilty verdict from a jury, the accused could always claim he had been railroaded. "When they plead, they acknowledge that it's all true," he said. "Many people who knew Wyllie couldn't believe that someone like him would do something like that until that day."

On Friday, February 10, 2005, Timothy J. Wyllie was set to appear in Superior Court to describe in detail before the judge his assault on Ann, as part of the plea agreement. It would be the first time Ann would see her abuser since she had been his captive pupil. It was also the first time she got to meet the law enforcement officer who helped put her tormentor away. She knew Mitch Kajzer's name, of course, and had seen him on TV. But they had never met face-to-face. Her parents drove her to Kajzer's office on the way to the courthouse. She walked in, dressed smartly in a winter coat, looked at him—and smiled. Kajzer took her in his arms to hug her, and Ann thanked the burly investigator for all that he had done. Kajzer admits he got a little choked up but shed no tears. Those would come later.

As they arrived at the courthouse, Kajzer tried to keep the conversation light. They joked about how well she was doing in school; Ann wanted to know about his gun and his Tazer. When she nervously mentioned that she had never been in a courtroom before, Kajzer smiled and said, "Come on—follow me."

She accompanied him down the hallway and up the stairs. Kajzer got one of the deputies to open an unused courtroom. She jumped up on the judge's chair. A little more relaxed now, Ann made her way back down to the courtroom where Wyllie was about to make his appearance. With Kajzer and her parents, she watched through an open door in a side hallway adjacent to the courtroom usually reserved for court staff. It was as close as Ann wanted to get, still uncomfortable being in the same room as Wyllie.

She stood no more than thirty feet away as her teacher, now forty-one, described how he had molested her repeatedly back in 2001. He spared few details, describing how he took pictures of her in various stages of undress, had sex with her and told her he would fail her if she told anyone. Ann stood there without moving. She just listened to Wyllie without saying a word. Then, when it was done, she turned, smiled and walked away. Outside, Kajzer gave her another big hug and congratulated her on how strong she had been. Cotter, too, was struck by her bravery. "She wanted to hear him say he did those things. It helped her hold her head up high and say to the world, See, I told you!"

Five months later, on July 20, 2005, Wyllie would make his final court appearance for sentencing. Though it was not required, Ann and her family decided that she should read a victim impact statement before the court. It was extremely rare for children to appear in sentencing hearings. Chief Deputy Prosecutor Ken Cotter had never seen it happen before, but he sensed that this girl was special.

Ann had told him earlier that she'd decided she wanted to become a prosecutor—and to take on child abuse cases as he did. "There was a sparkle in her eye," he said. "She saw a wrong and she saw justice. She got it. It's not going to make her whole, but it gives a sense a closure. People need to be accountable for what they did."

Still, this time, there would no standing in a hallway far away from Wyllie. "You don't have to do this," Kajzer told her, just before she walked into the courtroom. "It's probably going to be the hardest thing you'll ever do in your life. But if you do it, you're going to have such a great feeling afterward of what you accomplished."

"I understand that," she said, nodding.

Under the plea agreement, the judge was to sentence Wyllie to thirty years—not a day less or more. But family members—on both sides—wanted their say in court. Wyllie's mother was the first to speak. She apologized for her son's actions, telling Ann's family that "our whole family, our whole heart is breaking" for them. "I know what [Ann] is going through because I too was molested when I was young."

Ann's mother, for her part, had little room in her heart for forgiveness. "Instead of our daughter going out to play after lunch, or having fun with her friends at recess, she was being forced and coerced into remaining indoors, where you committed these sexual crimes against her that will forever have an impact on her," she told Wyllie. "We hope this case will serve as a wake-up call to our schools to do their jobs and protect our kids."

It was Ann, though, who held the court riveted when it was her turn to come forward and read her statement. She walked up to the left of the prosecutor, Ken Cotter. Wyllie stood just a few feet away on Cotter's right, dressed in prison greens, handcuffs on his wrists and chains on his feet. Cotter could see that Ann's hands were trembling, the paper with her handwritten notes shaking. It took her a few moments to get the nervousness out of her voice, but once she got going, there was no stopping the girl.

She began with a withering description of her ordeal at Wyllie's hands. "You were my teacher and you molested me. You hurt me . . . You pretended to care about kids, but all you cared about was yourself and your twisted, sick life. When it was my birthday—my birthday!— you didn't care. You saw it as another opportunity to attack me."

She berated him for not ending it when he had the chance. "When I told the police what you did, you lied . . . Like the coward you are, you blamed me. You didn't take responsibility. You didn't confess."

Then Ann turned to how the abuse had scarred her: "My life has changed forever because of you. When I close my eyes, I see you. I see you every day. I see you stare at me. In my life I have to be strong. Why? Because I know that there are wicked, evil people like you who like to hurt kids.

"The memories of what you did will always be with me," she continued. "But I am strong. I have to be. I am afraid of evil, but I will not back down in the face of it."

She concluded by thanking her parents, Kajzer and "all of the people who believed in me and worked hard to put you behind bars. These people care. They are not phony like you, Mr. Wyllie. They help kids."

It was one of the most powerful courtroom scenes that Cotter had ever witnessed. "She's up there, rock solid, reading that statement without flinching, and probably everyone in the courtroom has tears in their eyes."

By the time Wyllie himself spoke, it was almost anticlimactic. "I know that anything I say cannot come even close to saying how sorry I really am to Ann and [her] family," he said. "I just want Ann to understand that nothing that happened was her fault. It was all my fault. I've thrown away basically my life . . . I will be in prison for the rest of my life . . . I give the time because that's all I have to give," he said to a hushed courtroom. "I accept the punishment of the court."

(Wyllie's contribution was short-lived. In early 2007, he would appear before a Superior Court judge to ask for a new trial, claiming he was "misled" before his plea agreement.)

The judge wrapped it all up with a few terse sentences: "Thank you, folks. Defendant appears. Sentencing held. Guilty plea unconditionally accepted. Pursuant to binding plea, defendant sentenced to thirty years."

And it was over.

Outside the courtroom, Ann came running down the lobby into Kajzer's arms, joyful.

"You are so right!" she exclaimed. "Yes, it was hard, but I feel so great now!"

Chris Feller of NCMEC also got the chance to meet the girl she had helped. NCMEC staff studiously avoid meeting the children whose images flood their computers all the time. There are hundreds of them, and they cannot afford the emotional investment or the toll it would take. But Feller, by coincidence, was in town for the official opening of a new high-tech crime unit to be headed by Kajzer, so she made her way to the court. When introduced to the NCMEC analyst, Ann thanked her politely.

"No, thank *you*," Feller responded, "for being so strong and standing up to him. Because a lot of these kids don't want to speak out."

Prosecutor Ken Cotter had seen many victims of child abuse walk away from a trial—even a successful one—still shattered. But not Ann. "At that point she had worked through the hurt and pain. It didn't beat her down. And she didn't want these things to happen to other kids."

There was still some legal fallout from the case in the ensuing months. Wyllie faced federal charges for distributing child pornography and eventually got ninety months, to be served after he completed his three decades for abusing Ann. Her parents also sued the school board for not protecting their daughter. Her mother had hoped the incident would be "a wake-up call," but apparently school officials weren't listening. The school corporation's liability insurance company launched a defense of "contributory negligence," suggesting that Ann was partly to blame for not reporting the molestation for nearly two years.

Ann herself had transferred out of Walt Disney School once it became widely known what had happened. She enrolled in a private Catholic school. When things finally calmed down, Kajzer took a moment to speak to the schoolteacher who had first told him that Ann was a "troublemaker."

"Wasn't that her way of dealing with it?" Kajzer said. "She comes to school every day and is being sexually assaulted. What is a ten-year-old to do about that? Maybe act out and get sent to the office. That'll keep you from getting assaulted. Makes sense now, doesn't it?" In hindsight, the teacher agreed that the girl's behavior took on a different aspect.

Kajzer, meanwhile, had his hands full as commander of a bustling new High-Tech Crime Unit. Instead of being its lone member, he now had a staff of nine. His caseload grew from a handful at the start to over 100 in 2004 and 221 in 2005. Every child pornography case where criminal charges were laid ended with a guilty plea except one: the only man who elected to go to trial was convicted by a jury after just an hour of deliberations.

But Ann's case will always be special to him. To this day, he often reads her victim impact statement to the court at police training sessions he conducts across the country—and he still can't get through it without the hair standing up on the back of his neck.

"It was one of those cases that I would have worked forever," he said. "So many children never disclose what happened to them because they say, 'No one will believe me—they'll think I'm lying.' But Ann had the courage to go ahead. This could have been one of those cases of 'we can't prove it—sorry,' and unfortunately those cases happen every day. But Ann deserved better than that.

"All children do."

Eight

CHOICES AND CONSEQUENCES

I'll tell you right now, if it was your kid or my kid, you would want the police to do whatever they could to break down the door and rescue that child.
—DET. SGT. PAUL GILLESPIE, TORONTO POLICE SERVICE

It was not the kind of mail the postal workers in the small town of Alvesta, Sweden, were used to handling.

In fact, strictly speaking, it was not even mail. When they came to work one spring morning in 2004, they found among the piles of letters and packages several unmarked and unwrapped cassettes from a video camera. Playing the tapes to find out to whom they might belong, they discovered to their horror that the cassettes were filled with hours and hours of graphic images of child abuse. They immediately handed over the videos to the Swedish National Police, but the authorities could not make out the language spoken on the tape.

The Swedes took the material to one of the annual gatherings of child pornography investigators that Interpol had begun organizing. That year, the meeting was in Sri Lanka during a sweltering spring, and in a stuffy conference room they showed the tapes. Two of the attendees were Daniel Szumilas and Corinna Koch, investigators with the German Bundeskriminalamt (BKA), the federal police roughly equivalent to the FBI. "That's German," they said immediately. It was the start of a four-month quest across Germany as they raced to rescue four children in a single family.

"Normally a case like this would stop when police would say, 'This is not our language, this is not our problem, so we can't do anything about it,'" said Szumilas. "But in our business, international relationships are very important. We have a bond."

Szumilas and Koch were two of nine officers—along with a couple of civilian analysts—who made up the BKA's Child Pornography Unit. At the federal police headquarters in Wiesbaden, they spent hours reviewing the tapes they had picked up at the Sri Lanka conference: four cassettes with about four hours of abuse. Eventually they were able to sort out the cast of characters: there were two boys and two girls, evidently part of a family, because they would occasionally refer to each other as a brother or sister. The offender—either the father or some kind of guardian, named Frankie on the tapes—had one remarkable distinguishing figure: he had only one leg and wore a prosthesis.

The videos had been time-stamped and spanned eight years from 1995 to 2003. That led to one of the most troubling revelations. The more Szumilas and Koch studied the tapes, the more they became convinced that the eight-year-old boy being assaulted in the earlier tapes was the same person as the sixteen-year-old who was abusing his younger sisters in the newer videos. "We didn't know what to make of it, but we looked at it over and over again," said Szumilas. "The boy had just grown up: the victim becomes the offender." They later learned that the other boy, his brother, had also been trained to become an abuser.

Szumilas later discovered that the father was planning to destroy the tapes while on a vacation in Sweden, but his camera had been stolen. Szumilas could only surmise that the thief, once he saw the horrors on the tapes, had enough of a conscience to drop them in a mailbox, figuring that was the surest and safest way someone would find it and take action.

On the tapes the BKA officers could make out the faces of the offender and his four victims; they also used most of their first names. It was a good start.

Szumilas hoped Frankie's artificial leg would provide him with the next big clue. In Germany, almost every personal detail is usually stored on a government database somewhere. Some even keep medical records, including people who have prostheses; unfortunately, the largest of the five states that were the focus of the BKA's hunt was one of the few jurisdictions that did not keep such records. But there was one every town kept—the public registry. When you move in Germany, you are obliged to report the details of every member of your family to your new city. You also have to supply a photograph with your registration papers.

Szumilas figured that there could not be that many households in the country with a father called Frankie and four children with names matching those he had heard on the tapes. So the BKA team wrote to every town in the northwest—more than two hundred letters.

One week later, an official from one small town in the north called Szumilas's office. "I have a family here with these four names," he said.

"Send us some pictures," Szumilas replied, barely able to contain his excitement.

The photo was confirmation: they had found Frankie and his family. Szumilas and Koch contacted the local police and made the long drive to the town. For Szumilas, it was always somewhat nerve-racking to come to the end of a chase that had begun with pictures but finished with real people. "It's strange, because you get to know them very well, even if they are strangers," he said. "So it's a very good feeling to walk in there and recognize the victims and the crime scenes."

But the victims do not necessarily greet the police as their saviors. "It's not always people cheering and laughing," he said. On that day, the two girls, eleven and thirteen, sat at the breakfast table, clinging to each other and crying hysterically. "They look at you like, Why do you want to destroy our family? The offenders always tell the children that the abuse is normal. Some children don't understand that this is criminal and we have to take the father away." Szumilas also knew that the future was likely bleak for the children. Traumatized and twisted by years of sexual abuse, they now faced more years in a new foster family or worse, a government institution.

It was, Szumilas realized, just one of the consequences of the pursuit for predators that he and his international colleagues had undertaken. "You always have to keep in mind that you do the right thing," Szumilas said. "Someday the children will know that we rescued them."

For all their successes, there was one case that continued to haunt the BKA and their fellow investigators around the world. In Germany she was known as Schielendes Madchen, or "the Crossed-eyed Girl." In

America, her photos were known as the Angeli series. Pretty, with long blond hair, she was featured in pictures that were among the more popular for traders on the Web: she straddled a Harley; she lay across a hotel bed; she sat in a racing car at a game arcade, her skirt pulled high enough and legs parted wide enough to be revealing.

But no one could seem to identify her. And that became the obsession of one Canadian cop.

Whatever her real name was, it was obvious to Bill McGarry that the girl was being severely, consistently abused over several years by someone close to her. "You see the look in her eyes and you can tell she knew the person, that she was comfortable with the person, because in some of the pictures she was smiling," said the detective with the Child Exploitation Section of the Toronto Sex Crimes Unit. "But in some, she had a look so full of horror that it was almost like she was a zombie and the guy was basically having his way with her. She was helpless."

By early 2005, McGarry had spent almost two years trying to pinpoint a location for the young girl. Paul Gillespie, McGarry's boss, had given him some of the Angeli pictures after Gillespie returned from a European trip to meet with investigators doing work on image analysis. McGarry eventually collected over two hundred pictures of her, in thirty-five different environments. The earliest showed her at around five or six years old; in the most recent, she was perhaps nine or ten. "We're watching this little girl grow up," he said.

Growing up a prisoner of abuse. Her captor would tie her up in the basement for hours, force her to endure various sex acts and photograph them. In one set of pictures, she was naked, chained by her wrists and ankles to exercise equipment in a gym. "The guy had basically pried her open for the purpose of taking a picture," the cop said in disgust. "It was very, very disturbing."

As disturbing as the images were, McGarry's job was to get past his visceral feelings and find the girl. "Then a light bulb went on in my head," he said. Why not erase the disgust by erasing the victim from the pictures, he thought. "Imagine for a second you could just put your thumb over the kid. It's hard to look at the background when you have a kid sitting there, and 80 percent of the picture is exposed genitals. It's hard to get past that." With photo software, McGarry cropped out the girl's body, leaving a white, almost ghostlike, shape.

Now what was peripheral was central; what was just background for the abuser became the foreground for the investigator. "When you take away the victim, you see the surroundings," McGarry said. "That's where the clues are." The altered pictures made it easier on the police who had to stare at the abuse images for days on end; and it made it possible to share the pictures with outside agencies and civilians in the hunt for clues.

McGarry saw the advantage of that almost from the start when he began to analyze the pictures of the girl sitting on a motorbike. Riding the train home from work one day, he spotted a new Harley-Davidson dealership opening up. He went in later with a sanitized photo and asked if they could tell him anything about the bike. Within minutes he was surrounded by four excited mechanics as they brought their manuals and parts lists and argued over the fine points of bike physiology like zoologists analyzing a picture of a rare animal. They identified twenty-six points on the bike, a 1993 ElectraGlide, that made it unique—everything from a special clamp on the muffler to a custom air filter. Unfortunately, the picture was taken on the side where the serial number was not visible. McGarry checked with Harley-Davidson's head office in Milwaukee to find that there were about ten thousand registered owners for that model. Too large a pool to be useful, but McGarry hoped that if he ever found the abuser he could use the bike to prove his identity.

Next, McGarry tackled the pictures of Angeli in an elevator. There was a sticker on the wall next to her; he blew it up, hoping it might provide an address, but all he got was a blurred piece of paper. The logo and floor buttons told him it was a modern "Series 1" Otis elevator in a three-story building. He contacted the manufacturer; they estimated that there were about seventeen hundred possible locations in Canada and about ten times that number in the States. "Those were workable numbers, but it could take forever," McGarry said. "This kid could be an adult by the time I find her."

The detective's best, and last, hope lay in the pictures taken at her home. They were not only the most numerous but presumably they offered some of the surest pointers to her location. Slowly but surely, McGarry felt the evidence was pointing to the northeastern United States. The bricks on the outside walls of her home looked like any other building material to the nonspecialist, but McGarry discovered that to the discerning bricklayer they were as particular—and as geographically specific—as a fine wine. When he showed the bricks to manufacturers, they all agreed that they likely came from a company in Pennsylvania. McGarry also found out that bricklayers usually do not transport bricks from too far away, so he figured the house had to be somewhere in the region. He contacted the company, hoping for a list of their clients, only to discover that a recent fire had destroyed many of their documents. Another dead end.

In one photo, Angeli stood against a computer desk, her legs spread, one leg on the table and one arm behind her body. Behind her, through the window, McGarry could see a tree. He determined it was an American elm; a specialist pointed out that it had been struck by disease common to the northeastern snowbelt region; that put the house most likely not along the coast but somewhat inland. Vegetation in other piectures pointed to the same area. In one picture, the girl was sitting on her front stairs, a flower bed behind her. Once he figured out that the flowers were impatiens, McGarry joined an online chat group dedicated to enthusiasts of that annual. Identifying himself as a police officer, he asked if anyone could help him pinpoint the location of the flowers. He quickly heard back from a horticulturalist at the University of Pennsylvania, who then put him in touch with one of the world's leading experts on impatiens. She not only picked out the exact species and the companies that distributed those seeds in North America; she also determined that based on the height and other characteristics of the flowers the scene was almost certainly in the northeastern United States or southern Ontario.

McGarry was closing in on the girl, but he still could not pinpoint a state with certainty, much less a town. The case was beginning to dominate his life, taking up every moment of his thoughts on and off the job. He was becoming an expert on arcane subjects he previously didn't even know existed. In studying the bed coverings in one set of pictures of the girl, he had to determine if it was a coverlet or a duvet. "What's the difference? Well, one is four inches off the floor, and one isn't, and one is sewn in a particular way," McGarry said with a laugh. "Like, why do I need to know that? I don't even make my own bed. But when I call the manufacturer, I have to be as educated as I can about their product."

At his local Home Depot one afternoon to pick up some light bulbs, McGarry suddenly found himself thinking of the red hot tub in which he had seen the girl. He started questioning a salesclerk about hot tubs—what colors they come in, who makes them in flaming red, how widely distributed that model was. A couple of hours later, he sheepishly had to call his wife to explain why his simple errand at the hardware store had taken so long.

McGarry had started working on the Angeli file just a few months before the Toronto Sex Crimes Unit launched its mad scramble to find Jessica in the fall of 2003. Like everyone else in the office, he dropped everything he was doing to help rescue the girl whose very life seemed threatened by the increasing violence and brutality displayed in her pictures. Luckily McGarry and his colleagues solved the Jessica case in a matter of days. But with Angeli, it had been months and—despite the steady progress of clues—there had been no breakthroughs.

"You just can't throw your hands in the air and say, 'I think this is as far as I can go,'" McGarry said. He remembered turning to his fellow officers in the squad room one day.

"Come on, guys—there's got to be something else we can do!"

Gillespie shared his detective's frustration. The pictures of the girl's abuse were so popular that the Toronto cops were finding them on about half the computers they were seizing. With little hope of finding her through more cyber-sleuthing, they began to consider one of the more controversial tactics in the fight to rescue children trapped in the world of online abuse: releasing pictures of unidentified victims.

"How long do we let this go on?" asked McGarry. "If we release a photo of her, what are the inherent risks of doing that? Does she get hurt by the bad guy or killed? Does she disappear off the face of earth? Or does she get recognized by someone—and saved? Think of what this would do to a parent when suddenly the child's face is found on the front page of the newspaper. Are there options other than releasing her photo to the public?"

What they eventually decided to do would lead to a most unexpected result—and ignite a debate about how far police should go in their attempts to save children held prisoner by molesters.

* * *

If there was one country that was a showcase for the successful public distribution of victims' faces, it was Germany.

"It's always a problem, and you have to protect the children," acknowledges Daniel Szumilas of the German federal police, the BKA. He argues that the fear that an offender might further harm or even kill a child cannot paralyze police. "The abuse is real and we have to save the children."

The German police have released photos of child abuse victims and their offenders on a widely respected and widely watched national TV program, but only as a last resort and only after the police are satisfied that three criteria are present: the abuse must be recent and ongoing; it must be in Germany; and they have to be certain the case is unsolved. "We have a lot of child abuse pictures where we don't have a clue, but we don't show them to the media because then you do a lot of harm with no direct expectations," Szumilas said.

Once the three conditions are fulfilled, the police take the proposal to a prosecutor, and if he agrees, he applies to the courts for special warrant. "We get this warrant only if we've tried everything else and we have no other chance to solve the case," said Szumilas. Even then, the police release as few details on TV as possible, though they do state that the child is a victim of sexual abuse.

The results have been impressive. Since 1999, the German police have gone to the media three times with a child's face. The first time, the offender turned himself in within hours of the broadcast. In two other cases, relatives or a neighbor made a positive identification; in one of those incidents, the news was picked up by other German-language stations and rebroadcast in neighboring Austria, where a family recognized a German uncle as the suspect. "I know this harms the child in a way, because everyone knows that this child has been abused," concluded Szumilas. "But this is our final option."

But German successes have been matched by disasters in other countries when police agencies got media trigger-happy. One such case began with a lead from the U.K.'s Paul Griffiths. After a raid, British police came upon several CDs depicting some especially gruesome abuse: it showed children not just suffering sexual assault but also being drugged with needles, lying stupefied and passing out. One was a boy around eight, the other a girl around five. Griffiths could tell from the accents in the CDs and a magazine shown in one shot that the offender was from Australia. The images were sent to various Australian police forces, but nobody could find enough clues to narrow down a location any more precise than somewhere along the eastern seaboard, possibly Victoria, New South Wales or Queensland. There was a partial bumper indicating the type of vehicle likely used by the abuser but not its color; a tent seen in some of the photos was sold by too many manufacturers across the country to be useful. "We didn't know the child, we didn't know the offender, we had nothing that could clearly indicate where the child was," said Det. Senior Sgt. Jon Rouse, the operational leader of Task Force Argos for the Queensland Police.

Rouse is proud of his unit's mythological name, after a creature with a hundred eyes sent down by the Greek gods to protect a maiden, and of the scorpion that adorns the crest the team members wear. In Australia, Rouse explained, convicted pedophiles or child molesters are called "rock spiders" by other inmates, considered the lowest form of life. "The scorpion," Rouse says, "is the creature that hunts and removes them from the community." Hence the task force's motto: "Leave no stone unturned."

There is one line Rouse won't cross—and that's showing a victim's face, unless all other avenues have been exhausted.

The various police forces did have a clear picture of the offender's face, so preparations were made to distribute it on a national Crimestoppers program. Then all hell broke loose.

One of the state police agencies, without notifying other police forces, decided to release a series of stills from the video—not of the offender but of the girl—on a national TV show called *A Current Affair.* Her face was clearly visible; the program described her sexual assault at the hands of a middle-aged man. "I just nearly fell over," said Rouse. "I couldn't believe this media report was being done without consultation with anybody else."

If Rouse was stunned, the girl's mother was horrified and aghast. Like Rouse, she had been watching TV and suddenly saw a picture of her daughter on the screen; it later transpired that the girl's grandfather had been abusing her, unbeknownst to the rest of the family. After the mother of four from a town in Victoria notified police, a media circus ensued; reporters camped outside the girl's school. The family eventually had to move. Critics blasted the police for acting precipitately; there was even talk of charging them, since under Australia law any person who publishes material that could lead to the identification of a sexual assault victim could face jail time or a fine.

True, the girl and her abuser had been identified, but at what cost to her and her family? Within the police, there was much consternation. The state police erred, said one child abuse investigator, "by not looking at the graveness of approach of doing this and by going straight for the jugular and sensationalizing the story." It would have been wiser to go through "a number of graduated steps" before releasing the girl's picture, said Peter Crawford, the detective inspector who supervises Task Force Argos in Queensland: verify she is likely in the region, release the offender's face first, show her picture in limited distribution to school officials and care workers and then, if and when there were to be a public broadcast, keep silent on the nature of the sexual abuse. None of that happened in this case.

Finding acceptable guidelines for when and how to release photos of child pornography victims was also a pressing issue for the National Center for Missing and Exploited Children in the U.S. NCMEC was famous for its zeal in distributing photos of missing children as widely and as often as possible. There was an important distinction, however: these are already fully identified children, with names and addresses, who have been abducted—often by feuding parents—or who have disappeared. Even then, NCMEC distributes the photos of a missing child only with the permission of a parent or guardian.

The situation of unidentified children whose abuse photos are circulated on the Web is entirely different, said Michelle Collins of NCMEC. "It's very easy to say that if a kid is being sexually abused, don't you think we should do everything in our power to save that kid?" she said. "But it's not that black and white. Emotion has to slow down, and practicality has to step in to ensure that all investigative methods are exhausted, because the ramifications could be horrible."

To help police grapple with the legal and ethical complexities, NCMEC's board came up with a detailed, five-page policy guideline on releasing pictures to identify victims of ongoing child pornography abuse. It states that every effort should be made first to check with international, national and local police to ensure that the child has not already been identified. Next, police should try to narrow down the location where the image was produced. Then restricted inquiries to school officials, child protection agencies and prosecutors can follow. The central idea was controlled distribution, starting with the narrowest, most local area possible. "You expose the child in a limited way first to law enforcement, and then you expand the circle slowly," said Collins. "You don't start on TV. You start with the people who may have encountered the child before."

Collins disagreed with the criticism from some police quarters that NCMEC's restrictions obliged police to jump through so many hoops that a child's picture would never get extensive release. "I don't think they're hoops, I think they're solid investigative practice," she said.

But even the most carefully designed practices can fall short in a confrontation with the confusing reality of rescuing victims of child exploitation.

What frustrated the investigators trying to track Angeli was the brazen confidence of her abuser. He seemed so at ease that he was taking pictures of her in amusement arcades, at hotels and in other public locales. "He's committing these acts in some high-risk places," Paul Gillespie said. "It shows a lot of arrogance. He's obviously not too worried about getting caught."

His officer, Bill McGarry, had been posting news about his hunt for Angeli on Groove, the secure Internet exchange network that allowed child abuse investigators to swap leads and tips. The team had sent photos of her to American law enforcement agencies to see if anyone had other news. Gillespie even released a cropped photo of the girl to an ophthalmologists' association; her eyes showed some kind of slight malformation, and police were hoping that perhaps a doctor would recognize her as a patient.

By the start of 2005—two years into their investigation—Gillespie was considering a much broader distribution of her photo. He was aware of the controversy that the practice engendered within law enforcement circles around the world, but he has never been for half measures. "I understand the privacy issues, but the child has to wake up every day in a terrible, miserable existence," he said. So, when all else fails, he reasoned, why not release photos of Angeli the same way that police distribute photos of children who have been kidnapped or have gone missing?

"It's funny when you think about it," he said. "If you fear a child is missing, you put out their picture and do everything to notify the public and get help. In these cases, we actually have the crime scene photos; we have the evidence that our worst fears have been realized—and we don't do anything public about it?

"I suggest to you that the problem is that their picture is already out there on the Internet," he said, anger growing in his voice. "It's not like we're making this up. It's not like this is a private collection and we're the only ones to have it. These pictures are on the Internet, already open to the public."

What McGarry and the Toronto squad did not know was that as far back as 2003, a few months before they had begun their search on the Angeli series, a police sergeant in a Chicago suburb was doing some Web searches of his own. Sgt. Mike Zaglifa was carrying out the same kind of online undercover work that the FBI had pioneered: sometimes he pretended to be an innocent boy or girl, sometimes he pretended he was one of the predators. In his role as an Internet predator, he used the nickname billyboy7 and found himself chatting online with an active trader of child abuse images who called himself NkdSister—for "naked sister." The pictures of Angeli were a hot commodity on the Web, and NkdSister seemed to have an endless supply, which he was willing to trade for fresh material, as their chat logs revealed:

> NkdSister: Do you have anything good quality/new?
> billyboy7: i told you yes . . . you were going to send some
> NkdSister: Oh ya.
> billyboy7: Be a standup trader and I will trade with you
> NkdSister: I want skinny girls

Zaglifa had a bad feeling about NkdSister, he would later tell reporters. NkdSister was explicit in what he wanted—young girls ages eight to twelve, engaged in sex. He knew the names of the other popular series. Zaglifa could tell his new online buddy had been around. So he traced the Internet address of the man who was offering so eagerly the photos of this thin waif of a girl to the Pittsburgh area.

He passed on the details to the FBI, and that was it; he went on to the many other targets just as willing to send him their pictures of abused children.

Back in Toronto, the Sex Crimes Unit had come up with an innovative compromise around Angeli. Instead of moving right away to release photos of the unknown crime scene victim, why not start with photos of the unknown crime scene?

It was a bold gamble. McGarry used image software to airbrush Angeli out of the pictures her abuser had taken while on vacation somewhere, leaving just a photo of the bed in a hotel room, the amusement arcade and a fountain outside. "This is just an ugly fountain," Paul Gillespie joked. "But the thing is, it's a real unique ugly fountain."

The logic was to enlist the support of the public—through posters, TV and newspaper announcements and Web pages—to see if anyone could recognize the hotel where Angeli had stayed with her abuser.

Just before noon on Thursday, February 3, 2005, the Toronto police released a sort of Wanted poster of the crime scene. "Do you know where this is?" the headline read over pictures of the bed, arcade, fountain and elevator. The news media flashed the story not only across Toronto but around North America. "It's an awesome thing that they're doing," said Arnold Bell, head of the FBI's Cyber Crimes Unit when he heard of the Toronto gambit. "It's pretty cutting-edge stuff. We're watching it to see how successful it's going to be. And, if it works, we have no shame. We'll copy it!"

Back in the Toronto squad room, McGarry got a phone call within minutes from a man in Peterborough, Ontario, who had just returned from a family vacation in Disney World, Florida.

"That looks just like the hotel my wife and I stayed in," he said.

The man e-mailed the cop his vacation photos and a Web link to the hotel, the Port Orleans French Quarter Resort in Orlando. McGarry could take a virtual tour on the Web site, getting 360-degree panorama views of the hotel and its rooms. He was stupefied: "It was the same, right down to the bedspreads."

At a widely covered news conference the next day, Paul Gillespie thanked the public for this new, engaged role they were playing in trying to make the Web safer. "There is a real will and a hunger from people who are more educated about the problems that the Internet brings," he said. "This investigation is not over, but we now know where a crime scene was."

Bill McGarry allowed himself a glimmer of hope. Suddenly the "Disney girl," as the media had christened her, was real. Not a name yet. Not a home. But a real place visited by the girl: Orlando, Florida.

The Toronto cops passed on their file to their colleagues at U.S. Immigration and Customs Enforcement who had done such a comprehensive job on Operation Hamlet. The ICE investigators in Orlando, in turn, teamed up with the local police. They began combing through the hotel records, questioning staff, showing them head shots of the girl, hoping someone would remember her. But by the end of April 2005, three months after police had released the crime scene photos, the hotel leads had run dry. Except for the initial flurry of media attention—by then Paul Gillespie and his team had become stars of American TV and in newsmagazines across Canada and the U.S.—there had been little progress. Police were able to determine that the mystery girl had visited the hotel sometime in early 2001, but nobody could come up with a name for her or her abuser.

It was time to up the ante.

Paul Gillespie was itching to go all the way—release the face of the victim and hope that someone somewhere would identify her before her abuser decided to do her any more harm. "What is the cost of not doing that? I think we've been debating long enough. I think it's time we do something," he said.

The Americans were still cautious, so another compromise was reached. On Wednesday, April 27, at a joint news conference in Orlando, Paul Gillespie joined local police and ICE investigators to once again plead for public help. This time it was not just sanitized photos of rooms with no people. The police handed out photos clearly showing the face not of the blond girl who had been abused but of another little girl they called a witness. Dark-haired and fully clothed, she sat on a brown couch, the green trim on her tank top matching the cuffs on her denim shorts. The Toronto cops had seen those same

clothes on Angeli. The couch, gym equipment and floor in the pictures of the "Friend"—that, in fact, was how the photos were labeled
in the Angeli series—all matched those shown in the abuse images.
Clearly this dark-haired girl knew the victim. The cops could find no
evidence that the dark-haired girl herself had been abused, so they concluded it was safer to distribute her photos.

Even that half step drew fire from child advocates on both sides of
the border. At NCMEC headquarters, Jennifer Lee, the supervisor of
the Child Victim Identification Program, was appalled that the
tabloid papers had run lurid stories on child pornography showing
the dark-haired girl's face. "This is the centerfold of *The National
Enquirer*," she said, spreading out the newspaper. "The second it goes
to the media you lose control." Rita Karakas of Save the Children
Canada called the police tactic "an act of desperation." She warned
the media: "I'm quite concerned about [the publicity] because sexual
abusers kill children to eliminate witnesses."

But from some quarters there were calls for bolder action. "Show
us the victim," demanded Canada's *National Post* newspaper.
"Instead of pinning their hopes to one witness, police should release
a picture of the victim herself, inviting the assistance of countless
people who may recognize the child and know her name," the paper
said in a blistering editorial. "Potentially delaying the rescue of this
little girl any longer is inexcusable."

Two weeks later, the debate became entirely academic.

On Friday, May 14, Bill McGarry walked into the third-floor office
in Toronto Police headquarters. Everyone was standing in a huddle; it
was obvious something was up.

"You want to sit down," his colleagues told him. "They found
the girl."

"You're kidding me!" he exclaimed.

McGarry had long hoped they would locate the girl whose rescue had obsessed him for two years. In his darker moments, he had
considered the possibility that they never would find her; in his
darkest moments, he even feared she might turn up dead.

There was one scenario he never could have imagined.

As it turned out, she was neither dead nor still in danger. She had
in fact been rescued two years earlier by the FBI.

"Are you serious?" a stunned McGarry asked the other officers gathered in the squad room.

He took a deep breath. He wasn't angry, or even dismayed that he had spent so long looking for a girl that who already been found. He was elated that the girl was safe. But a huge question remained: how come they didn't know about it?

Slowly they were able to piece the story together.

Masha was her name, though she had been born Maria Yahsenkova Nickolayevna in a dreary southern Russian industrial town. Stabbed in the neck at age three by her alcoholic mother during a drinking binge, she was parked in a state-run orphanage so "scary and dangerous" she later recounted that she had had to hide her few toys and belongings "under my pillow because I was afraid they would be stolen." So in 1998, when an American man arrived to take her to the United States, she thought she had been saved. "He seemed nice," she said. "He gave me presents."

Matthew Mancuso was a divorced engineer and millionaire in his early forties who tried to offset his baldness with a dark mustache and long sideburns. He had paid a New Jersey agency thousands of dollars to arrange the adoption, specifically requesting a Caucasian girl under six. He picked the girl out from a videotape sent to him by the agency. From the day she arrived in her new home in America, Masha, by then five, realized that her hoped-for paradise had turned into prison. She asked if she was going to have a mommy, but the man told her there would be no mother for her. On her first night in her new home in America, she discovered there was also no bedroom for her. Mancuso made her sleep—unclothed—in his bed.

"The abuse started the night I got there," Masha said. "He molested me all the time. Sometimes he kept me chained in the basement. Because he didn't want me to grow up, he only let me eat a little bit of food—plain pasta, raw vegetables, no meat."

In the isolated ranch house in Plum Borough outside of Pittsburgh, the sexual abuse would continue for the next five years. Her adoptive father used a combination of rewards—like visits to Disney World—and punishment to force her to keep silent about his molestation.

"I knew it was wrong. I tried to tell him to stop, but he wouldn't listen," Masha later told a TV reporter. "I just waited until it was over. I made myself think of other things when it was happening.

"It's like he stole my childhood."

The end of her ordeal began in 2003. When Mike Zaglifa, the Chicago cop working undercover, tracked the Internet address of "NkdSister" it led to Mancuso's home. (The Toronto cops could take some solace that their geographic instincts had been right: The abuse had occurred in the northeastern United States; they had even picked Pennsylvania as the likely state.)

After Zaglifa notified the FBI, two agents approached Mancuso's home on May 27, 2003. They expected to find a prolific online trader. They were shocked to find a girl, pale and starved, sitting outside the house with the suspect.

"This is not good," one of them said to the other, according to a later account they gave to the media.

The FBI agents quickly separated the man and the child.

"It's about my secret?" ventured the timid girl, by then ten years old, hinting she had a dark tale to reveal.

Mancuso cried out for her not to tell the police anything, but it was too late. Five years of abuse and fear and horror and shame poured out.

"I finally had someone to talk to," Masha later told a TV audience. "It just all came out."

Now it was Mancuso's turn to be in chains. He was immediately taken into custody. The FBI seized his computer and found plenty of evidence of child pornography. Mancuso pleaded guilty and was sentenced to fifteen years in February 2004. Masha, for her part, was adopted by a woman named Faith Allen and began putting the pieces of her life back together.

But two strange things happened—or rather, didn't happen. For whatever reason, Mancuso was charged with the manufacture and distribution of child abuse images but never with the actual physical abuse of Masha. Perhaps police or the prosecutors felt that was unnecessary, given the long jail term he was going to serve anyway. Perhaps they wanted to spare Masha the ordeal of a trial.

The second shortcoming was easier to explain, but no less troubling. Masha's pictures, her full identity and the fact that she had been rescued fell through the cracks: her details were never reported to any central database in Washington—or if they were, they did not get filed properly and were never connected to the widespread and widely sought Angeli series. An official with ICE tried to put that breakdown into context for journalists when the discovery of the "Disney girl's" true identity made headlines: "A piece of child pornography doesn't have a label on it saying 'This child pornography was made by so-and-so,'" the spokesperson said.

Actually, more and more pieces of child pornography did have labels on them, thanks to the hard work of Michelle Collins and her team at NCMEC. They had a list of several hundred fully identified children, with details on where they lived and who manufactured their abuse pictures. Most of the children of Hamlet, after their rescue in 2002, were put on that list. Jessica, after police found her in 2003, was put on that list. Ann, after her teacher was convicted of abusing her and distributing her picture, was put on the list in 2004.

But not, apparently, Masha.

One problem was that there were multiple databases; at the time, the FBI, ICE and NCMEC all had their own systems, although in theory NCMEC should have been the collection point of all known victims. There was a deeper shortcoming in the system: the reporting of identified victims of child pornography was not mandatory; it was not even known among all police agencies. "Our system is only as good as the information that's put in here," says Jennifer Lee, a NCMEC supervisor. "What we've found historically is that a lot of the biggest cases are being conducted by local police departments. They have no idea that this child is all over the Web. They have no idea that we need to know about her." The NCMEC staff has resorted to combing newspaper reports of child pornography arrests and then cold-calling police agencies, telling them they should file the evidence with the national center so the identified and rescued children can be cataloged. "We get the word out different ways, but have we got it out to everybody?" asked Michelle Collins. "Absolutely not. With a child abuse investigation there is still no national database that everybody works on."

Indeed, shortly after Masha's story came to light, police agencies in the Clearwater region of Florida scrambled to save another girl thanks to a tip by the Toronto cops. From clues in online pictures, Bill McGarry and a colleague narrowed down the search for an abused girl to a specific area: they knew she was in an unknown house with a pool that was near a shopping mall with both a skating rink and a Macy's store. McGarry was advised that the police in Florida were even making preparations to put a chopper in the air to search for the residence. At the last minute, a bulletin with the girl's face was circulated among local police departments: an officer recognized her as a victim in one of his cases that he had never reported to NCMEC.

The sad truth was that it was easier for police to track a stolen vehicle than identify whether an abused child has already been rescued.

That's why two years after Masha had been found by the FBI, and one year after her abuser had been jailed, police in Toronto and Florida could be involved in a nationwide hunt for a girl and not know that she had been rescued. Only after the stir created when the Toronto cops released the photos of the hotel crime scene did American authorities begin to collect all the known pictures of Angeli from ages five to ten, and eventually a match was made with the girl, who had been rescued by the FBI in May of 2003.

With eighteen thousand police agencies in the United States and five hundred in Canada, there were bound to be overlaps and confusions. At least the Americans had a central database of abuse victims with NCMEC, even if it was not comprehensive. Canada did not even have a national registry of known child pornography victims yet; the RCMP was only beginning to set up a coordination center in Ottawa. Paul Gillespie hoped his pet project, the Child Exploitation Tracking System (CETS), would solve some of these communications problems, allowing police around the world to share information and compare leads. But CETS was far from fully operational when the hunt was under way for Masha.

"There's a disconnect," said Paul Gillespie, trying to explain how police on both sides of the border fumbled Masha's case. "We're doing our best to fix stuff, but it's a learning experience."

Masha's story renewed the debate within law enforcement circles about how far police should go in their efforts to locate a victim.

"You're dealing with the eternal moral dilemma here," said Jon Rouse of Australia's Task Force Argos. "What happens if we release the photo and the offender is then forced to kill the child and flee?"

In Masha's case, neither happened, fortunately—but an international police hunt with much media publicity had been undertaken for a girl who was already safe. For Michelle Collins, the situation reaffirmed the correctness of NCMEC's policy of slowly expanding circles of publicity: if law enforcement suspected that Masha was somewhere in Pennsylvania, you start there and carefully widen the net. Otherwise, if police plaster her picture all over the TV and the Internet, the risks of exposing the child to physical danger or a double-victimization were simply too high.

"It was all done with the best intentions, but you have to slow down for a second," she said. "You don't just start running around."

Paul Gillespie was equally adamant that police had to be willing to push the envelope and might not always have the luxury of waiting. "I'll tell you right now, if it was your kid or my kid, you would want the police to do whatever they could to break down the door and rescue that child. I have talked to countless victims and asked them, 'Had we been able to save you a year before at the cost of your family and friends being aware of the horrific things that happened to you, would you have rather us rescued you or would you have rather we'd left you in that situation to protect your privacy?' Not one has said anything other than 'Why did it take you so long? Why did you not come and get me?'"

As for Masha, she used her sudden loss of privacy to launch a very public campaign, turning the tables on the abusers. She decided to speak out to help other victims come forward, first granting a TV interview to a local Orlando station, with her face obscured, and then speaking to a few newspapers as well.

"I think it's wrong that he didn't get charged with half the things he did," Masha said of Matthew Mancuso, "and I don't think that should happen to anybody."

Masha told reporters that she had started counseling. She was even planning a trip to Orlando to "conquer it" but then decided to hold off returning to Disney World for the moment—she opted for Sea World instead. Meanwhile, her foster mother got in touch with the prosecutors in Allegheny County, where Masha's systematic rape had taken place. It was the federal authorities who had put Mancuso in jail on interstate child pornography charges; it fell to the state or local officials to charge Mancuso with the physical assaults on Masha. When the Allegheny County district attorney's office said they didn't think Masha was ready to testify, an angry Masha got on the phone: "I want to know why you dropped the charges," she said. "You didn't ask me, and I do want to testify."

Three weeks after Masha's story garnered national media attention, the district attorney's office announced that Mancuso would be charged with eleven new counts, including rape. Within two months, Mancuso pleaded guilty to child rape, incest and unlawful restraint for the abuse that had lasted over five years. He got thirty-five to seventy years, and he would not even begin serving those extra decades behind bars until he completed his original fifteen-year sentence.

Mancuso would never have faced the extra jail time for abusing Masha if the Toronto cops' very public search for her had not made headlines. In a strange way, they didn't so much find Masha as help her find herself. They had made her an international symbol of the unknown child abuse victim; then she decided to step into the limelight and put her abuser away forever. "That is something good that certainly came out of this—allowing her that knowledge that she'll never have to face him again," said Gillespie.

For Bill McGarry, the hunt for Masha was not two years wasted but two years of learning. It taught him "everything that I know" about image analysis, he said. "It turned our office around. We pioneered the technique of re-creating a crime scene by wiping out the victim's body. If you don't take risks and you stick with the same investigative techniques as in the past, you're limited to the kinds of results you got in the past. If you don't go outside the box to do something different, you're never going to know what kind of possibilities lie out there."

Putting Matthew Mancuso away for life also seemed to strengthen Masha's resolve to take risks. She was outraged when she discovered how much of her abuse had been turned into a commodity for trade by Mancuso. "I got much more upset when I found out about the pictures of me that he put on the Internet. I had no idea he had done that," she later said. "I asked our lawyer to get them back. He told me we couldn't do that. Then I found out that they would be there forever. That's when I got mad and decided to go public with my story."

On December 2, 2005, she took the initiative to appear on camera on ABC's *PrimeTime*. Her face on the screen for millions to see, she looked healthy and vibrant and had a wry smile on her face. "I think that it's wrong what he did," she said. "Some kids just give up and they don't have any faith. Even if they are afraid to tell somebody, no matter what they think is going to happen, [if they come forward] it's going to be for the better."

As he watched with his family from his home outside Toronto, it was the first time Bill McGarry had ever heard or seen Masha except in abuse pictures. "I couldn't believe it; she looked so different," he said. "This was a kid who had looked like someone from a concentration camp. Now she was looking more like a regular teenager. And she had become an advocate for victims."

If the abuse suffered by victims was unbearable, living with the memories could be just as hard.

Paul Griffiths knows of victims who have tried to destroy every photograph they can find of themselves as children. "But of course they realized there are still pictures that are out there, and they find that sometimes almost impossible to live with. Imagine a picture of your abuse is out there on thousands of computers and can never be erased."

So instead some try to erase it from their minds. Psychologist Dr. Sharon Cooper once interviewed a young girl on an American military base in Germany who had been abused over a period of two years by her father, who took more than five hundred pictures of his molestations.

The girl readily disclosed her abuse but not the pictures.

"Were there ever any pictures?" Cooper asked.

"I don't remember that," the girl said.

Guilt and self-blame play a big role in children's attempts to wipe out the memory of the camera. "They believe they were responsible," says Cooper. "Because, remember, in most of these pictures there is no one in the picture with them. No one sees the perpetrator. For the child the image represents her own self-image."

The children are not the only ones who cannot erase the memories of those pictures. The investigators who try to rescue them, in their own way, are equally haunted by the images they have to see day in and day out. "Just when you think you've seen the worst, you see something worse than that," said Bill McGarry.

Betsy Perino, the young ICE agent who took on the grueling Operation Hamlet investigation, gave birth and had two toddlers under age two by the time the investigation wrapped up. For her, the case struck too close to home. "It was extremely disturbing on a personal level when you have your own children," she said. She found she had to discard many names she was considering for her newborns because they reminded her of the case: "After you've worked a huge case like that, it takes up three-quarters of the names in the baby-naming book," she said.

It only got worse after she became a mother. "I don't let my hand off their legs in that shopping cart when I go to the store," she said. "I reached a paranoia level with my children. You don't want to look at every person as a threat. It was probably time to move on." Fortunately, she got a timely promotion and became a section chief manager of ICE's cyber crime unit, handling every immigration and customs violation related to the Internet—except child pornography.

Barbara Anschuetz, a psychologist who works closely with police departments in the Toronto region, says female officers are more prone to develop what she calls "symptoms of vicarious trauma" because women—especially new mothers—often exhibit a more nurturing personality. But men, especially fathers of young children, are hardly immune. One officer who worked for three years on the Toronto sex crimes squad back in the late 1990s left the child abuse beat in part because of the mounting stress: "I have become so over-protective of my children," he says. He enrolled his daughter in karate classes when she was five. "Instead of getting her a Barbie doll for Christmas, I'm buying her martial arts weapons," he says. "I'm not always going to be there. I want to give her as much protection as I possibly can."

Toronto detective McGarry, a father of four, had no intention of leaving a post he has become passionate about, but he is the first to admit it has influenced his family. "My wife hates it, because she thinks this job has stolen some of the innocence out of my kid's life," he said. "There are certain things we did growing up that I won't let my kids participate in."

Like sleepovers, for example. Even with neighbors or friends whom they know, McGarry is reluctant to let his daughter spend the night at someone else's house.

Anschuetz says that even the most traumatic event that police officers might have to endure—the fatal shooting of a colleague, or an innocent victim dying in their arms—is mercifully over in a few minutes or hours. Child pornography investigators, on the other hand, can spend days, weeks, even years staring at the same pictures of a child, watching her age under unrelenting abuse. "You're watching it, so you're taking on the pain of the child," Anschuetz said. "In videos, the sounds and the visual images are repeated again and again. The more one sees, the more one hears, the more you identify with the victim by knowing the child's voice, by knowing the child's name, the greater the risk of developing trauma."

It is all part of what the U.K.'s Jim Gamble calls "the corrosive impact" of the battle against child exploitation, which he sees affecting his investigators in London all the time: "You watch your own team. They work days and nights, they work long hours and sometimes you seem to be doing nothing but upsetting people." Almost all police departments insist on mandatory psychological checkups and counseling for their staff. Some agencies try to rotate people out of child abuse assignments after a few years, but many people resist. They are too committed to the cause.

Some veterans in the trenches, like the FBI's Emily Vacher, managed to build a wall between their hunt for predators and their personal lives. "There is nothing pleasant about this job. This is the worst of the worst," she admitted. But Vacher found her solace and sanity every time she put away a child sex offender. "Knowing that because of the work I did that guy is going to spend the rest of his life in jail and can't hurt another child ever—it kind of makes up for the pain you go through."

At NCMEC's headquarters, they formalized that kind of inspiration with a "Wall of Shame," a rogues' gallery of convicted abusers plastered along an entire wall of the office. "When I'm feeling down, I just look up at the board and think: 'You know, I could die tomorrow, and I know that I've made a difference,'" said Cristina Fernandez, who helps run the CyberTipline.

Down the hallway, supervisor Jennifer Lee looks at different pictures—those of the abused children—for a different source of strength and not stress. As she put it: "I just think to myself: I'm probably the only person who's looking at this picture who actually cares for the kid."

Nine

WANTED: "JOHN DOE"

For the first time, law enforcement has been able to charge an unnamed person for crimes against children. There is a warrant for the arrest of John Doe, despite the fact that agents don't know his true identity.
—*America's Most Wanted* TV BROADCAST,
FEBRUARY 21, 2004

Thomas Richard Evered walked up to the cop in the parking lot at the local gas station and grocery store near Missoula, Montana.

"There's a warrant for my arrest," he said.

The surprised officer ran Evered's name through his computer and came up empty.

"Your name isn't in the system," he insisted.

"Oh, I'm John Doe from *America's Most Wanted,*" Evered explained, almost proudly.

His picture had been broadcast nationwide that evening as one of the first suspects in an innovative FBI project to publicize abusers whose faces are known to the police but not their names. Their mug shots were widely distributed on the FBI's Web site and on the popular TV crime program, which, coincidentally, was hosted by John Walsh, the victims' rights advocate who worked with the NCMEC. The hope was that the public could help identify and find the predators. If there were too many ethical and legal time bombs involved in showing the full face of a child abuse victim, why not—in those rare cases where it was available—show the face of the offender?

"I loved the idea," said Emily Vacher, the lead agent picked to work on the project. "It goes back to what we did whenever somebody robbed a bank. We put the picture on the five o'clock news and said, 'Hey, does anybody know this guy?' So if the perp is brazen enough to leave his image on the Internet in an image of child abuse, why shouldn't we go after him the same way?"

But Vacher could never have predicted how quickly the arrests would come—and how nabbing Evered would lead her one day to the prison cell of one of the most dangerous serial sex offenders she would ever confront.

Its formal title was the Endangered Child Alert Program (ECAP). Faces of abusers were not plentiful on the Web, but some men could not resist boasting. "In some of the images we get, they don't make any effort to conceal themselves," said Arnold Bell, head of the FBI's cyber child unit. Other times it was accidental: a profile reflected in a shower head or a window.

The dangers in releasing these John Doe Wanted posters were greatly diminished compared with distributing the face of the victim. There was less chance of shaming or revictimizing the child. Oddly enough, if there was a peril in the John Doe gambit, it was to the abuser himself. If the authorities were wrong—and Operation Ore had seen at least a handful of cases of men tarred as child abuse enthusiasts when in fact they were victims of credit card fraud or had purchased adult porn—the consequences of such public exposure could be enormous. "We're always hyperconservative," says the FBI's Bell, insisting the bureau is certain the accusations are solid.

Vacher's first challenge was to choose the John Does. She got her first two guinea pigs from Corinna Koch, the German BKA officer who had worked with Daniel Szumilas in cracking the case of the mysterious post office videotapes. At one of Interpol's regular gatherings of child abuse investigators, the two women joined with other police officers, sitting around a conference table, exchanging new images that had appeared on the Internet.

"I think these are American," Koch told Vacher, as she handed her the files on two men. "See if you can find these guys."

Vacher studied the pictures and verified that they met the standards for the FBI's new program: they were current pictures of abuse with clear pictures of the abusers. She checked the FBI's database and with

NCMEC to be as sure as possible the cases remained unsolved. Then the hard legal slog began.

With a bunch of goodies from an Italian grocery store in Baltimore, she drove out to see her favorite Department of Justice prosecutor, Andrew Norman. Norman was laid up at home with a broken leg, courtesy of a parachuting injury. The damaged limb was an accident, but Norman's penchant for risky behavior was not. Vacher hoped that Norman would be just as willing to take a legal risk.

Vacher explained to the prosecutor that the *America's Most Wanted* TV show had agreed to broadcast the John Does on their show, but on the condition that the men could not just be suspects, they had to be officially under an arrest warrant. That was not going to be easy. Appearing before a grand jury and persuading a room full of citizens to indict a molester with no name, no address and no location for the crime was the legal equivalent of jumping out of a plane. It could be done, but you were taking a big chance every time. Norman decided to increase his odds: if he didn't have a name or address to show the grand jurors, he could work on the location.

"Why don't you go back to the office and see if you could find these pictures on the Internet," he told the FBI agent. "If you do that, it shows that there is a connection between the defendant's pictures and the federal district of Maryland."

Norman's logic was creative. To get an indictment, he could establish that the defendant had made or helped produce the abuse pictures, since his face was right in the photograph. Once it was proved that the picture was also easily downloaded in Maryland, regardless of where the suspect actually lived and committed the crime, he could try to show that the crime of interstate transportation had been committed in his jurisdiction. If the case went to trial, the FBI would already have the now-identified John Doe in custody, and by then presumably they would have even more proof that he had uploaded the pictures for distribution on the Web.

It worked, at least enough to get grand jury indictments for the first two Internet John Does. On the February 21, 2004, installment of *America's Most Wanted,* viewers saw two head shots of John Doe #1 and #2. Both were young men, with close-cropped hair. The script accompanying each picture read the same: "Agents have determined that

John Doe is an American, and that the movie of him having sex with a child was made recently, sometime in the last five years. For the first time, law enforcement has been able to charge an unnamed person for crimes against children. There is a warrant for the arrest of John Doe, despite the fact that agents don't know his true identity."

The first success was almost instantaneous—and surprising. Even before the show was over, a tipster called the *AMW* hotline. He knew the name of Internet John Doe #2—Scott Hayden. And he knew his address—Cell Block 2, Indiana State Prison, Michigan City, Indiana.

"I had no idea *America's Most Wanted* was so popular in jail," Vacher joked.

Hayden wasn't going anywhere soon. He was serving a thirty-year sentence for another, unrelated, child molestation. The FBI agents got on the phone with prison officials immediately; they printed a picture of Hayden from the *AMW* Web site and took it to Hayden's cell. Hayden confirmed that he was the man in the child abuse images.

Bolstered by their quick success, *AMW* and the FBI rebroadcast the picture of Thomas Evered the following week: Internet John Doe #1. Vacher was in the TV studios to help monitor the calls.

"A police officer wants to talk to you," one of the phone operators told agent Vacher that night.

"This is Bob in Lolo—" he said.

"Where's that?" Vacher interrupted him.

"Near Missoula."

"Forgive me, what state is that in?" Vacher said impatiently.

"Oh, we're in Montana," he said. "And we have your John Doe in our hands right now."

"I couldn't believe it," Vacher said later. "And it was true—it was him."

The thirty-nine-year-old truck driver from Montana had traveled the roads of the Midwest with a haul of child abuse images he picked up from the information superhighway. Thomas Richard Evered did not just trade in pictures, he also engaged in hands-on abuse of children. Evered's sister had been watching the broadcast and had immediately recognized her brother; she called her mother, who urged Evered to turn himself in. He agreed, but not before he drove out to a lonely stretch of road where he proceeded to run over his hard drive several times with his truck. "I pitched the carcass onto the sides of the highway," he later said. He smashed all his CDs and threw them into different garbage cans. Only then did he walk over to the cop at the gas station and turn himself in.

The third John Doe broadcast would also lead to success, but it would take somewhat longer than with the first two. When the FBI and *AMW* aired a grainy, five-second video of a man in early March 2003, no one could recognize the offender, but viewers were certain the images had been filmed inside the cab of a tractor trailer; in fact, they could name the make and model. Further leads from images seized from another abuser gave the FBI the man's name—Kevin Quinn—and a possible location in Texas. Brooke Donahue, the FBI agent in Dallas who had helped track down the Texas woman and the British man who were part of Burt Thomas Stevenson's online circle of abusers, ran the name through the driver's license and trucking employment records and found a match.

Quinn too had slipped through the cracks. While posted at a North Dakota air force base he had served two years' confinement in the mid-nineties after being found guilty of three counts of indecency with a child; the air force gave him a dishonorable discharge—but did not warn the police or the public once he was released. A loophole in the law did not require military personnel convicted in military tribunals of sex acts with children to register as sex offenders on completion of their sentence.

Once out of the military, Quinn teamed up with another trucker to abuse a string of young victims: four were from Dallas, three from Colorado; the youngest was only two. Quinn pleaded guilty to several federal sexual exploitation charges and was sent away for just over eleven years behind bars; his accomplice got seventeen years. Quinn later pleaded guilty to state charges of molesting children and got thirty-eight years—to begin after he completes his federal time.

Quinn's arrest confirmed Emily Vacher's worst fears. "With most of the John Does we had, there were multiple, multiple victims," she said. "So if a John Doe is still out there, he's probably still abusing either his kids or new kids. We needed to get him off the streets." Vacher was about to discover that in some cases, finding out the identity of a John Doe was the beginning, not the end, of the chase.

Following the psychologist Joe Sullivan's insistence on understanding the offender, the FBI agent knew that no matter how repugnant she might find the molesters she was helping to arrest, she could learn a lot by talking to them. "It is my personal belief that if you can catch one pedophile, you can catch another pedophile," she said. "Somebody knows someone or something about somebody else."

After the FBI picked up Thomas Evered—Internet John Doe #1— in Montana, they shipped him off to Baltimore, where both Vacher and the prosecutor Andrew Norman were based. "I could have said, 'Evered, you're going to jail for fifteen years, and I don't want to talk about it, I don't care,'" said Vacher. "But I spent hours and hours interviewing him. He helped educate me because he knows more about this than I do. What he did was repulsive. But if I learn a new trick, maybe that's going to help me solve another case."

Evered did not just offer the tricks of the veteran trader. He was also willing to give up a friend of his, a major producer of child abuse images, in return for a lighter sentence. The Montana trucker didn't cough up his pedophile partner's name immediately. All he divulged at first was that this was "a really bad guy—a pedophile who's in jail."

"Great," muttered Vacher, joking that that really helped narrow it down.

Evered, of course, had trashed his child abuse collection on the highway; Vacher sent a team out to look for the debris from the hard drive, but they came up empty. She had better luck on the Internet, though. The Web had perhaps become a pedophile's paradise, but it was also a vast archive of crime. It was from the German BKA that Vacher had first received the images showing Evered's face, and she got more pictures from Anders Persson at Interpol and FBI agents across the country: she assembled a large collection by looking for pictures with the same victims, the same background—a carpet or piece of furniture—or a common location: the same kitchen or bathroom kept popping up.

Vacher was intrigued because several of the pictures in Evered's collection showed another man who went to great lengths to mask his identity. "He was very, very careful," she explained. "He didn't allow his face to be in images except for one picture—and then he had his hand over his face."

Vacher cropped out all the sexual imagery in the photos and was left with a mangled head shot of the mystery man—not much more than an eye, a nose and a mustache. But the man's features were remarkably distinctive. The FBI agent then sent the cropped photo to a security officer she had met at the Federal Correctional Institution in Cumberland, Maryland, about 130 miles northwest of D.C. It was a complete whim; Evered's buddy could have been in any one of the nearly two hundred federal prisons scattered across the country, but Vacher started with Cumberland because at least she knew someone there.

The officer pulled all the photos of the sex offenders in the institution and, remarkably, found one face that seemed to match Vacher's photo. To make sure, he went out into the prison yard, holding the picture in his hand, and stared at the prisoner. No mistake—that was the man.

"You're not going to believe this," he said to Vacher on the phone. "I have your guy."

"Oh my God, oh my God!" was all she could say in response.

His name was James E. Reigle, a four-time-convicted child offender from Harrisburg, Pennsylvania. Once Vacher had Reigle's name, Evered obligingly filled in the details of their relationship. They had met in a chat room called "littleboysexpics" and actively began exchanging precisely that. Evered drove out from Missoula, Montana, to meet the older, more experienced abuser and witness his assaults on children. Reigle had guardianship over one boy, Alexander*; he had persuaded the boy's divorced parents to let their son stay at his home, which was in a better school district. Known as Uncle Jim in the neighborhood, Reigle had also befriended many other youngsters. "The rest of his victims were from the neighborhood or children of friends," said Vacher. The FBI agent estimated that between the two of them, Reigle and Evered had abused over thirty children.

In 2002, Reigle ran into a slight roadblock: he was sentenced to a thirty-seven-month federal prison term for possession of child pornography in another case and, on the state level, to a concurrent sentence for sexually molesting a Harrisburg boy. But prison seemed little more than a detour for the inveterate pedophile. Always the consummate planner, Reigle contacted his Internet buddy Evered by phone shortly after he began serving time. He had a favor to ask: take possession of his impressive collection of child pornography from his Harrisburg home and keep it in a safe place. You can copy it all, Reigle said, but I want it back when I get out.

And he was about to get out soon, Vacher discovered to her dismay as she was building a new case against Reigle in 2004. His prison time for his 2002 convictions was up in a couple of weeks. "I was racing against the clock because I didn't want him to get released," she said. "I would run the risk of losing him and I was afraid of what he would do."

At the federal prison in Cumberland, Reigle was counting down the hours. It was on a Wednesday that Vacher got an arrest warrant for his newly discovered offenses against the children in Evered's collection. By Thursday she was speeding to the prison, knowing that Reigle was getting set to walk out by Friday morning. When she arrived at the prison and sat down with the convict, he stared back at her, his striking blue eyes not giving away any fear or hint of concern.

"Do you know why I'm here?" she asked.

"Yeah, you're here about Evered," the prisoner replied. "I saw him on *America's Most Wanted.*"

Vacher didn't disabuse him of that notion right away. She started pulling out thirty-one photos depicting Evered's assaults on children. Reigle, leaning forward on the table, calmly identified his friend and even some of the children.

Then, seventeen minutes into the interview, Vacher pulled out a new batch of pictures: images showing Reigle's abuse of Alexander and other victims. "It was textbook," she recalled. "His demeanor completely changed, and he was shifting in his chair."

When the FBI agent placed in front of the prisoner the picture of him with his hands over his face, he blurted out, "That's not me." Vacher had not even had time to ask him if it was him.

"If that's not a red flag, I don't know what is," she later remarked.

She then showed him pictures from his home, and again he said too quickly, "That's not my kitchen."

Finally, Vacher pulled out an image in which one could just make out the abuser's bald spot on his head, a bit of his bright blue eyes and a few moles on his face. She pointed to Reigle's face and then to the picture: "Look—mole, mole, mole, bald spot, blue eyes."

The color drained from his face. Vacher allowed herself a small smile. "Oh, and by the way," she said, "I have a warrant for your arrest, and you're not leaving here."

Reigle tried to maintain his composure as he got up to leave. But as soon as the guards got him around the corner, they later told Vacher, the convict's knees buckled under him.

Reigle knew what he was facing. He had four previous convictions in state and federal courts for child molestation and pornography stretching back to 1983; but while he was in prison on the last of those convictions, a special "two strikes and you're out" law had been enacted for people convicted of two serious sexual offenses against children. By the time his trial got under way in late 2005, Reigle was looking at jail for the rest of his life.

Still, to keep him in jail, Vacher and the prosecutor Andrew Norman faced several challenges in gathering evidence against him. The only proof they had that Reigle was in a conspiracy with Evered was the latter's word—and the testimony of a self-confessed pedophile was not going to be enough to sway a jury. Evered maintained that he kept Reigle's collection with him at all times during his cross-country travels—no doubt a convenient way to both look at it regularly and keep it safe. But he was also committing a federal offense by constantly transporting the child abuse images across state lines. Luckily for Vacher and Norman, Evered's trucking logs showed that one of his routes took him through Maryland—for only eleven miles—but it was enough to lay the conspiracy charges against Reigle and Evered in the state where the FBI's Innocent Images project was centered.

It would be harder to prove that Reigle had been directly involved in the production of the images—and the hands-on abuse of Alexander and others. Vacher would have to nail down the time and location of the assaults and the identity of the victims. In one image, on a refrigerator door behind a boy, Vacher could make out a magnet with the date 1997. In another picture, a *TV Guide* lay in the foreground. She couldn't read the date but could see the cover photo. She found a Web site with the cover of every issue of the magazine and matched the one in the image to the July 27, 1999, issue, featuring the TV cop Dennis Franz. Now she could frame the abuse over a span of at least two years.

She then confirmed the location with mortgage records and land deeds, tracing the house Reigle had occupied during those years. On a trip to the home, Vacher found that the countertops in the kitchen had been redone, but the layout matched exactly what she had seen in the photos. Other pictures of abuse were taken in a bathroom painted a shocking red; the bathroom had been redecorated and repainted white, but Vacher took off the top of the toilet tank and found some of the same red paint on the wall behind.

Combining the clues in the pictures with the dates from the land records and a copy of Alexander's birth certificate that she later obtained, Vacher was able to prove that the boy could not have been older than thirteen at the time the abuse had taken place—and that, in fact, the pictures showed him aging through many years of abuse, starting as a young child.

Facing that mountain of evidence, Reigle's lawyer was eager for a plea bargain. But the FBI and prosecutors would settle for nothing less than life. Reigle had little choice but to gamble on a trial.

He had a losing hand from the start. His co-conspirator, Thomas Evered, testified against him. Even in the picture in which Reigle had shielded his face with his hand, the jurors could make out his nose, mustache and one of his eyes. Quipped one of the courtroom clerks, "Even Ray Charles could figure out it was Reigle."

In one video, Reigle was not in the shot but was busy filming—and talking. The prosecution compared the voice on tape to Reigle's and got a match. Then, to seal the case, they brought in some of his victims. In the image with his hand covering his face, Reigle was performing oral sex on a boy. Now, Alexander sat in the witness box and told the jurors, "That's me and that's Mr. Reigle." In all, Vacher was able to persuade three of his victims to testify.

Finally to drive home the extent of the harm, the prosecutor had the U.K. investigator Paul Griffiths fly in to testify about the early availability of the Alexander series of pictures produced by Reigle. "I wanted to impress upon the jury that these pictures, once they're on the Internet, go all over the world," he said. "The damage to the child is irreparable."

Still, even with all the evidence, Andrew Norman knew that convictions were never a sure thing in a jury trial. There was a shaky moment when a juror wrote a note to the judge. "Did the children resist?" the juror wanted to know. It was a heartless and foolish question—and legally irrelevant, since no child under the law can give consent to rape. Still, Norman found it unsettling. "That was very disturbing," he said. "I was worried that we might have an idiot on the jury."

After four weeks of testimony, on December 8, 2005, the jury found Reigle guilty on all six counts relating to the abuse of ten victims. As the jury foreperson read out the verdict, Vacher glanced at the man to gage his reaction: "Nothing," she remarked. "He knew it was coming. It was as if the jury had just said, 'Free pizza for everyone.'"

"I think you should be in jail for life!" the mother of one of the victims cried out in court when the verdict came down.

That's exactly what he got when the judge handed down the mandatory sentence a few weeks later—life behind bars. A month afterward, Thomas Evered, the John Doe who had snitched on Reigle, got ten years, followed by lifetime parole. "What that means is that until he stops breathing, if he does anything wrong, he can be locked up again in federal prison," said Andrew Norman.

Almost all the "John Does" had been captured within days, if not hours, of the TV broadcasts. But there was one case that lingered, unsolved, for almost a year

On July 7, 2004, a federal grand jury in the Western District of Missouri had indicted "John Doe #4" and charged him with distributing child pornography over the Internet. The charge singled out "sadistic and violent conduct" against a young child. The suspect was described as a white male, approximately 180 to 190 pounds, with brown hair. *America's Most Wanted* broadcast a fairly clear picture of the man, along with close-ups of a scar and tattoo on either arm.

But no one called. No tips, no leads.

"He's been out the longest," said a frustrated Arnold Bell, head of the FBI's cyber crime child unit. But no one in America seemed to know who this man was—because, as it turned out, he wasn't in America.

Fortunately, the FBI and Interpol had taken the precaution of circulating the series of graphic pictures featuring John Doe #4 to police agencies around the world. In the spring of 2005, members of Toronto's Sex Crimes Unit came across new pictures and a video of the same abuser in an Internet newsgroup. Detective Ian Lamond blew up a corner of a movie poster in the background of one of the pictures and discovered the words were in French. Then, through a window in another photo he could make out a distinctive railing on an outside staircase, common in one major city in Canada—Montreal.

The Toronto Police forwarded the information to the Quebec provincial police, and to the RCMP's recently created National Child Exploitation Co-ordination Centre in Ottawa. An investigator from the center recognized a young girl in the photos from an old tip that had been passed on to Canada's own CyberTipline, which was operating out of Winnipeg. The leads were enough for Quebec police to confirm the suspect's identity and location. On June 24, 2005, police, armed with a search warrant, seized about 1,000 DVDs, CDs and computer disks at the man's home. They also were able to rescue the girl whose exploitation he had been documenting online—his own daughter.

It was a gratifying example of how far police had come in terms of image detective work and cross-border cooperation. By the middle of 2005, just over a year after the launch of its John Doe initiative, all but one of the suspects had been captured.

Still, the FBI knew the scope of this program would be limited. Of all the millions of child abuse images on the Web, the bureau had found fewer than half a dozen with a clear view of an offender's face. There was also a growing realization in law enforcement circles that going after men like Reigle and Evered, who swapped and produced the pictures and videos for their own pleasure was not enough.

There was a pressing need to go after the money men who were making millions from the booming commercial trade of child exploitation contraband.

PART THREE **PREDATORS, INC.**

Ten

FOLLOW THE MONEY

*What's scary is when organized criminals understand there is money
to be made, and they don't care what the product is.*
—ERNIE ALLEN, EXECUTIVE DIRECTOR OF NCMEC

S enator Richard Shelby is not a man to be trifled with.

As the senior United States senator from Alabama and chairman at the time of the powerful Banking, Housing and Urban Affairs Committee, he is the kind of politician who can call the captains of commerce and industry around a table and get them to listen. Which is what he did in the summer of 2005. "It came to my attention that child pornography was an international growing business, and they were using our modern financial networks to collect the money and pay for it," he said.

On July 20, Shelby hosted a meeting on Capitol Hill with the representatives from leading banks, credit card companies and payment services. He boomed out his disgust in his no-nonsense Southern accent: "If people were buying heroin and cocaine with their credit cards, people would be outraged," he told the financiers. "This is worse. Much worse."

Shelby's analogy was apt, because, like the illegal drug trade, the commercial exploitation of children needed two things to succeed: a strong demand and a criminal network that could deliver the product. But there was one important difference. Neither the Medellin drug cartel nor the local street pusher takes Visa or MasterCard. Child porn sites do.

"I believe financial institutions ought to have higher standards and some things that they won't do for money," said the Republican senator. "Because you can always look the other way, close your eyes and say this is just a transaction. But this is more than a transaction. This is the exploitation of the most vulnerable people, our children."

Much of that exploitation, of course, was going without any money changing hands, as huge amounts of child abuse images were being traded free on the Internet among its enthusiasts. Certain hard-to-get images or missing pictures in a popular series—like Masha's photos or the Hamlet club ones—attained enormous trading value and gave their holders impressive status among their pedophile peers. But the motive was still collecting pictures, not profits.

Yet crime, like nature, abhors a vacuum. If there is money to be made on the Web, organized criminals and unscrupulous business-men will jump in. One study by the Internet Filter Review, an American business analysis Web site, concluded that "child pornog-raphy generates $3 billion annually." Higher figures were tossed around at U.S. congressional hearings, but getting a precise figure on child porn profits—much like exact statistics on the number of children abused via the Internet—was nearly impossible.

What was clear, though, was that while law enforcement was scrambling to get a grasp on the hordes of abusers seeking personal pleasure, tracking down merchants intent on profit was going to be an even more daunting task. "You have some of the most vicious organ-ized crime gangs coming out of Eastern Europe and Russia," said Senator Shelby. "They'll stop at nothing."

At forty-five, Carlos Ortiz had seen his share of financial crime. As deputy chief of the United States Attorney's Office for the District of New Jersey, he supervised work on government fraud, commer-cial crime and the Organized Crime Strike Force. Before that he had been a traveling prosecutor out of Washington, D.C., tackling a lot of criminal tax cases, where he learned how to sniff around compli-cated money trails. For all his number crunching, it was the numb-ing cruelty of child abuse that stuck in his mind. "You can't even imagine what's physically possible," he said. "I remember one image of a little girl—she's crying and her face is red, and it's horrible. Who subjects someone that young and innocent to something like this? Who enjoys this?"

The suffering of children struck a deep chord inside Ortiz because he had witnessed it himself: he and his wife lost one of their twin boys three days after he was born, and the surviving child needed special care. "I'm very sensitive to a child who is intentionally exploited," he admitted. "Because of that life experience I feel the need to protect children."

Early in his career, he had to prosecute a man who posted pictures online of the rape of a seven-year-old girl in his family. At trial, the sentencing judge did not want to see the images.

"You know, Your Honor, I understand that this is difficult to look at, sickening," said Ortiz in court. "But you have the opportunity to see the type of abuse perpetrated on this child firsthand." The judge hesitated for a moment, then slowly opened the binder in front of him to look at some of the pictures quickly.

"You know what? You're right," he said. "I could not have imagined it was this bad."

The defendant got fifteen years.

As a senior prosecutor, Ortiz began to see child pornography take off as a money-making extravaganza. There were pay-for-videocam sites, membership sites and bulk download pages, all offering simple and easy payment with a major credit card. "The more I heard about it, the more disgusted I got," Ortiz said. "You had Web sites that were advertising this stuff like they were selling cars."

Never one to shrink from a challenge, Ortiz brought it up with his bosses. "Why aren't we following the money? Why isn't anybody going up the chain?"

"Look, if you want to give this a shot, give it a shot," he was told. Not that his bosses' response would have made much difference. "I was not going to take no for an answer," Ortiz said.

He reached out first to Maria Reverendo, an IRS agent he had teamed up with on public corruption cases. They brought in John Johnson, a postal inspector who had been tracking child pornography for some years, as well as Susan Cantor from the Newark office of Immigration and Customs Enforcement who had experience in fraud and money-laundering investigations.

In early 2003, Ortiz and his team went to the FBI's Innocent Images task force to get the latest in investigative techniques and to see what they knew about commercial child exploitation Web sites. That was standard procedure. But what they did next was something no one in law enforcement had done before in a systematic way: they approached the credit card companies. Ortiz set up meetings with Amex, MasterCard and Visa security executives for what evolved into a two-way exchange that would change the way cops and corporations tackled child abuse online.

"We made them really aware of what was going on," Ortiz said. In return, said John Brady, MasterCard's senior executive for fraud management: "We gave them a good understanding of how the credit card system worked."

The answers are not as easy as they may seem. Many people assume that when you buy something online and pay with a credit card—whether it's a book from Amazon.com or child abuse images from a dubious Web site—the credit card company pays the seller and then collects the money from you. A simple three-way deal that should be easy to trace. In fact, it's a lot more complicated than that. For starters, it is not the credit card companies but banks that issue cards to consumers and businesses. Getting your own merchant account can be lengthy and costly, so small Mom-and-Pop operations can bypass that stage by going through intermediaries, known as process servers or aggregators. These third-party payment services allow your business to essentially piggyback on their merchant account; they handle your credit card collections for a generous cut of each sale. Convenient for Mom and Pop, but also handy for a businessman running a pornography Web site. He does not apply directly to Visa or MasterCard or a bank for the right to use their logos and payment system; he can go through multiple partners to shield the true nature of his operations.

"With the layering and anonymity, these guys thought they were unstoppable," said Maria Reverendo. "Even though we were gung-ho and ready to go, it was going to be incredibly difficult."

Once they got their heads around the complexities of online finances, Ortiz's team had to figure out a way to investigate them. The first problem was speed. It was all too easy for a child porn provider to set up a business identity, get a merchant account and then if they started getting hassled to simply close up shop, come up with a new name and Web site and find a new credit card broker. By the time investigators could begin the legal paperwork, the money trail would have long gone cold.

"Unless you're able to move quickly, these guys are going to stay a step ahead of you," said Ortiz. "What we needed to do was establish a mechanism where we got information in real time."

At MasterCard John Brady stepped in to help. Ortiz soon got the other major credit card companies—and later some banks—onboard to open up their books quickly when presented with the proper warrants. Normally it would have taken months; Ortiz got it down to hours or days.

Now the Newark team was ready to make purchases of child exploitation images and follow the financial footprints. Finding the stuff for sale wasn't hard. "I just Googled 'child pornography,' and I got gazillions of kids' photos for sale," said Cantor.

But they didn't need just any photos; to make their case, they needed to find a company that was processing its credit card sales in the United States.

It was easy to miss the nondescript building near the Fort Lauderdale beach on Sunset Drive just off East Las Olas Boulevard. A simple note on the door said, "Please ring bell," but there were few visitors to the offices of Connections USA.

Inside, a handful of employees worked quietly, busy on the phone or opening mail. The Florida company had initially run a string of legal online and telephone dating services. Arthur Levinson, a successful local businessman, was the company president, but the man on the scene who called the shots was the chief executive officer, Eugene Valentine, from nearby Hollywood. Valentine knew everything about Connections USA's operations. He knew that among the thick files the company kept on all its customers and clients, one file labeled "Regpay" contained only a few names and sheets of paper. Valentine also knew that despite the scant contract details, Regpay was his biggest client, making millions by selling child abuse images.

Regpay was based in Minsk, the capital of Belarus, one of the shaky new republics formed after the collapse of the Soviet Union where the Russian mafia and other organized crime bosses had become the new czars. Yahor Zalatarou, a twenty-seven-year-old well-educated entrepreneur raised by an engineer and a teacher, was the company president. His partners included Aliaksandr Boika, a computer expert in his early thirties who served as the technical administrator; Alexei Buchnev, twenty-eight, a skilled translator who was identified as the marketing director; and one woman, Tatsiana Sienko, twenty-five, the administrative and financial assistant.

The Belarusian gang operated a network of unabashedly graphic and degrading child abuse sites. One of their Internet addresses, Redlagoon.com, offered a portal to the "underground pedo world," and Regpay made no secret of its underage offerings: "Until they grow up," its advertisement said, "get closer to the innocent passion." Four other Web sites with names like lust-gallery.com and lolittles.com— operated from Belarus but hosted by Internet service providers in the United States and elsewhere—promised buyers "all girls under 14." Regpay also processed payments for at least another fifty third-party child-abuse sites.

Regpay originally had called itself Trustbill, but after getting hit by two cease-and-desist orders from the Michigan attorney general's office in the summer of 2002, it did what so many dodgy distributors do—it simply changed its name. Its loyal customers signed on with their credit cards to get access to the thousands of child abuse images, and Connections USA collected the money. After taking an 11 percent commission, the Florida firm shipped the money offshore. And there was plenty of it. Valentine would later acknowledge that he knew of at least twenty-nine wire transfers to Regpay from June 2002 to June 2003, totaling at least $3 million.

Regpay's Redlagoon.com happened to be one of the first child abuse sites that the ICE agent Susan Cantor came across, and it soon became apparent that Regpay was a major player in the market. Ortiz's investigators noticed that regardless of which site they started at, they often ended up paying Regpay for the purchase. "It was incredible: page after page of Regpay showing up," said the IRS's Maria Reverendo. "That's how we became aware how big they were."

The credit card companies were aware of Regpay's proliferation. The problem was that the Regpay name did not show up on any of their merchant client lists. There must have been a front company offering Regpay a layer of protection. Only by clicking to pay for the child porn purchase could the companies discover who was collecting the money for Regpay. But of course the credit card companies couldn't legally buy child abuse images.

But the cops could. When they made their controlled buys of Regpay's products, they found their credit card statements showed a charge under the name of Iserve. A corporate search of that name led to the Florida-based operation called Connections USA. Now Ortiz's team had what they needed for a made-in-America prosecution: a major distributor pushing child abuse images on the Web and pulling in millions via a U.S.-based company.

Working with the credit card companies and the banks, the Newark investigators began making regular purchases and monitoring the money flow. Connections USA did its banking with Morgan Stanley Trust. Ortiz served the financial firm with the proper legal paperwork, but he took care to make the case a money-laundering one, thus ensuring that the bank could not inform its client of the investigation.

The money, Ortiz discovered, flowed from Morgan Stanley to the Deutsche Bank in Germany and then to an Aizkraukles Bank account in Latvia owned by Regpay's operators. A steady stream, then a gushing tide, of porn profits. "When we got the bank statement, you could see that it started slowly, then the amounts of money in the system exploded," said Ortiz. In late 2002, Regpay was pulling in about $100,000 a month; then it doubled to $200,000 and by the spring of 2003 they were moving $700,000 to $800,000 every month.

The Regpay money men would later all deny that they had any direct role in the manufacture of the child abuse images, but investigators were not convinced. Ortiz said that with a little more digging they were able to discover that while Regpay was moving money for hundreds of child pornography sites owned by other companies, the top five moneymakers were sites they ran themselves. "So 23 percent of all the money they were moving stayed with themselves."

Still, the Newark investigators resigned themselves to the fact there was little chance that they would ever get the crime figures in Eastern Europe. "Realistically, we thought we could take out the American side," Ortiz said. "No one is ever going to get the guys in Belarus. That's a pipe dream. Not gonna happen."

*   *   *

It was still hot late into the evening, as only a June night in Florida can be. Hotter still because so many people were packed into the hotel conference room for the briefing: more than eighty federal officers— ICE agents, postal inspectors, IRS enforcers—plus local police troops, getting ready for the raid on Connections USA.

"It was huge," said Susan Cantor. "For the first time, we realized how big this was going to be."

For several weeks, Cantor and the other investigators had been gathering and collating the evidence. By the time they flew down to Florida, they had identified all the Connections USA employees and put together packets on each one. "We had a very meticulously laid out plan—how it was going to be executed, all the interviews that needed to be conducted—because we needed to find out every piece of information."

By six the next morning, June 4, the teams were ready to roll. They swooped down on the offices on Sunset Drive and the homes of the company executives. Not surprisingly, the initial reaction from the senior staff was to feign ignorance. "Their story was 'We weren't doing anything wrong,'" said Carlos Ortiz, who was on hand for most of the interviews. "We were told, 'It's the bad Russians. It's the bad guys offshore. We're shocked and we had no idea.'"

That story began to fall apart when investigators found that the Regpay file was suspiciously thin—as if they were trying to hide any incriminating information—compared with the amount of detail Connections USA had for its other accounts. "This is your biggest customer; this is the only thing you're really doing now," Ortiz pushed them. "How do you not know them?"

The biggest break came when Arthur Levinson himself, the company president, agreed to cooperate. Insisting that he knew nothing about Regpay's child pornography activities, Levinson later pleaded guilty to a much lesser financial crime of structuring transactions to avoid reporting requirements. But he gave Ortiz's team something better than information: he gave them his e-mail identity. That prompted the Americans to take a gamble: Regpay had been playing online hide-and-seek for years. Why not turn the tables and pull an online scam on the Belarusians? The Regpay people had never met or spoken to him, so here was a chance to run a sting operation against the Minsk money men. "It was pie in the sky, in a way, but we figured let's give it a shot," said Ortiz.

The timing was perfect because, by coincidence, at the moment of the arrests Levinson's company owed Regpay a little over $1 million. The ruse was simple: an undercover agent acting as Levinson would send an e-mail to the Regpay bosses, informing them with much embarrassment that there had been some legal setbacks and he could no longer wire them large amounts of money. But he desperately wanted to make things right with his best customer. He offered to hand them $35,000 in cash that he had at his home when he met with them face-to-face to discuss future business ventures.

To play Levinson, the team recruited a former assistant attaché for ICE in Moscow who not only spoke fluent Russian but also actually looked like Levinson. Then a delicate dance of geography began: the Belarusians, naturally, wanted to meet only somewhere they felt safe; the Americans were desperate for a country with which they had an extradition treaty. The fake Mr. Levinson first proposed London; the Regpay executives balked and countered with Moscow. In the end, both sides settled on Paris, and a luncheon meeting was set for July 30, 2003, at the exquisite restaurant of the Hôtel Concorde La Fayette, a thirty-four-story tower overlooking the Champs-Élysées.

Police staked out the restaurant in true spy-movie fashion. Susan Cantor was pretending to have lunch with two other undercover agents at a table nearby. French officers were stationed throughout the hotel. Until the last minute, the Americans did not know who would show up from Regpay. It turned out that the president of Regpay himself, Yahor Zalatarou, came, along with his translator and marketing director, Alexei Buchnev. Over drinks and fine food, the fake Arthur Levinson assured the Belarusians that he was lining up a new credit card process-ing firm that could handle even more volume with less hassle. Buchnev in turn stated that there were no serious competitors to Regpay in the market and that they "could process up to $2.2 million per month."

On cue, the agent playing Levinson excused himself and stood up to go to the restroom. That was the takedown signal, and the French police officers swarmed in. "It was fabulous," said Cantor, who watched from a few feet away the arrest of the men she had been tracking for months. "They took them right down, to the ground. The look on their faces? Shock. They were shocked."

Two days later, the third man in the Regpay triumvirate fell: Customs records indicated that Aliaksandr Boika, the Regpay software expert, was vacationing at a hotel on the northeast coast of Spain. Police moved in to cut short his holiday. Spain and France soon extradited all three men to the U.S. The last thing the three men from Minsk ever expected was that their flourishing worldwide trade in pictures of innocent children would land them in a cell in Newark, New Jersey.

Back in the States, it was time for Connections USA to cop a plea or join their Belarusian comrades for a couple of decades behind bars. "They denied, denied, denied, until they finally came around and saw the light," said ICE agent Cantor. Eugene Valentine, the chief executive officer, pleaded guilty in federal court in Newark to a conspiracy to launder money for Regpay and was facing seven years in prison.

With all the top Connections USA executives convicted, Ortiz worked out a corporate plea for the firm itself: the corporation agreed to plead guilty as a company, dissolve itself and forfeit over $1.3 million. The harshest penalties were reserved for the Belarusian gang responsible for the widespread distribution of the child abuse images. Buchnev, the marketing man, folded first, pleading guilty to conspiracy to distribute child pornography, for a potential twenty-year prison term. The two senior administrators, Zalatarou and Boika, held out until the last minute. Then on February 28, 2005, the day before jury selection was to start, both caved and pleaded guilty to money laundering and conspiring to distribute or advertise child pornography.

Back home in Belarus, they would have been inconvenienced by only a fine or at most five years in prison. In the States, they were facing between forty and fifty years in prison; even with a plea they still had to settle for twenty-five years and a $25,000 fine each.

As one of the prosecutors at the sentencing hearing put it, "These two defendants will spend their adult lives in prison because they care more about money than the lives of innocent young children."

* * *

The money men were now behind bars, but that didn't mean the Newark investigators were finished cleaning up the Regpay financial empire. There were, after all, all those tens of thousands of eager clients who had run up credit card charges totaling several million dollars.

To pull in their fortunes every month, Connections USA and Regpay had to be systematic, organized and computerized. Good news for the businessmen until they got caught; bad news for their customers, because credit card payments leave a nasty trail of evidence. On the company's computer servers, the forensic examiners found names of some ninety thousand Americans—what they purchased, when, and of course their home addresses. About half of them were Americans; the others lived in twenty-nine countries from Australia to Hong Kong to Italy.

Unlike the delays in the wake of the Landslide investigation, this the American authorities moved quickly before the evidence grew stale. ICE agents prioritized the customers, ignoring those who had made just a single or occasional purchase. They looked for repeat clients who subscribed to the sites more than three times; people whose jobs or lives gave them direct access to children; and finally suspects with criminal records. The 330 people arrested represented an all-too-typical cross-section of ordinary citizens: a Mormon camp counselor, a minister at an all-girls school in New Jersey, a seventh-grade teacher in California and a Catholic priest in New York who stored his abuse images on a computer in the church rectory. When police raided the home of a pediatrician from Chicago, they found two computers with more than three thousand images of children as young as four; he got five years in prison.

The raids conducted in New Jersey struck a little too close to home for Susan Cantor. On Rosh Hashanah, one of the holiest Jewish holidays of the year, she found herself sitting in her local synagogue two rows behind a man she knew was about to be arrested. "I'm watching him, knowing that he's going to jail in a couple of months," Cantor said. She was so uncomfortable that she left the synagogue. Sam Cynamon, of Millburn, New Jersey, was a wholesale pool equipment company owner and by all accounts a loving husband who cared for his ill wife, and a devoted community member who rushed to the scene of the Twin Towers on 9/11. But he was also a Regpay customer and got a two-and-a-half-year sentence for his illegal purchases. "You think you know a person, but you really don't," said Cantor. "It could be the guy sitting next to you in your office."

There were hundreds of other clients around the world. ICE dubbed the international fallout from its Regpay investigation Operation Falcon. At Interpol's headquarters in Lyons, police from more than a dozen countries gathered as ICE handed out detailed dossiers on CDs for each suspect—names, credit card numbers, addresses, and the type of child abuse images they had purchased.

One of the largest groups came from Australia, where the Americans handed over the names of seven hundred suspects to the Australian Federal Police (AFP). By March 2004, the AFP's recently formed High-Tech Crime Centre launched Operation Auxin to handle the file, aiming for a "national day of action" in September to hit targets across the country. But there was an uneven response from police agencies. Some states relied mainly on a "risk matrix" to pursue only the potentially most dangerous offenders. Jon Rouse and his aggressive Task Force Argos in Queensland disagreed. There was nothing wrong with prioritizing the targets, they concluded, and removing the known high-risk people first. "But everyone has to go," said Rouse. "The worst offender will probably be someone who is not even known, with no criminal history."

The end result was that the Queensland police executed warrants on all 127 of their targets; their sweep accounted for more than half of the national criminal charges in the case. The Regpay consumers arrested by Rouse's team included teachers and school crossing guards. The images they found on one computer allowed them to identify and rescue eight children who had been abused.

In a repeat of the Landslide fallout, one former police officer facing forty-six charges committed suicide. He was not the last Australian caught up in Regpay to take his life. At least six other suspects across the country who had been named by the police killed themselves, prompting police in some jurisdictions to stop publicly identifying their targets and to provide contact numbers for counseling services to those people they arrested. But Peter Crawford, the detective inspector who supervised Task Force Argos, was firm: "We didn't get the wrong persons. We got the right people," he said. "There's a lot to lose there. Go to jail, you're not going to be a hero."

What bothered the Task Force Argos members more was how slowly and sporadically their country had responded to the challenge of Regpay. Operation Auxin was Australia's version of Landslide—a wake-up call for police to get their act together. "It was our lesson," Rouse concluded. "Australia was ill prepared for this, across the board."

Still, worldwide, the Regpay probe led to the arrest of more than twelve hundred people. For the Newark team, there was a deep sense of accomplishment in opening new frontiers of investigation for law enforcement. "It's a very satisfying feeling to know you've taken down a major organized crime organization," said ICE agent Susan Cantor. "We knew that if we followed the money, we would be hitting where it hurts—in people's pocketbooks."

The investigators had only scratched the surface. Regpay president Yahor Zalatarou reportedly pocketed only about $20,000 to $50,000—fueling speculation that a big chunk of the millions Regpay was pulling in went to unknown higher-ups, who were presumably now free to operate under a different name. Zalatrou's American lawyer told *The Wall Street Journal* that there were "levels of hierarchy above him."

Susan Cantor agreed. "Are there other Regpays out there? We absolutely know there are." Indeed, *Pravda* newspaper reported that the head of the high-tech crimes unit of the Moscow Central Directorate for Internal Affairs concluded that income from Internet-based child abuse formed a "considerable part of the black market," offering organized crime about $30,000 in illegal income each month for every Web site they operated.

Prosecutor Carlos Ortiz had hoped other district attorney offices and police agencies would get the message: "Regpay was further evidence that this was now becoming a problem of organized crime," he said. "Organized crime had seized on this as a way to make money and was doing this aggressively." In the months that followed the Regpay busts, Ortiz helped put together two quick, smaller-scale financial probes of child porn operators—in part to further drive home the point that these types of investigations could be done.

Unfortunately, in the following years, there were few serious attempts to launch other Regpay-like investigations in the United States that went after the big money, although the Regpay case would inspire British police to go after the profiteers of porn. "It's incredibly difficult to make those financial cases," said Maria Reverendo. "There is still a fear of the unknown and going into that whole uncharted territory."

Clearly, prosecutors and police were not going to be able to do this on their own. If exploiting children was becoming big business, why not recruit big business in the fight?

The big bucks being made exploiting little children had not gone unnoticed in Washington. Ernie Allen, NCMEC's executive director, was frustrated. "I wanted to focus on the economics, to see if there was a way to strangle the flow of money," Allen said. "Because the reality is that children have become a commodity. It has become an industry."

So when Senator Richard Shelby asked Allen for a briefing on how organized crime was moving into the child exploitation business, the NCMEC leader jumped at the chance. Allen made several points to the then Republican chair of the Senate banking committee about why it was easier to make money from children's exploitation compared with more traditional sources of revenue: "Children are plentiful and there is easy access," Allen said. "The production of child pornography is cheap, and there is a huge consumer market for it. There's basically no risk, unlike with guns or drugs."

Allen's prognosis was bleak: "What's scary is when organized criminals understand that there's money to be made, they don't care what the product is. The dollars are huge. Financial transactions are increasingly moving offshore. How do we stop the transactions?"

Senator Shelby wanted answers to those questions when he berated the representatives from the banks and credit card companies on Capitol Hill in July 2005. He told the financial institutions to report back in six months on what they planned to do about it. "Could they be blind to what's going on?" he asked with more than a hint of skepticism. "At the end of the day, the financial people have got to want to cut this out; they have to want badly not to make money on this. They're making money off it now."

"It took a long time for people to wake up to this problem," admitted Robert Alandt, the vice president at Visa International responsible for Global Acceptance Compliance Programs.

Once they were made aware, Visa moved into action. But stopping a porn merchant from using your world-famous credit card system meant you had to find him first—and that was not as easy as it sounded. Visa had set up a child pornography monitoring program as far back as February of 2002. Called "spidering," this electronic search had as its goal spotting Web sites using Visa's brand or logo to peddle child abuse images. It can be slow going. Every day Visa scans through about a million Web pages looking for misuse of its brand; in four years, the company had tracked eleven hundred problem Web sites and cracked down on about one hundred merchants or payment service entities.

Meanwhile, over at MasterCard, John Brady had been talking to Carlos Ortiz in the wake of the Regpay convictons. "That was a really successful case," he told Ortiz. "But we can do more."

"With limited resources, law enforcement can't get all these guys— there's too much out there," concluded Ortiz, who by now had moved into private practice with one of the largest global law firms, DLA Piper. "We started meeting informally and coming up with some ideas of how we could do this."

If cooperation had worked on an ad hoc basis for sidelining Regpay, why not build a permanent structure that could get business on board in the fight against child exploitation? That's what happened on March 13, 2006, with the official launch of NCMEC's Financial Coalition Against Child Pornography, bringing together eighteen of the world's most prominent financial institutions and Internet industry leaders. On paper, at least, it was an impressive alliance. From the Web world came America Online, Microsoft and Yahoo and eventually Google; the three major credit card giants American Express, Visa and MasterCard signed on, as did major banks such as Bank of America, Chase and Citigroup.

"We've set a goal to eradicate commercial child porn by 2008," said Ernie Allen, though he conceded that target was ambitious.

"Choke the money," he said, "and you choke the supply."

Indeed, the financial coalition made some early progress. Under a pilot program over the summer of 2006, NCMEC created a secure mechanism to allow its analysts, law enforcement, and the financial institutions to exchange leads. The CyberTipline received 422 reports of commercial child pornography and identified ninety-nine unique commercial child porn Web sites with names like "Elite Child Porn" and "Loli-Virgins." Every single one of these Web enterprises offered multiple payment methods for the purchase of illegal images.

And therein lay the dilemma—there were so many ways to pay on the Internet. Perhaps the only thing that flowed faster across the Web than child abuse images was money. The coalition could boast that it had on board the companies that process 87 percent of the business in the United States, but that still left gaping holes in the worldwide markets for the porn peddlers to exploit—notably in the shadier financial netherworlds such as Russia. "You can write as many laws as you want, but unless you really systematically enforce those laws, it's going to be difficult to patrol the Net," said Ruben Rodriguez, the director of law enforcement affairs for NCMEC's new sister organization, the International Center for Missing and Exploited Children (ICMEC). A street-smart D.C. cop for years, Rodriguez was tapped by the FBI to work on Asian organized crime and Panamanian drug smuggling, and by the late 1980s he was using computer databases for complex investigations at the bureau. He became the first director of NCMEC's Exploited Child Unit before moving on to help ICMEC track the money trail.

Rodriguez traveled to Latin America, Asia and Europe to drum up support for a financial crackdown on child exploitation, but he encountered stiff resistance in Russia. Little wonder. "Some of the members of the board of directors of some of these Russian banks were organized crime figures," said Rodriguez.

Law enforcement told Visa the same thing, warning that Russian organized crime had infiltrated the financial sector. "We had a few banks in Russia that came back to us and said we basically have every right to have clients sell this material," Visa's Robert Alandt said. So Visa pushed back, fining three Russian banks—Alfa, the Prima Bank and the Joint Stock Bank—a total of $300,000 for refusing to stop merchants from using Visa to collect child porn payments. The banks eventually buckled.

The financial coalition had another problem, closer to home. Increasingly, the illegal Internet traders and distributors were turning away from traditional credit card payments to newer, more anonymous Web-based schemes like E-gold. These so-called digital currency systems operate largely outside the regulatory system. Anyone can open an account with E-gold, perhaps using a fake name; you buy units of E-gold using a wire transfer or a (possibly stolen) credit card. Unlike opening a bank or credit card account, buying E-gold does not require verification of identity. You then transfer the E-gold units to a seller (who could just as easily be distributing child abuse pictures as car parts), who simply changes the E-gold back to regular money with the same anonymity. E-gold claimed it had about 3.6 million accounts with a daily business of over $8 million.

In late December 2005, FBI and U.S. Secret Service agents raided the Florida offices of E-gold, carting away documents and computer files. The agencies declined to comment, citing ongoing investigations, but at least one Department of Justice source said there were elements of child pornography involved in the investigations. A month later, the Justice Department demanded that E-gold forfeit more than $800,000 in two of its accounts. In a lawsuit filed in federal court, the government alleged the company was operating "an unlicensed money-transmitting business." The case is still before the courts.

E-gold, for its part, decried what it called "the unfounded charges and adverse misleading publicity." The company's founder, Douglas Jackson, said he was particularly struck by the dangers of online child abuse when he attended a NCMEC conference. He insisted that his company had cooperated with the police whenever contacted about child abuse investigations, and he even made sure E-gold was one of the first companies to join the financial coalition.

That did not convince some of E-gold's competitors. "It's a bit like inviting a burglar to the policemen's ball," said one senior executive from a rival credit card firm.

One didn't have to be much of a cyber-sleuth to find out how eagerly a certain clientele was flocking to E-gold and similar operations. "Credit cards are old school in the online world; everything is moving toward E-gold and other forms of payment that are totally anonymous," said one posting on May 3, 2006, in the "alt.fan.pretty-boy" Internet chat group. An advertisement in the "alt-sex.incest" group was even more explicit:

We are offering REAL CHILD PORNO delivered on
CDs . . . Since it is a high risk for you to pay by credit
card and dangerous for us to accept checks we'd like to
offer you to use E-gold payment system. You open an
anonymous account with them (they do not verify any
contact information) . . . There is no need to mention
what is this payment for.

It seemed that when it comes to moving money clandestinely—just
as they had been doing for years moving millions of pictures and
movies illegally across the Internet—the online child abusers always
manage to stay one giant technological step ahead of the law.

Eleven

TOURISTS ON THE PROWL

The shit has hit the fan . . . Woody's been arrested in Thailand, you've got to get rid of your computer hard drive, you've got to get rid of your disks.
—E-MAIL MESSAGE FOUND ON THE COMPUTER
IN LONDON, ENGLAND

"Here you are king and dreams do come true," the hotel boasted on its Web site.

But aside from the slogan, the plug for Castillo Vista del Mar in Acapulco was deliberately understated. Everything was simple, alluring and tactful. The prospective visitor would send in $175 as a down payment, and then the American who ran the business, Tim Julian, would forward the client head shots of a few young Mexican boys to choose from.

After a month of careful e-mail correspondence, once Julian was convinced that he had a reliable customer, he allowed him to reserve a room, with payment sent by regular mail—no credit card or online banking that was easy to trace. A Spanish-speaking American named Robert Decker signed on as the innkeeper, picking up the clients at the airport—they came from the U.S., Canada, Sweden and Britain—and introducing them to the boys they had bought and paid for.

"It was a business, a guesthouse, a safe house for men to come down from the United States to have a place to go with a boy," Decker would later testify. "A safe place where they wouldn't have problems."

Think of it as Priceline for pedophiles, the Expedia of the child exploitation world, where a predator can find a package, pick a victim and pay for that trip. If some entrepreneurs like Regpay saw a way to make a fortune marketing pictures of abused children, others realized that there was money to be made from selling direct access via sex tourism. Nothing stopped the eager Western pedophile from traveling on his own to Asia or Latin America or any other location where the children were poor and desperate and the laws lax or nonexistent. But there were the inevitable hassles of knowing where to go, where to stay and how to avoid legal headaches. So naturally, some enterprising child molesters realized they could offer their services and expertise to like-minded travelers—for a fee.

"Tim Julian was a pedophile himself, but he was also a business-man," said Perry Woo, who headed the child sex tourism investigations for U.S. Immigration and Customs Enforcement. "He was going to match demand and open business."

A convicted child molester—he had raped a child back in 1989—Tim Julian hailed from Hammond, a small town in the extreme northwest of Indiana just over twenty miles from Chicago and the cold winds of Lake Michigan. Maybe that's why he favored the sunnier climate of Acapulco.

Mexico was the perfect spot for American sex tourists, close to the States but blessed with weak laws on child abuse, an easily corruptible police force and plenty of desperately impoverished children. "There was an abundance of children, of homeless boys on beaches," said Woo. "They didn't want to participate, but it meant everything from new shoes to meals."

The boys, ranging in age from eight to sixteen, were usually homeless urchins or runaways, often addicted to drugs. Boys like thirteen-year-old Jesus Santiago, who said he had sex with Decker "and many more whose names I don't remember. I want to forget it." The reason was simple: "I was told I would never be hungry again," Jesus later said in court. Some of the boys worked on the premises, but the beachside resort had all the appearance of a normal vacation tourist spot. Molestation was never out in the open. "These people took good care to disguise the operation," said Woo.

But not forever. It eventually unraveled through a four-year investigation led by ICE's Perry Woo, working together with U.S. postal inspectors and a Customs team across the country. The arrest of two men running a photo shop in Dallas, which also served as a child pornography production center, led to the discovery of videotapes of them molesting boys in Mexico. E-mail and phone records turned up the name of Tim Julian, among others. "It took a couple of years to follow the targets, follow e-mail trails and interview individuals across the country," said Woo. By late 2002, Mexican federal police were tipped off about Robert Decker; they canceled his visa and would have kicked him out of the country if he did not agree to leave for the States voluntarily.

"He insisted on bringing his computer—a desktop," Woo said. "Big mistake."

A mistake because customs officials do not need a warrant or even an excuse to search and seize someone's belongings. So when Decker was sent by Mexican authorities to Laredo, Texas—the nearest point of entry—he was promptly arrested for possession of child pornography. "We did a thorough computer forensic exam, and that's when we broke open the case," said Woo.

Decker was held in a Laredo jail for a year, where his fellow inmates included several Mexican nationals less than pleased that their new houseguest had assaulted Mexican boys. "He had a rough time," is all Woo will say. Whether it was his grim jail time or the prospect of spending even more years behind bars unless he squealed and made a deal, Decker agreed to testify against his partners. He got ten years for possession of child pornography instead of two or three times that sentence for orchestrating a sex tourism operation.

Following up on Decker's leads, agents traveled to Utah, Colorado and California interviewing customers, compiling a potential target list of thirty men in the U.S. alone. But prosecutors decided to focus most of their energy on nailing the top organizer, Tim Julian. Woo discovered that, enterprising businessman that he was, Julian was not only sending Americans to Mexico to abuse boys, but he had also shipped at least one boy back to an American. Decker had helped to smuggle the child into the States for one of Julian's former roommates. When Woo called on the Indiana home of the man, Louis Accordini, the young Mexican boy himself answered the door. Accordini got one year for harboring an illegal alien since he too agreed to testify against Julian.

By August 2002, Woo had enough for an arrest. Within six months, Julian went on trial, and after just four days a jury found him guilty for having sex with minors and for transporting a Mexican teen to Indiana for immoral purposes.

Meanwhile, Decker coughed up another name of a major client who had also helped finance some of the hotel's operations: Stefan Irving was a former pediatrician for the Middletown school district in New York who lost his license after a conviction for attempted sexual abuse of a child in 1983. According to court papers, in one poem found by investigators when he returned from one of his trips to Mexico, Irving compared his male victims to "small mangoes piled at the door."

"Unique. Unripe. So pretty, each one," he wrote.

It was Irving's poem, along with the habit of Castillo Vista del Mar offenders of taking pictures of themselves in front of Acapulco's mango trees, that gave Operation Mango its name. In the end, though, what Irving had written was a one-way ticket to prison hell. He went to trial seven months after Julian did, and on February 13, 2004, Irving was sentenced to more than twenty-one years in prison. Two weeks later, Timothy Julian, who had had such big dreams for his Castillo Vista del Mar resort, got his sentence: twenty-five years behind bars in a federal prison with precious little sunshine and no ocean view.

In all, agent Perry Woo's investigation into sex tourism led to eight arrests in the U.S., ten in Mexico and the rescue of about thirty children. When Woo went down to Mexico to look for some of the boys who had been abused at the Acapulco beach resort, he was able to find only four of them. Two testified in the States, including Jesus Santiago, who at thirteen had bartered sex for food but at age eighteen flew to Manhattan to help send Stefan Irving to prison. Jesus by then was living with his aunt in the central state of Hidalgo, going to school and working as a door-to-door water distributor.

Some of the other boys who were captive at Castillo Vista del Mar were not so lucky. "We combed the streets of the Acapulco underworld," said Woo. "One had become a pimp. One was missing, a drug addict. Two had been found decapitated on the beach."

After the success of Operation Mango, Perry Woo got promoted to national program manager at ICE headquarters, overseeing the agency's burgeoning child sex tourism operations.

For Woo and other investigators, it was becoming clear that travel-ing sex offenders were playing a key role in the cycle of production of child abuse images on the Internet. "Before you can take pictures of the child, you have to find and abuse a child," said Woo. "They know that U.S. laws are strong and being strengthened, so they travel to regions where they can exploit children and laws are lax." They photo-graph and videotape the child, then build Web sites to sell the pictures or trade them in chat rooms, and the cycle of abuse accelerates.

A survey by End Child Prostitution, Child Pornography and the Trafficking of Children for Sexual Purposes (ECPAT), a respected international human rights group headquartered in Bangkok, reported that Americans account for a quarter of the business in the world's global sex industry, which involves about two million children. But they were hardly alone—English, Canadian, European and Australian men flocked to the beaches and brothels advertised on the Web.

Mexico remained popular, but as American and local authorities cracked down, word spread about other, more forgiving countries in Asia. Eric Franklin Rosser, the first child predator to be placed on the FBI's Ten Most Wanted fugitives list, was charged with a crime com-mitted not in America but in Thailand. He made a videotape showing his assault of an eleven-year-old girl there. That earned him a spot on the FBI's top-ten criminal hit parade just after Christmas in 2000. Within two months he was arrested in Thailand, but he was released on bail and disappeared. He underwent liposuction, had cosmetic sur-gery done on his face, and then traveled to Europe before returning to Thailand, where he was rearrested in August of 2001. This time, he served a two-year sentence there before being extradited to the U.S., where he pleaded guilty and was sentenced in October of 2003 to more than sixteen years in federal prison.

Thailand was proving equally popular among British predators. Men like Robert Errol Wood, a twenty-four-year-old Web page designer from Dewsbury, West Yorkshire, found the pickings easy in Klong Toey, the largest slum in Bangkok. More than eighty thousand people cram into narrow alleyways and ramshackle huts. The smoke and smell of cooking fills the air. Children, many in torn clothing and patched sandals, race around on bicycles or chase balls. There is a con-stant din of pots clanging, vagrant dogs barking and babies crying. It is a poor community but also a vibrant one. Its people are proud of their ability to survive and friendly to strangers—perhaps too friendly.

Wood took advantage. He bribed young boys between the ages of seven and thirteen who eked out a living selling flowers on the street. "His victims were among the most vulnerable," said Father Joe Maier, a priest who ran a school and community health center for the children in Klong Toey. "They live in desperate conditions, and a dollar can be a fortune to them." Some of the children called him "Uncle," but Uncle would take the boys back to a rented apartment where he assaulted them and then took pictures to post on the Internet. Using the online nickname "Woody," he boasted of his escapades to his buddies back home.

Paul Griffiths had first come across Wood when he was still working as a Manchester police officer. It was the spring of 2002, and Griffiths had just received a brand-new series of abuse pictures that came with a distinctive name burned into the bottom corner of the images: Woody.

"He was posting them straight to the newsgroups on the Internet and signing them, which is fairly rare," said Griffiths. "But he was looking for kudos." Griffiths did some digging in the archives   of search engines—which often keep cached copies of old Web postings— and found some messages that Wood had posted using the same e-mail address. He found one with an IP address he could trace back to a U.K. Internet provider. When police went knocking on his door, Woody had left the country.

Wood was that new breed of twenty-first-century world traveler: the sex tourist who goes to the third world not just to abuse children but also to use the Internet to spread the tricks of the trade. "The chats on his machine showed that he was advising people where were the good places to go and not to go," said Griffiths. Griffiths began collecting pictures and chat logs that proved Woody was abusing young boys in Bangkok—he just didn't know exactly where. And he knew he couldn't break the case alone. For years, Thai authorities had turned a blind eye to sex tourism; after all, Bangkok's reputation as a "sin city" brought in much-needed tourist dollars. Pressured by local human rights groups and Western governments, Thailand began to crack down on at least the child end of its sex trade. ECPAT International made Bangkok the center of its operations and lobbied hard for changes. Airlines and hotels ran powerful advertisements warning that tourists abusing children for sex was illegal.

Thai police, too, had shaken off their historical apathy on the issue, and several dedicated officers were doing their best to hunt down predators. Paul Griffiths reached out to several Thai police investigators who flew to England for a strategy conference on the Wood case. Griffiths showed the visiting police Woody's snapshots from outside Bangkok's Grand Palace; one Thai officer recognized a palace guard he knew. In the pictures Wood took of the boys in his apartment, they could make out some buildings through the windows—and the lead Thai officer on the case, Police Sub-Lieutenant Nathapan Sresthputr, was fairly certain he recognized the neighborhood.

Once back in Bangkok, he canvassed the streets and soon discovered a British man who matched Wood's description had lived there but had since moved. Sresthputr then mapped out the fastest route from Wood's apartment to the local bars frequented by sex tourists; the path took him through intersections where street kids hung out, selling flowers and sweets.

"He knew where Woody would go to pick the boys up," said Griffiths.

It didn't take long for Sresthputr and his men to find boys who knew Woody; he even located some of the victims in the online images. One of the boys had startling news: Woody—perhaps tipped off by inquiries back in England that police were on to him—had left that day for the airport. The cops dashed to Bangkok's Don Muang airport but could find no mention of Wood on the passenger manifests of flights to England. Griffiths was getting worried: the police knew Wood's visa was running out, but perhaps he had given them the slip. Thai officials then decided to check all flights, guessing that Wood might fly home through an indirect route. This time, his name did pop up—and Robert Errol Wood was arrested before he boarded a plane to Dubai.

"The shit has hit the fan," e-mailed a panicked pedophile from America known only as JoeJoe Biggs. "Woody's been arrested in Thailand, you've got to get rid of your computer hard drive, you've got to get rid of your disks." JoeJoe may have heard from Woody about his planned flight from Bangkok; he certainly could have read the local news agencies' reports of his arrest on the Web. He had sent the urgent message to one of Woody's regular correspondents back in London, but it was too late. Police had already arrested the man and were reading JoeJoe's message as he typed it. They found more pictures of Woody's Thai travels on the London man's computer.

Fearing that Wood's victims might be silenced by being paid off— or worse, killed—by some of his associates in the Thai pedophile world, British officials at first wanted to extradite him to face charges back home. But in the end, the Thai authorities came through. On November 25, 2003, the Web designer from West Yorkshire stood shell-shocked in a Bangkok courtroom as the judge sent him away for forty-two years—one of the longest sentences ever imposed on a sex tourist. When he heard the translation of his sentence, a furious Woody banged on the table and shouted abuse at the judge. The outburst earned him an extra two months.

Thailand continued to flourish as a destination for child abuse tourists, but Woody's harsh sentence and a new resolve by at least some Thai police officers to go after the foreign predators pushed them to look for fresher terrain.

They found refuge just across the border in neighboring Cambodia, encouraged by Web sites that promote it as a pedophile's dream vacation destination. "Traveling sex offenders have easy access to children, mostly acting with complete impunity," said Aarti Kapoor, a barrister who got her first job at twenty-four, working for a child rights group in Cambodia, and spent the next four years there. "Since the Thai crackdown, a lot of these guys have come over to Cambodia." One of the world's poorest countries—with half its fifteen million people living on less than $1 a day—Cambodia has an estimated thirty-three thousand child sex workers, according to the UN.

"The judicial system is very corrupt and inefficient," said Kapoor. She noted that there is no law in Cambodia that spells out child pornography offenses or specific offenses against children; men accused of assaulting underage children can often buy false documents on a street corner to boost the age of their victims. "Anyone can fake a birth certificate," she said. "It's just about money, and you can buy anything in Cambodia."

Kapoor cited an incident in December 2004 when police raided an infamous Phnom Penh hotel that was little more than a brothel, arresting eight suspected traffickers and putting more than eighty women and girls under the care of a non-governmental organization (NGO). But just a day later, a mob attacked the NGO shelter to recapture the women and children and force them back into the sex trade. Even when police seemed willing to take on the traveling sex offenders, they were hopelessly out of their league. Kapoor recalled at least two occasions when local officers came to her with laptops they had seized from tourists. "They did not even know how to turn them on," she said.

Initially, Kapoor despaired of seeing any improvement. While charities or NGOs reported Western tourists on the prowl, foreign embassies seemed more concerned with protecting their own citizens than the children in poor countries. Things began to change in 2003, when ICE started cracking down on American abusers. Then Jim Gamble lent the considerable weight of the U.K. police, as part of his efforts to build a new police agency to coordinate Britain's global assault on child exploitation. Gamble himself traveled to Cambodia, and for the gruff commander who had survived bloody street fighting in Ireland and the mountains of horrific child abuse on display in Operation Ore, it was an unsettling but ultimately uplifting experience.

"To see the true hardship in which those children live, it makes you think in a whole different way," he said. In a country where too often "the size of your wallet determines the size of your sentence," as Gamble put it, he was determined to change the balance of forces. "The only way to make a difference in Cambodia is to do it high profile," he said. So Gamble sent in teams of about twenty experts from the U.K. on three occasions, training social workers to help child victims and teaching forensic specialists to gather evidence in sexual assault cases. Gamble's officers worked alongside Cambodian police to help them nab the abusers.

Joe Sullivan, the psychologist who specialized in helping police understand the "spiral of abuse" of child sex offenders, was one of those experts. He found street children giving out business cards with e-mail addresses and Internet bulletin boards advertising specific details on the best brothels. With a group of international human rights investigators, he visited the impoverished village of Svay Pak, notorious for its child sex brothels. An undercover camera recorded the action as a pimp brings them down an alley and into a filthy shack where a seven-year-old is put on display for purchase. "Yum, yum, me good," she says, putting her finger in her mouth. Fortunately, she and more than thirty other underage victims were rescued, but Svay Pak continues to flourish as a sex-trafficking center.

Some sex tourists did not get quite the warm welcome they expected. Gary Glitter was an ostentatious, if fading, glam rock star who was jailed in Britain in 1999 for having thousands of child abuse images on his computer. After serving half of his four-month sentence, he headed off to what he doubtless hoped was a safer haven in Cambodia. But he was kicked out of the country, only to return and buy a house before being expelled again in late 2004, after spending several nights in jail. Glitter, whose real name is Paul Francis Gadd, fled to neighboring Vietnam, where by 2006 he was condemned to another three years in prison for abusing two girls, ages ten and eleven, in his home. British police flew to Vietnam to examine his seized computer to see if they could locate any more victims. They warned him that he would face jail in England if he ever returned to his home country.

Still, Glitter remained the famous exception among the thousands of lesser-known traveling sex offenders. "We get some of them, but very few," said Hamish McCulloch, the assistant director of Interpol's Trafficking in Human Beings Sub-Directorate. One problem, McCulloch said, is that international regulation and cooperation is spotty at best. Australia, for example, allows for registered sex offenders to be pulled off airplanes if they are traveling to notorious sex tourism locales, but most countries have few restrictions. While many countries send the names of convicted drug traffickers to Interpol, few forward any information about known sex offenders.

It was just one example of the incomplete and often contradictory array of laws around the world that made the pursuit of online predators that much more complicated.

Twelve

WEB OF LAWS

You can't paint every sex offender with a broad brush and think our society is safe. That's just not accurate.
—Rachel Mitchell, Arizona state prosecutor

Two hundred days in prison—or two hundred years. Depending on which side of the U.S.-Canada border you live, there can be a world of difference in jail time for the same crime against children.

Robert Rehill, a thirty-one-year-old from Sudbury, Ontario, was found with 256 files of child abuse on his computer, including thirty-two videos. In May 2006, a judge sentenced him to seven months behind bars. Just a week later, south of the border, the Arizona Supreme Court upheld the conviction of Morton Berger, a fifty-two-year-old father of four and a history teacher with no criminal record, for possession of twenty pictures of child pornography. There were no allegations that he ever touched or molested a child. But under Arizona law, the mandatory minimum for simply possessing a picture of child abuse is ten years—per picture. And the time is stacked, not running concurrently. Twenty pictures, two hundred years.

Berger appealed, arguing it was "cruel and unusual punishment." After all, Arizona's minimum sentence is equal to or greater than the maximum in forty-four other states. But he lost his state case and next sought a hearing before the U.S. Supreme Court.

The extreme range in sentencing is just one of the incongruities in the judicial battlefield of online child exploitation, where the crime is global but the punishment local—if legislation even exists in any particular jurisdiction. A study in 2006 by the International Center for Missing and Exploited Children (ICMEC) found that more than half of the 184 member countries of Interpol—95 states—had no legislation at all that specifically addressed child pornography. Not surprisingly, the list included destinations popular among traveling sex offenders, such as Cambodia, Thailand, Singapore and Malaysia, as well as other well-known tourist hot spots such as Fiji, Grenada and Jamaica.

Even among the countries that do have some laws on the books, half of them do not define child pornography in national legislation or criminalize the possession of child abuse images. A quarter of them—twenty-seven states in all—do not spell out computer-facilitated offenses. In fact, only five countries—the U.S., France, Belgium, Australia and South Africa—met all five of ICMEC's standards for comprehensive legislation: laws that (1) single out child pornography, (2)clearly define what child pornography is, (3) include computer offenses, (4) criminalize simple possession and (5) make it mandatory for ISPs to report child abuse images.

"There is still an enormous lack of awareness and also a lack of comprehension about what the problem is," said ICMEC's Ernie Allen.

When it comes to child pornography offenses, there is not even agreement on the most basic questions: When does a "child" cease being a child under the law? How old does he or she have to be before being able to consent to sexual relations?

The United Nation's Convention on the Rights of the Child—the most widely ratified of the world body's human rights treaties—defines a child as a person under eighteen. While not spelling out an "age of consent," it declares children under eighteen must be free from sexual abuse, pornography and prostitution. ICMEC also recommends eighteen as the legal age of consent; the norm around the world is closer to sixteen, but in many countries it is much lower.

The question is far from academic. In April of 2004, the RCMP in Moncton, New Brunswick, arrested a thirty-eight-year-old man from Pennsylvania while he was alone with a fourteen-year-old girl in a motel room. They charged him with luring her over the Internet and with sexual assault. If proven true, such charges could bring decades behind bars in the States, but in Canada, police had to let the man go when the girl told police she had agreed to be with the man. That's because at the time the age of consent in Canada was fourteen—one of the world's lowest. Chile and China also set the bar at fourteen; Spain and Japan and other countries fix thirteen as the legal standard. There can be wide variations within a country: in Australia, it hops between sixteen and seventeen, depending on the state. Some American states like Iowa and South Carolina permit sex between consenting teens as young as fourteen; in other states like Oregon and Wisconsin it is illegal until the age of eighteen. In Canada, pornography laws set the age limit at eighteen, meaning it is legal to have sex with a younger teen but not to photograph the act.

Many societies, quite rightly, do not want to criminalize sexual behavior among teenagers. Surveys indicate that anywhere from 30 to 50 percent of teens under the age of sixteen have engaged in some form of sex, most in consenting relationships with other teens. Strict age-of-consent laws applied blindly can have devastating consequences. A disturbed resident of Nova Scotia named Stephen Marshall went on a shooting rampage in Maine in April of 2006, after he took it upon himself to hunt down sex offenders whose names he had found on the state's public registry. One of the victims he gunned down was a man whose only crime was that at age nineteen he had slept with his girlfriend, who was just two weeks shy of her sixteenth birthday and therefore not of legal age to have consensual sex.

That's why experts say it is better to talk about "the age of protection" rather than age of consent. David Butt is a former prosecutor who has worked closely with Paul Gillespie of the Toronto Police and is now the world general secretary of ECPAT, the international advocacy group that fights child exploitation and sex trafficking. He proposes a sliding scale that moves from complete protection to complete freedom, matching a child's journey to maturity. Society can criminalize sex with a child under a certain age it deems fit, such as thirteen. At the next stage, fourteen- and fifteen-year-olds should have the right to "pursue their awakening sexual development, but that development should take place in the safety of a social environment limited to their peers in age," Butt suggested. For these young teens, there should be a five-year window for consensual sex partners: for example, a nineteen-year-old could have sex with a consenting fourteen-year-old. For teens sixteen and over, the same rules for consensual sex would apply as with adults—providing there is "no exploitation, abuse of power, trust or authority."

"Protection is a concept, not a cut-off year," Butt explained. "It means protecting children from predators but also protecting them from the state." He was gratified when, in June of 2006, Canada's new minority Conservative government brought in legislation that explicitly talked about "the age of protection," raising the age of sexual consent to sixteen from fourteen and including a near-age exception of five years.

"It's about creating the right balance," said Butt. "We have to protect children at an important yet vulnerable time in their sexual development while letting them do what they have always done with their peers: awaken sexually."

Not only is there little consensus on the legal definition of a child, there is also a wide disparity on how to classify crimes against children and how perpetrators should be punished.

In Australia, until recently, child pornography offenses were absent from the criminal code altogether. Police were reduced to laying charges under the film and literature classification rules. Operation Falcon, the widespread arrests that came in the wake of the international fallout from the Regpay probe, helped force federal and state governments to take the issue more seriously. By 2005, it was a national criminal offense to possess and distribute "child exploitation material," perhaps the most accurate legal formulation in the world to describe the abuse images.

Still, a gap still existed between the law on the books and the law in the courtrooms. An investigation by one newspaper in New South Wales found that two years after the Regpay arrests, only fifteen of the more than one hundred men charged in the raids were in jail, despite the fact that most of them had been convicted. Many of the offenders merely got suspended sentences or fines instead of jail time. Figures from the Bureau of Crime Statistics and Research indicated that stealing a car was five times more likely to land someone behind bars than looking for child abuse images online.

In the U.K., prosecutors and the courts also had to scramble to keep up with the Internet crime wave. For years, online sex offenders were charged under a 1978 Protection of Children Act, which was ancient by technological standards, or under a scarcely more modern

1988 law that likewise predated widespread use of the Web. That law offered penalties of only six months maximum for possessing abuse images, and charges had to be laid within six months of the offense, making it a near impossibility, given the backlog in police computer forensics.

"We had to think outside the box," said Esther George, a policy adviser with the Crown Prosecution Service.

By 1999, the prosecutors scored a legal coup of sorts by getting the courts to recognize that simply downloading an image was the equivalent of "making" a picture—a more serious crime with longer jail terms—since the offender was in effect creating a new picture on English soil in his hard drive. A 2001 reform brought in tougher sentences, raising the maximum punishment for possession to five years.

But it was not until the Sexual Offences Act of 2003 came into being that Internet crimes in the U.K. related to child abuse were finally codified and more severe penalties spelled out. A new offense was added to cover grooming, making it illegal to arrange to meet a child under the age of sixteen with the intent to abuse him or her. For the first time, the law also hit at traveling sex offenders. "In the past they were able to act in the relatively secure knowledge that they were immune from prosecution by the U.K. authorities," said George. "No longer."

Still, it was easier to change the law than to change people's thinking. When a twenty-three-year-old doctor appeared in a Scottish court in 2004 to plead guilty to downloading what the court termed "sickening" images of young boys, he was let off with a reprimand—no jail sentence or even a fine. The judge noted that the offender planned a career working with elderly people, and not pediatrics, as if that somehow changed the nature the offense. In another case involving grooming, a judge gave a man who had lured and assaulted a girl of twelve a conditional discharge because he felt the chat logs showed she was "a willing participant."

The situation was even worse in Canada, where the sentences handed out for Internet-related child abuse offenses were appallingly lenient. More often than not, Canadians charged with simple possession of child abuse images would get conditional sentences to be served at home: no jail time, no mandatory treatment.

So some judges got creative. Judge Gerald Morin, a Cree from Saskatchewan who worked his way up from a small community with no high school to a seat on the Provincial Court, once found himself at a bail hearing for a nineteen-year-old from a local reserve facing charges of possessing child abuse images. "I remember when the elders would say that people who take pictures are stealing your spirit," he said. "What could be more true than taking pictures of a young child like that?" Morin took an exceptionally hard line, refusing bail; the defendant eventually pleaded guilty. "It's the difference between doing what is right sometimes, when the law is not all there," the judge said.

The law certainly was not there for other victims. When Sergio Martinez, thirty-five, lured an eleven-year-old girl to his east-end Toronto apartment by claiming to be nineteen in a Web chat room and then attempted to rape the girl, he faced a possible maximum sentence of five years for luring and ten years for the attack. The Crown asked for ten to twelve years. The judge gave him twenty-one months.

Courts—and jails—seemed to be nothing more than revolving doors for some offenders. Blair Evans was a married father of two and a scientist at the National Defence Research Establishment in Shirley's Bay when he was arrested for downloading 20,000 pictures of child pornography. He got eight months for the offense. By 2002, he had moved to Toronto and was arrested again; this time he got two years. One of his conditions of release was that he could not use a computer with access to the Web. By 2004, he was at it again. Paul Gillespie's team tracked him down to a university computer, active in the "100%PreTeenGirlSexPics" chat room. This time he got forty-seven months, believed to be the longest sentence ever handed out in Canada for possession of child pornography.

Even when a judge leaned toward a harsher stance, the effort seemed doomed. When the Quebec Court Judge Dominique Wilhelmy sentenced a father to ten years for raping his two-year-old daughter and five years for distributing images of the assault on the Internet, she called it "the worst crime in the worst circumstances." But in a stunning reversal, in June 2006, the appeal court said the man should be spared the maximum punishment because, as one judge put it, "there was no violence, such as gagging, threatening or hitting the child." The appeal judges also gave the man credit for having no criminal record except for a juvenile charge. That exception happened to be his sexual assault on a six-year-old when he was seventeen. His sentence for the abuse to his daughter was reduced to nine years.

A recent federal law finally imposed minimum mandatory sentences for child pornography: distribution can get you ninety days to one year; possession will put you away from fourteen to forty-five days. Hardly a deterrent to frighten offenders from taking those first steps down the spiral of abuse.

"What is that saying about how we value children?" asked David Butt. In Canada, he notes, jail for child-abuse-related offenses is discretionary, but a conviction for an attempted bank robbery—even with no weapon used and little cash taken—almost automatically means jail time.

"We routinely see penitentiary sentences for a totally insured loss for a multinational banking corporation, but far less for someone who has ruined a child's life," he said. "The calculus is fundamentally out of whack."

The calculus was perhaps a bit out of whack the other way in America. No other Western country prides itself as being as tough on crime as the U.S. Sexual crimes in particular receive lurid attention from tabloid papers and TV. Conservative politicians and Christian evangelical preachers are not above exploiting the issue as an excuse for gay bashing. But for all the noise and fireworks, there is often more heat than light in the U.S. in tackling how best to keep children safe from predators.

There is much the world could learn from the U.S. legal system when it comes to protecting children. American judges are more aware than most that trading in child abuse pictures is not any less a sexual crime than a hands-on assault. In the aftermath of Operation Hamlet, a forty-four-year-old man from Spokane, Washington, pleaded guilty to taking pictures of his three-year-old daughter and exchanging them with one of the ringleaders, but he insisted he never physically abused the girl.

"You just told me that what you did was not bad, not evil, that you are not a rapist," said the U.S. District Judge Oliver W. Wanger. "What you did is bad; it is wicked and it is evil."

The man got seventeen and a half years in prison as part of his plea agreement.

Even in law-and-order America, there are some anomalies. In some states such as California, possession of child abuse pictures is still only a misdemeanor. At least eight states do not make it a crime to use the Internet to entice a child for sexual activity, and some states reduce the offence to a misdemeanor if the child is between fourteen and seventeen.

The much-vaunted sex offender registries also had gaping holes. NCMEC notes that though there are nearly 600,000 registered sex offenders in the United States as many as 150,000 of them are "lost" by failing to comply or by taking advantage of the confusing array of regulations. For example, the law did not require armed forces personnel convicted in military tribunals of sex acts with children to register as sex offenders on completion of their sentences—a flaw that let the John Doe suspect Kevin Quinn fly under the radar for several years.

That loophole was closed in a wide-ranging reform known as the Protect Act of 2003. The new law also tackled sex tourism, doubling the minimum sentence from fifteen to thirty years and removing the need to prove intent. "In the past, we had to show that the purpose of travel was premeditated to have sex with a minor," said ICE's Perry Woo. "Now we just have to prove the offense took place." Americans who engaged in sexual activity abroad with a child under eighteen—regardless of the legal age of consent in the countries they visited—could face charges in the U.S. While only a handful of sex tourists were nabbed before the new law came into effect, since 2003 ICE has arrested nineteen American traveling sex offenders—half of them for crimes allegedly committed in Cambodia.

Three years later, in 2006, Congress passed the Adam Walsh Child Protection and Safety Act—named after the son of victim's rights campaigner John Walsh—with even more far-reaching changes. For starters, the law created a national public sex offender registry and mandated consistent sex offender requirements in all states. Businessmen who profited from child abuse faced a minimum of fifteen years and a fine of $500,000 or their gross profits, whichever was greatest.

And, as always, American legislators loved to heap on the jail time. The one-size-fits-all solution seems to be: throw the book at them big-time and then throw away the key. The act created new minimum mandatory sentences or lengthened existing ones, leaving judges little flexibility. The punishment for the production of child pornography was set at fifteen years for a first offense and twenty-five years for a second. Aggravated sexual abuse of children warrants a minimum sentence of thirty years.

The prison years for predators kept piling up. Paul Whitmore, one of the instigators behind the international ring of abusers unraveled in Operation Hamlet, was offered a plea deal of about thirty years to life, so he figured he had nothing to lose with a trial. Bad choice.

Jeff Dort, the San Diego deputy district attorney, was not looking forward to the proceedings. "The judge in this case actually had barf bags, just in case someone lost their lunch during my opening statement," Dort said. Whitmore seemed to take pleasure in watching his handiwork again, smiling as some of the abuse pictures were displayed on a screen in the courtroom.

He wasn't smiling, though, on November 30, 2005, when it took more than an hour to read the verdict for the dozens of accusations. Whitmore was found guilty on fifty-one felony charges, including bondage, sodomy, sexual penetration, oral copulation and multiple victims. On February 9, 2006, an unemotional Whitmore stood to hear his sentence: 467 years to life in state prison.

Whitmore, not surprisingly, has launched an appeal.

A sentence of four centuries makes headlines and no doubt provides some moral comfort to the victims. But it also runs the risk of giving the public a false sense of security.

Lars Underbjerg, the Danish police officer who started Operation Hamlet, was obviously pleased that someone like Whitmore was going to pay for his crimes. He also wondered if there was a danger in being simplistic about the solutions. "If you tell me that we should take all pedophiles and put them in jail forever and then we are all safe, I could say the same about cars: take all cars off the road and no one would be killed in traffic. But we don't do that," he said. "We are not going to strand all the pedophiles on an island, or shoot them. So does that mean there is nothing you can do? That's not true."

Underbjerg raises a problem that few American politicians, prosecutors or police can voice publicly for fear of being branded "soft on
crime." The average jail time in America for child sex abusers is not a
few centuries but closer to eleven years, according to a *Time* magazine
report—and even shorter in most other countries. "The harsh reality
is that not all these guys will go to prison and not all will stay in
prison," said the U.K.'s Jim Gamble. "So when the offenders come
out, how can we keep the public assured?"

Dispatching all offenders indiscriminately to interminable jail sentences may actually make things more dangerous, not less. "The blunt
instrument of a harsh jail sentence is the worst means of addressing this
problem," said Ken Greer. Greer is a public defender in Nova Scotia
who frequently has to represent accused child molesters and child porn
collectors. "These offenders need to be dealt with individually."

He cites the case of a former client, a disturbed man in his mid-
twenties. Sentenced to two years in federal prison on child pornography charges, he was raped on four occasions, once by several men
at one time. "He was socialized even further into a world of forced
sexual gratification and violence," said Greer. "When he completed
his sentence, he emerged from the institution stigmatized, traumatized, victimized and with no greater insight into his condition or
the means by which he could control it."

Some offenders are unrepentant sadists who should be kept
behind bars, Greer, the father of four girls under the age of twelve, conceded. But others may suffer from diminished intellectual capacity,
drug and substance abuse or mental disorders. No one can be forced
to take treatment once incarcerated, be they in Canadian, American
or British prisons. Offenders often choose to serve all their time
rather than seek treatment and get a better chance at parole because
they fear the ridicule and abuse heaped upon child molesters behind
prison walls. Inmates charged with child abuse crimes will usually
not advertise it—signing up for treatment can be asking for trouble.
Greer argued it would be more effective to give some offenders a
community-based sentence with mandatory treatment: if they refuse
treatment they know they will be immediately incarcerated for the
duration of the sentence.

Those views cannot be easily dismissed as the predictable complaints from a defense lawyer, because they are echoed by the hard-line prosecutors from Arizona. Remember, that's the state where getting caught with a single picture of child pornography means a minimum decade-long prison term. But while the case of the high school teacher who got sent away for two centuries grabbed national media attention, underneath the radar Arizona authorities were actually a lot more inventive.

The state allows some offenders to take a lesser plea: for example, for attempting to obtain child abuse images rather than fully possessing them. That means the person may receive a shorter prison sentence and probation. The catch, however, is that a strictly supervised probation term must be followed for the rest of his life.

And strict it is—all the way down to a specific rule that the offender must wear underwear at all times he is in public. The other fifteen Sex Offender Terms and Conditions of Probation stipulate that the offender cannot have any contact with children—even in his own family—or date someone who has children without written permission from the authorities; must not "go to or loiter near schools, parks, playgrounds" or "possess children's clothing, toys, games"; and— perhaps most important—must "submit to any program . . . to assist in treatment."

In effect, Arizona uses the stick of decades behind bars to force offenders to take the carrot of lifetime treatment and surveillance. It appears to be working.

"Lifetime probation is an extremely successful program," says Rachel Mitchell, the senior prosecutor in charge of the sex crimes bureau at the Maricopa County Attorney's Office. She has sent more than her share of predators to jail but would just as soon see some of them getting the help—and the supervision—they need. "You can't paint every sex offender with a broad brush and think our society is safe. That's just not accurate," she said.

Indeed, a study showed that only 2 percent of those in the supervised probation program reoffended. "That's phenomenal," said Mitchell. "Clearly, it works to have them on probation for the rest of their lives and to have them in treatment."

International statistics indicate the Arizona experiment is not the exception. Dr. Karl Hanson is a clinical psychologist and a senior research officer with Public Safety and Emergency Preparedness Canada in Ottawa. He has tracked studies of about twenty thousand sex offenders from around the world. He found that on average the recidivism rate among sex offenders who received no treatment was about 17 percent for new sex offenses after five years out of prison—a statistic far lower than a frightened public has been led to believe. But it dropped even further, to 10 percent, for those who received treatment of any kind. Yet to date, Andres Hernandez's treatment program in Butner, North Carolina, is the only one in the U.S. federal prison system.

"Treatment is sadly lacking," Hanson said.

Turn on a TV these days and you'll see public service announcements for victims of rape, spousal abuse, children's help lines, drug clinics, alcoholism and erectile dysfunction. But if a man feeling troubled by his urges to have sex with children wanted some guidance, where would he turn?

When the Vermont child abuse program called Stop It Now! opened its doors in 1992, the first caller was a man with a simple message: "Hello, my name is John and I need help." Fifteen percent of the nearly seven hundred calls to the helpline in subsequent years, according to the Stop It Now! Web site, were from self-identified abusers.

Mark Langham, the pedophile from Edmonton, Alberta, sought help in Canada after his first two arrests in his late teens. But he was struck by the contradiction that he had to commit an offense before treatment options opened up. "Say you're a pedophile and you've done nothing but voyeuring or looking on the Internet at child pornography and you want to get help," he says. "There is nothing out there for you. Nothing whatsoever! Now isn't that kind of fucked up?"

Langham is honest enough not to blame anybody or anything but himself for his actions. "I don't blame the Internet—I blame myself. I put no blame on my wife or on the kids, it's all me. I made the choice to turn on my computer and go into those porn sites. No way my computer can control and tell me where to go."

And he is honest enough to realize there is no magic cure. "I'm going to have fantasies every day for the rest of my life. I can choose to challenge them in my head and think, Okay, that's not appropriate. That's not what I want to do anymore."

For seven years he was able to control his urges, until he slipped again into the abyss and began a cycle of abuse that would eventually send him—and several of his partners in his pedophile ring—to prison for many years. His message to other pedophiles is simple: "There is no cure. You're this way for life. Get help before anything happens."

Experts like Joe Sullivan agree. "We know from the statistics that the criminal justice system is not effective in reducing the number of children who are sexually abused," the U.K. psychologist said. "We need to encourage offenders to seek help and to deal with their problems."

Treatment programs typically offer offenders a mix of drug therapy and psychological counseling—both of which have impressive success rates. At the Royal Ottawa Hospital's Sexual Behaviours Clinic, Dr. John Bradford and his colleagues have treated more than four thousand people since 1980. In the early years, about 20 to 30 percent received drugs, but today closer to 80 percent get some kind of pharmacological treatment.

Most of Bradford's patients receive what are called selective serotonin reuptake inhibitors (SSRIs)—anti-depressants best known to the public in forms such as Prozac and Zoloft. But doctors found SSRIs also reduced sex drive and lessened obsessive thoughts and compulsive behavior among pedophiles. For more severe cases—such as child killers—the Ottawa clinic administers powerful anti-androgen drugs that dramatically reduce testosterone levels and block receptors in the brain. "It suppressed deviant sexual fantasies and arousal, which is exactly what you want," says Bradford. "In at least one study that we did it actually reversed the pattern of arousal so pedophiles no longer had sexual preference to children—they had a preference for adults. That is a dramatic turn of events, a cure as opposed to a treatment— provided they remained on the medication."

Bradford's clinic also offers all of its patients a relapse prevention program, usually in the form of group counseling. Started in 1982, the groups still have some people who attend regularly after twenty-four years. Follow-up statistics from Bradford's clinic indicate that recidivism rates for men treated for abusing their own children was down to a remarkably low 6 percent; for extra-familial abusers it was about twice that at 12 to 13 percent.

In England, Joe Sullivan was having equal success in a program that favored getting offenders to help themselves at the Wolvercote Clinic in Surrey, where he began work in 1995. "Without a doubt there are individuals who should be incarcerated for the rest of their lives," said Sullivan. One case he handled was a convicted abuser who continued to fantasize about abducting and murdering children. "We have to protect society from such people, but not all sex offenders are like that," he said. "You can't make someone change if they don't want to change. But there certainly are some sexual offenders who don't like what they do and would dearly like not to be doing that."

Sullivan and other like-minded psychologists around the world treat child sex offenders in much the same way that rehab centers handle alcoholics or drug abusers: people have to admit that they face an incurable but treatable sickness; they have to accept that their sexual attraction to children is wrong; and they have to learn coping skills to control their urges. Wolvercote took in 305 patients in seven years. Over 80 percent of them did not reoffend. But when its lease ran out, plans to move the center failed because of fierce local opposition—including bomb threats—from worried neighbors. Wolvercote, the only clinic of its kind in the U.K., was forced to close in 2002.

That knee-jerk reaction came in for sharp criticism from a surprising quarter—a child abuse victim. Shy Keenan shot to prominence in England when, frustrated after years of failing to get authorities to treat seriously her allegations against her stepfather, she took her story to BBC's popular *Newsnight* program. The TV investigation eventually led to her stepfather's arrest for a series of sex attacks on her and other children dating back to the 1970s; he was jailed for fifteen years. Keenan then went on to form Phoenix Survivors to campaign for victims' rights. Named "Britain's Children's Champion" by a leading charity in 2003, she lobbied cabinet ministers and confronted predators online. She also took on what she saw as the public's "head in the sand" approach when it came to forcing the shutdown of treatment centers like Wolvercote.

"Do you want this dangerous bloke on the street, or do you want him in a controlled atmosphere where he is monitored by people who know what he is and what he does?" Keenan said. "The protestors ended exactly the kind of treatment that pedophiles need—they need control."

In the United States, too, politicians—and some unenlightened police leaders—promoted scare tactics instead of solutions. The hysteria that depicts child sex offenders as "monsters" has reached epidemic proportions. Seventeen states forbid child sex offenders to live near schools, which does makes sense. But Georgia enacted a new law that forbids convicted offenders to live or work within one thousand feet of a schoolbus stop, a situation being challenged by civil rights groups, because in effect it bars offenders from living almost anywhere in the state. Several towns or communities in Texas, Kansas and Georgia have explicitly gone that extra step, passing laws that expressly forbid child sex offenders to live anywhere in their area. A new law proposed for California would make Los Angeles and San Francisco virtually off limits to offenders.

But the problem with the "not in my backyard" panic when it comes to child sex offenders is that it obscures the uncomfortable truth that the predators you most have to worry about are the ones who are already in your backyard: the overwhelming majority of children are abused not by a stranger but by someone they know. When Congress was patting itself on the back for pushing through the Adam Walsh Act to crack down on and track sex offenders, a key promoter of the reforms—widely praised as "one of the primary authors" of the legislation—was none other than the Republican Congressman Mark Foley, later disgraced for sending sexually suggestive e-mails to teenage boys who had worked in Congress.

It is far too easy for lawmakers to push for more and more punishment or banishment—as if hiding a problem behind bars or in some other city or state eliminates it. That kind of simple-minded "out of sight, out of mind" policy does little to protect children in the much more complicated world of high-tech predators.

PART FOUR **NEW FRONTIERS**

Thirteen

TECH WARS

We're at the stage where the smallest, most detailed piece of information sometimes has the largest impact. Some out-of-the-way information, buried somewhere, in fact can turn a case from a loser into a shining win.
—DON COLCOLOUGH, AOL'S DIRECTOR OF
INVESTIGATIONS AND LAW ENFORCEMENT AFFAIRS

Sometimes they get sloppy. Or just plain stupid.

In one series of child abuse images submitted by the Connecticut State Police to NCMEC, the molester had digitally imprinted the first and last name of his young victim in his movie, making her—and her abuser—relatively easy to find. In Germany, a twenty-year-old man turned himself in to the police—along with his ample child abuse collection—when he got spooked by the Sober computer virus in 2005. The virus came with a spurious warning, "We have logged your IP address on more than 30 illegal Web sites," scaring the man into confessing his crimes.

Such slipups are rare. After more than a decade of guerrilla warfare hiding from, sparring with and learning about law enforcement, the online abusers were getting better and bolder. "The bad guys are sophisticated," said Carlos Ortiz, the prosecutor who took on the Regpay conspirators. "They're organized. They know what they're doing. They're young and computer savvy."

The online predators and producers of child abuse images have several advantages over investigators chasing them, not the least of which is that they are not constrained by laws. The police—unlike their undercover counterparts in drug squads who are allowed to carry or trade in small amounts of contraband to lure criminals—are forbidden to exchange any kind of child exploitation images. Online undercover agents like the FBI's Emily Vacher or Scotland Yard's Jim Pearce can misrepresent themselves only to the extent that they do not have to tell their targets—until their arrest—that they are law enforcement.

Their targets, on the other hand, make use of false identities, stolen credit cards, pirated Internet signals and illegal downloads. It is hardly a fair playing field.

The players, not just the rules they play by, are also unevenly matched. Most investigators in this field are ordinary police officers who have become computer experts, and even then they often do not have the time to keep up with the latest software and Web-browsing developments. On the other side, many child molesters are either computer professionals or they live and breathe the Internet, spending long hours boning up on the latest techniques.

When police first came across Burt Thomas Stevenson's pictures of his daughter Jessica in 2003, they noticed that he had blurred a few of them to obscure his face or identifying features on her clothes. At the time, that kind of attention to detail was rare. Over the years, investigators began to find more and more examples of offenders who were catching on. "They're blurring the background, and they're hiding their faces," Vacher noted. In one recent set of pictures uncovered by ICE agents in the States, two little girls lie asleep in a bed. A pile of letters on a table in the foreground has been carefully blacked out. The predator took the care to cover up the buttons on the TV remote control—presumably knowing that the police could try to trace a brand name or local store—as well as the labels on all the videotapes on a shelf in the background. He even drew black patches over the girls' eyes, making them nearly impossible to identify.

At Visa International, Robert Alandt and his security team were also noticing that the porn merchants were getting shrewder. To make test purchases of child abuse images on sites they were probing, Visa's investigators would sometimes use special credit cards that looked just like real ones but were not issued by banks—and hence not valid to complete the transactions. The entrepreneurs caught on, and in private chat rooms and Web discussion boards they started circulating lists of such cards that could not be trusted. Merchants are also setting up dummy purchases to hide their operations. "They ask you to buy ring tones for your cell phone or software that has no real value, and then, as a part of that purchase, you're given a code or a password to go to the site that actually has the abuse material," said Alandt.

The traders and producers of child exploitation material are also getting more adept at finding new ways to access and store their bounty. "In the old days, when you did a search warrant on one of these guys, the most important thing for you to walk out of there with was the desktop computer tower," said Emily Vacher. "Now there are thumb drives and wireless drives. You saw a Swiss Army knife in the drawer, you didn't go for it. Now you do—it could be a storage device."

Cell phones and other portable personal devices may soon replace stay-at-home computers as the main way people log on to the Internet. More than thirty countries in the world now have more cell phone accounts than people; most mobile phones today come equipped with cameras and Web browsers. NCMEC started getting cybertips when technicians repairing cell phones discovered the same kind of child porn images previously found by computer repair shops. "It's the immediacy that makes cell phones so attractive," said NCMEC's Jennifer Lee. "It can be live. It's instant, and it can go from cell phone to cell phone. Phone to e-mail. Phone to iPod. Based on chats that we read by the predators, [such immediacy] is really exciting to them: their buddy in New York is actively raping his daughter, taking pictures of it and sending them to his buddies in California."

Cell phones are much more disposable than computers; you can buy a throwaway model and lay down some cash for a pay-as-you-go service, in effect wiping out any trace that Internet service providers can usually provide to police for their connected customers. Most ISPs keep some kind of record of their clients' Web activity for at least a few weeks; the situation for the phone companies is murkier. "What happens to images sent via cell phone?" asked Lee. "Are they automatically deleted from the phone? If so, are they retrievable? Does that cell phone company keep them? Who knows?"

Both in terms of access and storage, the increasing popularity of the wireless Web poses the most immediate technological challenge to law enforcement. There are about nineteen million notebook computers sold in the United States alone with wireless access and at least three million access points where you can log on, far away from your home or office—and much more discreetly. The FBI agent who started the agency's Innocent Images program back in 1995, when people relied on excruciatingly slow dial-up connections to get online, marvels at how much easier it is today for a predator. "I'm going to drive up to some neighborhood that's got a wireless access plan, and I'm going to trade my child porn and drive away," she said.

Most people don't secure their home wireless network, so it's easy for someone to "borrow" your connection for a child pornography trade; an IP trace would make it look as if you had downloaded the illegal material. Entire cities are planning to offer free wireless access, making it almost impossible for police to trace an IP address.

Tech-savvy child porn enthusiasts are also using "wi-fi" technology to hide their material in case they get busted: a favorite trick is to stash a wireless hard drive inside the walls of a home, where unsuspecting police would have trouble finding it. Some, like Australia's Task Force Argos, now carry the latest high-tech tools. "Our search teams are equipped with wi-fi detectors when we go into a house," said Jon Rouse, "so we straightaway look for a wireless network as soon as we go in."

In the tech wars, both sides keep getting craftier and craftier.

If you're trying to stop offenders from producing and swapping child abuse images, it helps if you have sophisticated image databases and recognition tools. But around the world law enforcement was bumping up against the limits of technology and the lack of global coordination.

In the U.S., there are two major child abuse image databanks that accomplish two different tasks. In Alexandria, Virginia, NCMEC does not store pictures but only their hash values. The main purpose is to spew out information to law enforcement quickly. "Ours is fast, it bangs out reports and it is easy," says Michelle Collins. But it does not do facial recognition. Collins's analysts have to rely on their own memory and intuition to pick up matching faces or objects in the background.

In Vienna, Virginia, at the Cyber Crimes headquarters for ICE, they have collected close to 200,000 images in a database that uses a

European software-recognition program. It can find similar shapes, colors and objects, but it also cannot match faces. "The NCMEC system is very good for quick return to get information back into the field," says Claude Davenport, who supervises the ICE program. "Ours is for a more in-depth analysis, such as searching similar backgrounds." For example, the ICE database can match two different victims sitting on the same bed; or take the same outside veranda of a home and find all the pictures featuring a child in that spot.

In England, the police rely on Childbase, developed by a Vancouver company, to spot not just shapes and objects but also faces. It started with 280,000 images in 2003 and has grown substantially since. Paul Griffiths likes to enter a lot of new pictures into the system himself so he can study—and hopefully remember—them. The software is robust enough that it can cope with slight changes in someone's appearance, such as facial hair, hats and glasses. But it still might fail to return a match for the same face if two pictures were shot at different angles or with different lighting.

Neither Australian nor Canadian police have their own image databases yet, but they're hoping to cherry-pick from the best ideas already in operation elsewhere. "We're the new kid on the block," said Garry Belair at the RCMP-run National Child Exploitation Coordination Centre. "We'd like to have it all." He hopes to build a database that will combine hash values with shape and facial recognition software.

Meanwhile, at Interpol headquarters in France, they use the same software as ICE to catalog and scan more than half a million images from around the world. The problem is that none of these databases "talk" to each other, in part because the various software applications are not compatible, and in part because not all agencies are completely willing to share their data.

"We're not a one-stop shop yet, and that's a big problem, because police have to ask at many different places," admitted Interpol's Anders Persson. The Toronto cop Paul Gillespie, as usual, was more blunt: "We still don't have a common portal, one place to look," he said. "Right now I have to pick up the phone to call Interpol, call NCMEC, call ICE, call England. Give me a break. That's ridiculous."

*   *   *

You would think that the easiest way to win the tech war against the online predators would be through the Internet service providers (ISPs). After all, every single image of an abused child on the Web has to get there by passing through an ISP: no access to the Web, no online child exploitation. If airlines or railroads were found to be negligent by helping their customers transport bags of cocaine or looking the other way while passengers smuggled children, there would be outrage. Yet the attempts to impose some kind of responsibility on the companies who provide the e-mail services, Web pages, chat rooms and communication backbone that fuel the child porn trade have been uneven at best.

It requires a delicate balance between what is technologically feasible and democratically acceptable. Repressive states, of course, can simply impose strict controls and censorship on the Web within their borders—and even then, intrepid Internet surfers can find loopholes. No other democratic country has been as successful as the U.K. in securing the cooperation of industry, child rights groups, the government and the police to block child exploitation sites before Web surfers get a chance to see them. Someone in the United States or Canada might type in the address of his favorite child exploitation Web site and the page would pop up with no problem. But an Internet user in the U.K., typing in the same Web page coordinates, would simply get a message that the page was "unavailable."

Founded in 1996, the Internet Watch Foundation (IWF) brings together more than seventy Internet companies and organizations in a cooperative venture to clean up the Web. Its headquarters is in a modest two-story house in a small village just outside Cambridge, surrounded by small farms and prim cottages with gardens full of white and red tulips. On the second floor, six people sit at computer screens, trolling the Web for child exploitation content.

It does not look very high tech, but this is is perhaps the world's most sophisticated watchdog agency for child abuse images. Through a hotline reporting system, citizens, law enforcement or companies themselves can determine which Web sites, newsgroups and other Internet locations that they feel are hosting illegal content. In its first year of operation, the IWF handled 615 reports; a decade later it processed 27,750. The sites are reviewed by IWF staff to see if they violate Britain's child protection laws. If so, the IWF then issues a "notice and takedown" alert to the ISP and also forwards the information to the police for further investigation. There is no law that forces ISPs to report known abuse sites to authorities, but cooperation is high. "There is a willingness here to find this stuff and get rid of it," said Adrian Dwyer, the hotline team leader. "The companies do it because they want to—generally in a matter of hours—because of our unique standing: we sit nicely in the middle between law enforcement and industry."

Their success is stunning. More than thirty-one thousand Web sites found to contain potentially illegal child abuse content have been blocked; even more impressively, the Web sites hosted in the U.K. plummeted from 18 percent of the reported child exploitation material in the IWF's first year to a minuscule 0.2 percent today. Major providers like British Telecom incorporate the IWF's information into what they call a Cleanfeed system, which blocks known child abuse sites from their customers.

Naturally, that means some of the hosting of abuse material has just moved elsewhere, where the IWF is powerless. The foundation says that of all the confirmed child abuse content it has found in the past decade, 20 percent appeared to be hosted in Russia and 50 percent in the U.S. One particularly pernicious Web site, for example, has been reported ninety-six times since 1999, but it keeps popping up in different corners of the globe. "It is obviously Net aware, so it moves from country to country, server to server," said Dwyer.

The notion of a small team of people huddled in an office making lists of banned sites deemed to be unsuitable for Web surfers appeals to police and child protection agencies but is anathema to civil liberties advocates. Still, the allure of the IWF approach is growing. In late 2006, the Canadian Internet industry announced plans to implement a similar system in Canada. The big test, however, will be in the U.S., where unrestricted Web surfing is seen as the epitome of free speech. NCMEC formed a new Technology Coalition—made up of AOL, Microsoft, Yahoo and other big players—which pledged $1 million to develop technology that can "detect and disrupt the distribution of known images of child exploitation" on the Web.

Whether such a program could pass a legal challenge in the United

States is another question. In 2004, the U.S. District Court of the Eastern District of Pennsylvania struck down that state's law that blocked access to Web sites accused of carrying child pornography as unconstitutional, violating the First Amendment. But the First Amendment is designed to protect citizens specifically from the government infringements on their rights. In theory, there is nothing stopping a private corporation from setting its own rules and restricting child porn on its services.

Indeed, at least one major American company, AOL, has been quietly using the IWF's list of problematic Web sites for years to purge suspected child abuse images from its system, thanks largely to one executive who has taken a personal interest in the tech war against child abuse.

Sometimes evidence of a crime can turn up in the strangest places. Just ask AOL's top tech sleuth, Don Colcolough.

When a couple of hitmen in Texas roared up to their target in their car, shot and killed him, then ran over him for good measure, a piece of paper fluttered out of their vehicle as they sped away. It turned out to be a printout from Mapquest, one of the Web's most popular geographic sites, owned by AOL. There was enough of the Web address printed at the bottom of the page that when investigators contacted AOL, the company was able to help trace who had done the search.

"I think crime in America has stayed the same; you just do more of it on the computer these days," said Colcolough. As director of AOL's Investigations and Law Enforcement Affairs, he is used to all kinds of requests from police and prosecutors. Murders, fraud, bank robberies—almost any crime has some kind of computer connection these days, and as one of the largest American Internet companies, AOL frequently has its hands full.

It was Colcolough who first assisted the FBI back in 1995 in what became the first Innocent Images case.

The Web—and online child abuse—was still in its infancy back then. AOL had only a million customers; Internet access was clumsy and slow via telephone dial-ups. And most of the pictures were simply sent as attachments to e-mails. Don Colcolough at the time was a new AOL manager whom the company had recently named to handle its emerging security problems. Colcolough jokes about how he got the posting within the relatively new company. "They asked, 'Who wants to handle our security?' and nine others stepped backward. I got the job," he said. "Child porn was starting to be my number-one issue. But at first we really didn't know how to deal with it. We were nervous."

Everything was new and clumsy: the FBI didn't really understand how the Internet e-mail system worked; AOL was wary about law enforcement infringing on customers' privacy rights. Eventually, with the proper court orders, AOL was able to help the FBI shut down one of the earliest online pedophile networks.

Since that time, AOL has mushroomed into a multi-billion-dollar behemoth offering high-speed services to tens of millions of Americans. AOL no longer dominates the Web-connection business the way it once did, but through its news and video Web sites, Netscape, ICQ, Mapquest and other products, it still handles at least a quarter of the daily Internet traffic in the U.S. AOL's director of investigations ends up devoting about half his time to the problem of online child abuse.

To help law enforcement, AOL drew up a training manual on the best way to file subpoenas. "Here's the data we have, here's what we don't have, here's how long we keep it and here is how you get it," Colcolough explained. "We've done the hard part for you." He is a regular lecturer at the FBI Academy in Quantico, the U.S. Naval Justice School and at various training centers run for prosecutors by the Department of Justice.

"With some other companies it is more of a battle than partnership," said the FBI's Emily Vacher, who is often on the phone to or in constant e-mail contact with Colcolough. "Don is always there for you."

When Colcolough and AOL heard about the U.K.'s IWF program in the late 1990s, they imported the watchdog agency's list of abusive newsgroups and Web sites to screen out illegal content. "We're not required by law to do it, but we thought it was the right thing to do," he said.

While blocking Web sites is not mandatory in the U.S., reporting them to authorities is. Since 1999, federal law has required ISPs in

America to notify NCMEC of any suspected online child pornography they discover on their service. But compliance has been spotty. No one knows exactly how many ISPs operate in the U.S., but of the estimated two thousand or so, fewer than three hundred have registered with NCMEC, though the major companies that dominate the market have signed on. But there were no written rules that clearly spelled out just how detailed those ISP reports have to be or for how long they should keep their records.

Colcolough, for his part, was troubled by the vagueness of the regulations and the passivity of the industry. As spam filters improved, customers and Web users stopped complaining as much as they used to about the abusive images or invitations they were receiving in their inboxes. "For us to say, 'Wow, we're not getting reports of child porn anymore, so child porn must have gone away; we must have solved that problem!' is a hollow victory, if you ask me," Colcolough said. "In my opinion, the problem is just getting deeper."

So he and his team came up with something called the Image Detective Filtering Process (IDFP). Instead of relying on customer complaints, AOL could proactively and automatically locate known images of child pornography moving through its system, delete them and then route a report to law enforcement via NCMEC. Colcolough's team spent six years studying, nurturing and tweaking the system. The first year was devoted to working out the legal hassles: for starters, they had to get special permission from the Department of Justice and the FBI to study how to identify and track child pornography. AOL then developed its own database of hash values similar to the system used by NCMEC and law enforcement, where a numerical value is assigned to known images.

Colcolough and his colleagues took the next four years to integrate the IDFP into AOL's massive system. He had to make sure it did not degrade the performance and speed of AOL's e-mail and Web sites, and he had to be sure there were no false positives: they wanted to stop as many porn traders as possible while making sure that Granny still got her pictures of the kids at summer camp.

Finally, in the summer of 2004, Colcolough, his technicians and senior executives sat in the war room at AOL's sprawling campus nestled right next to Dulles airport outside Washington, D.C. They were ready to throw the switch. Within minutes, the IDFP caught its first transmission of child pornography. An AOL user tried to send a known child abuse image to his pal, but it got zapped. "The e-mail arrives, but the photo file does not," Colcolough explained. Undeterred, the porn trader tried sending the same attachment forty seven times. "We were all in this war room saying, 'He's going to do it again,'" Colcolough recounted, his head bobbing as if he was following a tennis match. "Here it comes. There it goes. Intercept. Forty-seven times."

Colcolough's automated IDFP system could produce amazingly swift and far-reaching results. On December 28, 2004, AOL notified NCMEC that an AOL user had attempted to upload a single illicit image to his AOL e-mail account. Within eight days, NCMEC had contacted the local police, who obtained a search warrant and arrested Mark McGarry in Clovis, California. The investigation led to the identification of thirty-five other people; in his plea agreement, McGarry—a youth softball coach—admitted that he had also abused a young female.

After about a year and half, AOL moved into phase two of its program, tracking and blocking not just attachments but also offensive images embedded inside e-mails. Each time AOL tightens the electronic vise, it takes a while for the porn traders to realize what's up, and then they migrate to other ways of transmitting their stash. That's fine by Colcolough: "If I don't get you today, I'll get you tomorrow," he said. "You just have to screw up once."

In late 2004, Colcolough got a call from a discouraged police officer in Westchester, New York. An eleven-year-old girl disclosed to her parents that for the previous two years she had been having sexual intercourse with an older man who lived a few blocks away. Aside from her word—and the testimony from her parents that she had been not herself for the past two years—the police had little to go on.

The girl claimed she and her abuser had kept in constant touch through AOL's instant messenger. She had one of his screen nicknames in her buddy list, but that was still not enough proof. The suspect, who had a PhD in computer science, had recently wiped his hard drive clean. He had deleted all his AOL screen aliases (the company allows users to have several) except for his master account; he had erased all his buddy lists and e-mails. Then he reinstalled AOL.

The computer expert had eliminated all traces of his ties to the girl—or so he thought.

"Don, is there anything we can go through?" the New York investigator pleaded. "This is our last straw. We can find nothing."

Colcolough was suspicious. "He's going through the process of deleting screen names, deleting buddy lists. Something's up." But how to prove anything when a computer whiz had taken great pains to hide his trail?

Time to pull out an "Easter egg." In the computer world, Easter eggs are hidden surprises layered into programs—usually games—that give users a bonus or extra benefits. Colcolough walked the investigator through a series of keystrokes and mouse clicks to uncover one such prize inside AOL's software.

Click on Help. Next, in the dropdown menu, select About America Online. Then hit the control key and E. That displayed the error log—a file that AOL technicians use when customers call to help them diagnose what could have gone wrong. Because of a quirk of programming, that's also where AOL stores a list of unsuccessful attempts to send instant chat messages.

Colcolough was taking a gamble, but a reasonable one. The one thing the abuser probably could not simply erase was his obsession with the girl. After she had cut off all Internet ties with him, he was desperate to reach her. He could not very well drop by for a visit or call her. He was enough of a computer expert to know that he could not e-mail her because AOL would keep e-mail logs for a month. So instead he kept trying to see if she was online by clicking on the Find function in AOL's instant messenger. He kept getting an error message telling him she was not online.

Each time that happened, AOL recorded it in the error message log—a file buried deep in the hard drive. "He didn't know about it. The girl didn't know about it. The New York investigator didn't know about it," said Colcolough.

But Colcolough knew about it—and told the police officer.

On the other end of the phone there was silence. Then "Wow!" The file showed that of the last twenty error messages, almost all were attempts to reach the girl. Colcolough instructed the officer to open up the full file where AOL stores up to a thousand error messages—

and there were hundreds of attempts by the man, every few minutes, for days on end, desperate to reach the girl.

"That little piece of proof revitalized the case, empowered that little girl," said Colcolough. "We're at the stage where the smallest, most detailed piece of information sometimes has the largest impact. Some out-of-the-way information, buried somewhere, in fact can turn a case from a loser into a shining win."

When that evidence was presented to the computer expert with the PhD, he folded and pleaded guilty.

For Don Colcolough, it was just another skirmish in AOL's tech war. The evidence—at least the evidence stored in the vaults of AOL's computer records—doesn't lie. "My vision is not to solve this over weeks and months but over a long period of time," said AOL's director of investigations, taking a longer, if more optimistic, view. "We win a battle, then we lose a battle, but it's a war we can win."

If there is a command center where the legal and technical strategies in that war are plotted, it is the Department of Justice's Child Exploitation and Obscenity Section (CEOS) in Washington, D.C. There, a squad of eleven prosecutors works on some of the biggest or most complicated federal child pornography cases. In the center hallway, right next to the door marked "Evidence Room" is another door labeled "Coke Machine." The sign reads unapologetically, "We need our caffeine."

The CEOS lawyers get a boost from geeks as well as Coke. There are almost as many computer forensics specialists here—seven members of a High Technology Investigative Unit—as there are people with law degrees.

"We needed a capacity, an engine to go after the cases that nobody else was going after," said the CEOS chief, Drew Oosterbaan. He started by hiring Jim Fottrell to serve as the forensic chief. "He knows the inside of a computer better than anybody," said Oosterbaan, "especially those guarded corners where the evidence of child pornography will be."

Fottrell had been working as a systems administrator at U.S. Customs headquarters, but when Internet crimes exploded, his expertise suddenly had a new appeal and he moved to the Department of Justice. On the simplest level, CEOS's High Technology Investigative

Unit can help prosecutors faced with a defendant who claims his computer was infected with a nasty virus or invaded by a sneaky hacker. Like any other defense, it is either true or it is not—and a forensics exam of a computer should be able to prove it one way or the other.

Technically speaking, a Trojan horse virus—such as SubSeven, Netbus or BackOrifice—can allow a hacker to gain access to your computer over the Web without your knowledge. "These viruses give me complete control over putting files on your computer and getting files from your computer," said Fottrell. He knows of at least one case where a man used a Trojan to plant indecent images of children on the computer of a another man who was having an affair with his wife. No use charging someone if he is not at fault for what is on his computer; but at the same time, no use letting an abuser go because of sloppy hard drive detective work. Fottrell was called in when a man claimed the SubSeven virus had allowed someone to plant child abuse images on his machine. But Fottrell's analysis showed the man had firewall software installed and configured to neutralize the SubSeven virus. Fottrell even restored a mirror image of the defendant's computer in his office and tried to connect from another machine running the SubSeven Trojan but was successfully blocked. Then the CEOS investigator searched through the logs on the man's computer to find Yahoo chats with his programming buddies in which he expressed interest in using the SubSeven virus to spy on a cheating girlfriend.

"Not only does he know what the SubSeven virus is, he knows how to use it," Fottrell concluded. The man was convicted.

But Fottrell and Oosterbaan also wanted to go the offensive against the online abusers. They put together a team of young, plugged-in computer probers by doing the reverse of what most law enforcement branches had done in the past. "The FBI and other agencies basically take special agents and try to teach them the technology," Fottrell said. "It's much easier to take people with technical savvy and teach them the law. Web programmers and developers know where the evidence is, where the locked files are kept—because they wrote the programs."

Programmers like Lam Nguyen, a former PriceWaterhouseCoopers developer. One of Nguyen's first assignments was to build a better mousetrap to catch the high-tech offenders using Internet Relay Chat (IRC) file servers, commonly known as FServes. FServes allow someone to turn his computer into a sort of massive, automatic storage database where people can upload and download files. For the child porn distributor and collector, FServes are like a superstore of Web abuse: why go to your small corner shop when you can browse through aisles and aisles of the latest goods? "You can go in there twenty-four hours a day, seven days a week," said Oosterbaan.

The logic was obvious: instead of just going after the bottom feeders, the low-level traders exchanging a few files through e-mail, the Washington office could help coordinate attacks against the bigger— and nastier—players. But FServe cases can be hard to prosecute because of the forensic challenges. If police arrest someone running an FServe, he is likely to have gigabytes of data stored on his computer. Most police agencies have huge backlogs in their forensic laboratories as it is. Even if a seized hard drive with Fserve logs moved to the top of the list, those logs are so massive that it could weeks to sort through them. Yet Internet providers keep their records for only a short period, so by the time prosecutors issue subpoenas to collect the data needed for a wider case, the evidence may be lost.

So Nguyen wrote a program—it did not take him longer than a week—that would do a lot of the forensic work automatically. He can plug in a seized hard drive and scan the FServe files; his program then reorganizes most of the information into easy-to-read tables. Next, it runs through the IP addresses and isolates the ones that are American-based. It can also create a separate table for each suspect with a detailed upload and download folder.

One of the first major FServe cases tackled by the CEOS team happened to end up in their own backyard. Someone calling himself BruceDC was explicit in promoting his FServe in the IRC chat rooms: "Free credit to boys under 16 with camera or willing to chat on the phone." From October 2004 until January 2005, BruceDC offered up more than eleven thousand images and movies, with such titles as "torture12.jpg," showing a prepubescent girl in a bondage pose being sexually assaulted or "gerber24.jpg," which depicted a toddler.

When authorities executed a search warrant on the Washington home of thirty-four-year-old Bruce Schiffer, they found not only several computers—and the details of plenty of his trading partners—but also more disturbing material. In his bedroom were two boxes of cataloged correspondence he had with about 160 prison inmates, most of whom "had either sexually assaulted or murdered children," according to the Department of Justice. Schiffer visited a number of the convicts, some of them multiple times. In his letters, he discussed his "desire to rape children"—preferably boys between six and sixteen. He also wrote in detail about taking in runaways and "making use of them." Authorities also found a clown suit and a printed-out Mapquest route from his place of work to a boys' shelter.

Bruce Schiffer pleaded guilty on October 14, 2005, to a single count of using his computer to "advertise, transport, receive and possess" child pornography. He got twenty-five years. "It's chilling," said the CEOS chief, Drew Oosterbaan. "This guy was fantasizing about murdering children."

Always eager to stay technologically ahead of their pursuers—and out of jail—the online predators have proven themselves to be imaginative and resourceful, pushing into new frontiers with such cutting edge Web technologies as the Freenet.

When a University of Edinburgh student named Ian Clarke came up with the idea of the Freenet and launched it in 2000, his laudable goal was to create a way for political dissidents, contrarians or pretty much anyone who did not want to be hemmed in by laws to communicate with one another away from the glare and scrutiny of the official Web. The Freenet "lets you publish and obtain information on the Internet without fear of censorship," according to its official Web site. "Without anonymity there can never be true freedom of speech." Distributed free of charge, the software has since been downloaded more than two million times. Clarke's seminal article on his invention was the most cited computer science paper of 2000, and he was selected as one of the top hundred innovators of 2003 by MIT's *Technology Review* magazine.

Criminals can spot a good idea as fast as ordinary citizens—in fact, usually faster. Money launderers, terrorists and child sex enthusiasts quickly began crowding out legitimate users of the Freenet. "When I first discovered the Freenet, there was political stuff in all the countries like in China where you can't really discuss things openly," said Det. Const. John Menard of Toronto's Sex Crimes Unit. "Now, bit by bit, those users have slowly dropped off."

Even the Freenet organizers seem to acknowledge the problem. "While most people wish that child pornography and terrorism did not exist, humanity should not be deprived of their freedom to communicate just because of how a very small number of people might use that freedom," the Freenet Web site states. If you don't want your computer "to be used to harbor child porn, offensive content or terrorism" when connected to the Freenet, they offer a simple solution: "You should not run . . . Freenet."

But the child sex offenders do run it—and that meant John Menard had to run after them. Menard is one of the younger breed of cops who takes to technology like a teenager to an Xbox. At twenty-nine, when he married a Catholic woman and decided to convert, he spent long hours in the evening studying the Bible for his catechism classes. During the day, he spent equally long hours studying a different kind of scripture—the inner workings of the exploding Freenet. He is one of the few police officers who understands it and has deeply penetrated it, and his diligence has paid off in helping law enforcement around the world bust important cases.

Freenet is an anonymous peer to peer (P2P) network that allows people to chat, send files and host Web sites. Unlike most P2P programs, such as the now-defunct Napster and its successors like Limewire, there is no centralized server that stores anything. Each individual computer hosts the locations of the files, but the Freenet operates in such a diffuse and well-hidden fashion that even individual users do not know what is on their computers. For example, with traditional file sharing, if you want to illegally download a song, you log on, your computer looks for other computers on the network that have what you want and the two computers connect. Usually, the persons—or at least the computers—doing the uploading and the downloading are clearly identifiable. In more sophisticated programs like BitTorrents, the song or movie you are after is not taken from a single computer but from "bits" of that large file spread across many computers. But even with BitTorrents, you know the name of the file—for example, the latest episode of *The Sopranos*—and you know where you are getting it from.

Freenet takes the "bit" idea one step further. If you want to upload a picture or movie of child abuse, it takes a file, breaks it into many pieces, encrypts them and stores them randomly on computers connected to the Freenet. No one knows what is on their computer; the Freenet directory on their hard drive looks like a collection of garbled files. The uploader has a key that he can distribute to friends; to download the desired file, you put in the key and Freenet will go out and look for all the missing pieces. Only when all the pieces have been retrieved and stored on your computer will Freenet decrypt the file and reassemble the child porn image.

"The Freenet has been created in a way to make tracing an individual user nearly impossible," Menard said bluntly.

The untraceability of files is a predator's dream but a police officer's evidentiary nightmare. If an investigator downloaded a child abuse image from the Freenet and got a search warrant for a suspect's computer, it would be nearly impossible to decrypt the files. Even if he succeeded, he could never prove what was transmitted or that the user knew about it.

Not surprisingly, what Menard called "the higher-end producers" of child exploitation material have flocked to the Freenet, where they feel even less inhibited than they do on the regular Web—and that's saying a lot. For example, one extensive collection of violent abuse is called Uncensored Preteen Hardcore. To drive the point home, its organizers ask politely: "Please don't put softcore to this list."

The Freenet, though, is more than the Web's underbelly, where the darkest and dirtiest of child abuse thrives. It is also a bustling marketplace, where pedophiles come to exchange tradecraft and technique. "There is one producer who is abusing his daughter," Menard said of someone whose postings and chat he has examined in detail. "He writes a guidebook on how to use children. He knows how to cover his tracks. He knows how to keep pictures and erase the metadata and the evidence in the background so we can't find him. And he teaches all the other people."

Pedophiles discuss all kinds of tips and strategies with impunity on the Freenet: how to groom seven- and eight-year-olds, for example; how to approach them and how that strategy differs from twelve- or thirteen-year-olds. One extensive guide available on the Freenet is regularly updated and currently at its fourteenth edition. "It provides access through content and links to social, political and pornographic resources for pedophiles and sympathizers," the Web site states, plus a collection of female child pornography conveniently categorized using the five age levels of the Girl Scouts of America (Daisies for ages five to six, Brownies for six to eight and so on).

At first Menard was frustrated by his inability to crack the Freenet and figure out a way to trace its users. He contacted the best "white knight" hackers—experienced tech junkies who sell their hacking skills to corporations, the government and the military—but came up empty. So he decided if he could not beat 'em, he'd join 'em. He uses the Freenet as a training school, picking up the best skills and tricks from the enemy. He succeeded in infiltrating well into the ranks of some of the most active Freenet child pornography groups. "The neat thing about us being in the Freenet now is that we built up confidence," he said. "These guys wouldn't in their wildest dreams believe we are police officers."

Menard has used that access to the uncharted corners of the Freenet to download the missing pieces of puzzles other investigators were trying to solve. It was Menard who found important pictures in the Jessica series that helped police rescue her. It was on the Freenet that the Toronto cops found a video of a young baby being abused to help Spanish police break up a child porn ring.

And Menard's access to the Freenet would eventually play a key role in a high-tech hunt that would test how far police had come in their technological race to keep up with online predators, a global game of infiltration and intrigue that came to be known as Project Wickerman.

Fourteen

TAKING DOWN THE WICKERMEN

*—I'm getting worried . . . Did you guys hear they took down the
room on WinMX?*
*—Stop spreading bullshit. No one has taken any rooms down on
WinMX.*
—For real. Check CNN. Not trying to scare anyone but it's true.
—Holy shit!
—Yep.
—ONLINE CHAT IN "KIDDYPICS & KIDDYVIDS"

I t started in a no-tech way, with a conversation between two children
overheard at a ball hockey game.

"I didn't get any candy this week," a woman in Edmonton, Alberta,
heard a nine-year-old girl say to her younger brother.

"You don't suck Daddy's peepee," the six-year-old replied.

Shocked, the woman told the children, "Don't be talking like that!"

"Well, that's the truth," the children said, rather matter-of-factly.

The woman was bothered enough by the incident in May 2005
to call Children's Services, and a child abuse investigation was
launched. The two siblings gave a full disclosure that their father,
Mark Langham, had been sexually molesting them, along with two
other children under the age of twelve.

Langham had not had a run-in with the law since his two assault
charges as a teenager. He sought treatment and settled down with a
woman who already had two young children. "I believed in treatment
but it didn't work," he said. "Well, actually it worked but I chose not
to follow it. I made the wrong choice."

When Langham went to pick up his stepchildren from school on that spring day in 2005, he was told Children's Services had come for them—and he realized he had been caught. "I knew right away," he said. "I knew exactly what had happened."

Langham was taken into custody for alleged child abuse. But when police found a computer at his house hooked up to a Webcam, that opened up for them a new avenue of inquiry: Internet offenses. They called in Detective Randy Wickins, assigned to the province's new Integrated Child Exploitation (ICE) unit, which brought together the RCMP and local forces. The police laid out for Wickins what they had.

"Let me at it," he said eagerly, drawing up a search warrant for the computer. On site, he did a quick preview of the hard drive—enough to see hundreds of child abuse images, including pictures of Langham's children.

"We knew we had a fairly significant investigation," Wickins said. "But we had no concept of the size of it."

Back at the station, Langham had spent three hours "in the tank," as he put it, stewing in the holding cell. Strangely, he felt sadness, but also relief. "I didn't have to look behind my back anymore."

And anger: "I was pretty pissed. I'd lost everything I had worked for—my family, my life. What did I do?"

"I have done so many heinous crimes to children and the fact is I'm not going to change, no matter how much therapy I get. No matter how much a parole officer watches me," he said, raising a finger to his head, "they can't get in there."

Langham made the fateful decision that he would tell the police about his secret online network of fellow pedophiles. "It wasn't an attempt to cleanse my soul," he insists. "I've done all this harm; now maybe I'm going to start to change something."

He had already been candid with the sexual assault investigators but now he seemed open to widening the door to a broader inquiry. "If I could talk to a detective who deals with child pornography, I got a fair bit I could tell you," he told police.

Wickins leaped at the chance. "I was jumping out of my boots," he said. Wickins, like his FBI counterpart Emily Vacher, was one of those investigators who, rather than being repulsed by the idea of meeting an abuser, relished it. "Most police officers or members of the public would say, 'I want to eliminate them from the face of the earth,'" Wickins said. "My perspective is that I acknowledge the evil they have done, but, holy cow, could I learn a lot from these people!"

That was the beginning not only of Wickins's own education into the modern world of online child exploitation but also of an international probe that would push police into new technological frontiers, cracking computer codes and infiltrating a high-security Internet underground that spanned several continents.

It was midnight by the time Det. Randy Wickins got back to the police station and walked into his first meeting with Big_Daddy619, Langham's nickname in the Internet chat rooms he frequented.

"I want a color TV and cigarettes," the prisoner said. "And can you get me on *Oprah?*"

"I'll work on that," the Edmonton police officer replied, pretty sure he could handle the first two requests but dubious about becoming a TV agent.

Wickins told him up front that there were no deals on the table. Langham, who pleaded guilty to sixteen counts of sexual assault and child pornography charges, got a fourteen-year sentence in July—an unusually long punishment in Canada. But it was clear he wanted to cooperate. Langham gave the cop access to his buddy list on his MSN and Yahoo instant-message accounts, information that would soon prove instrumental in tracking fellow abusers in the States and the U.K. He also told the investigator about a series of secret rooms accessed through a powerful file-sharing software called WinMX.

"He's opening the door for me to come into his world," Wickins said, "a world no police officer has entered."

WinMX was one of the more robust and popular peer-to-peer programs that allowed Internet junkies to easily trade music, videos and chat. The crackdown on illegal downloads by the recording industry led the company that made WinMX to shut down its official Web page, but an ardent group of supporters kept it going, building patches and improvements and effectively driving the program to the dark fringes of the Web. In the hundreds of "rooms" hosted and controlled by secretive administrators, Web surfers could do and say as they wanted. In each room, you could see what other members had stored on their shared folders on their hard drives, select what you wanted and download it.

"Oh my god, I just went bonkers," Langham says of when he first discovered WinMX. He had seen plenty of pictures of child abuse but never the variety and amount of videos that filled the WinMX vaults. "I started talking back and forth. That's when I started meeting some of the guys."

As "Big_Daddy619," Langham began hanging around in several of the rooms dedicated to incest as well as one labelled "Kiddypics & Kiddyvids (Adult Chat)." What was special about "the guys" in his WinMX club, he soon discovered, was that many of its members abused children live while online, streaming the torture for others to watch on a Webcam. It didn't take long for Langham—equipped with a late-model Webcam and with access to two children he could exploit at will—to move up in the ranks and become one of the room administrators. "I wanted to get the high status," he says. "It gave me a sense of belonging—now I had lots of friends. Hundreds of friends. I know it probably sounds pretty sick, but this is what I lived for. It was my ultimate glory."

Even an experienced investigator like Wickins was repulsed by what Langham was telling him. "This was not picture traders. These were real children in real homes that were being tortured," he said. "We couldn't just sit back and not do anything."

Realizing the case now had potential targets worldwide, the Edmonton detective contacted the RCMP's still-fledgling National Child Exploitation Coordination Centre (NCECC). Investigators flew out to Alberta and worked briefly with Wickins, gathering information and tips before returning to their homebase in Ottawa. Over the summer, Wickins continued his meetings with Langham, but he was growing increasingly concerned that leads needed to be followed quickly.

On September 8, he decided to move on his own to test how solid Langham's allegations were. BigDaddy had boasted that he would often meet his friends in the WinMX room, then exchange live video feeds through Yahoo or MSN instant chat. At the top of Langham's Yahoo buddy list Wickins found the username Af9572.

Why is that contact name familiar? he asked himself.

Then he remembered that in Langham's collection, he had seen numerous files labeled "af972daughter1," "af972daughter2," and so on. Wickins drew in a breath: he realized the girl in those pictures was associated with the mysterious man on Langham's buddy list. With the password that Langham had provided, Wickins logged on, blocked all of BigDaddy's other buddies and waited for Af9572 to respond.

Within minutes the man connected and fired up his Webcam. "Where you been?" he asked Big_Daddy619, and Wickins invented a story about a broken Webcam. In the video feed he was receiving, Wickins could see a girl around twelve years old walking around in a pink nightie. For eleven minutes, the two men chatted—long enough for Wickins to grab an IP address from Af9572's Webcam transmission.

"Gotta go," wrote Af9572, suddenly ending the chat.

"I'm bouncing off my chair," recalled Wickins, excited that he had captured the man's IP address, which indicated that he was talking to someone in the U.K. "Great, we got this guy."

But it would quickly turn darker.

Moments later, Af9572 was back online. This time, the girl was right close to the camera. The man's hand came into the frame; he lifted her clothing and exposed her buttocks and underwear. "I'm thinking, Oh my God, what's happening here?" said Wickins.

The man grabbed her hips and pulled her toward him. She got away briefly, and the man's erect penis was exposed to the Webcam.

"Nice—do you miss seeing this?" he said. Then he grabbed her again and pulled her onto his lap.

Wickins was alarmed. "My heart is pounding. I'm thinking, I can't watch this. I can't do this. I wasn't looking at some movie. This was life—right now. This child was going to be raped in front of me."

Wickins was shaking. He came up with an excuse—"Someone's come home, got to go"—and terminated the connection. Still unnerved by what he had witnessed live on the Webcam, the detective quickly drew up a complete report, including Af9572's IP address, threw it on a CD and couriered it to the RCMP's NCECC in Ottawa. By accepted protocol, they were tasked with passing on international leads to the proper authorities.

It was 10:30 P.M. London time when Paul Griffiths, the U.K. cop who had cooperated so closely with the Canadians and the Americans in the past, got the call. He had been working long into the night on another case and was just two minutes away from leaving. The RCMP officer at the other end was a bit surprised, expecting to leave a message on voicemail. So he ran down the case with Griffiths and passed on the IP address. It was too late for Griffiths to act on the information, but first thing in the morning he made the request with the Internet company for the IP trace.

The good news was that it only took a few hours; the even better news was that the computer used for the Webcam transmission was located in London. The police raced to the house by late afternoon.

Back in Edmonton, it was 11 A.M. when a tense Randy Wickins got a call from an RCMP colleague in Ottawa. "Randy, I've got some bad news," he said, and the Edmonton detective's heart sank. So many things could go wrong in an international child abuse case.

"You're not going to the U.K. to testify," the RCMP officer said with a chuckle. "He confessed and the girl disclosed everything."

Indeed, the thirty-five-year-old man whom the London police had found at the home with the Webcam-equipped computer readily admitted that he had been abusing his twelve-year-old stepdaughter. Within months he would be given an indeterminate sentence on sixteen counts of assault and pornography—meaning that his case would have to be reviewed before he was ever released.

"I was flying high," Wickins remembered. "In fourteen minutes of chat with a guy, we documented an offense being committed, and within hours a child is rescued. It just doesn't get any better than that."

But Wickins hoped it would get better—and bigger—because the arrest of Mark Langham's Internet buddy Af9572 showed something else. "I realized our source is right," Wickins said. "Everything he is telling us is true. That was just more proof that we needed to act on the information we had."

By November of 2005 there was still little national initiative forthcoming on the file from the RCMP. "I can't believe they dropped the ball on this," said one officer close to the case. "They should have been able to see the potential."

Wickins picked up the phone to call his friend Paul Krawcyzk, one of the hard-nosed investigators in Det. Sgt. Paul Gillespie's Child Exploitation squad at the Toronto's Sex Crimes Unit.

"I can't sleep at night," Wickins told his colleague as he went on to brief Krawcyzk on the horrors he had discovered about WinMX. "He went ballistic," Wickins recalled.

"Randy and I agreed that we couldn't wait for anybody else to act," Krawcyzk said. It was typical of how much things had progressed in the battle against online child abuse: two experienced detectives from opposite ends of the country felt confident enough to investigate a high-tech global network with no prospect or even likelihood that the suspects or the child victims would be in their own country, much less their own cities. It didn't matter. "We've got to save some kids," said Krawcyzk.

On November 17, Wickins forwarded to Toronto the e-mail addresses from Langham's buddy lists. Five days later, he showed Krawcyzk how to enter the WinMx chat rooms, specifically the one called "KiddyPics & KiddyVids." On November 28, the Toronto cops were ready to begin surveillance on the room. Some of the most active participants—administrators and busy traders named Chevman and MOH, for Master of Horsemen—were immediately apparent. "We were trying to get a feel for the players, see who the regulars were," said Toronto Det. Const. Scott Purches, who had joined Krawcyzk on the case.

Between them, Purches and Krawcyzk had spent far too many dreadful hours trolling through the Web's underworld of child pornography chat groups, but they sensed this WinMX crowd was special, a breed apart. "You could tell the organization was different from what we'd ever seen," said Purches. Many Web sites and chat rooms favor and in fact thrive on anonymity: you go in, trade your stuff and get out. But WinMX was like a seedy bar where the regulars all knew one anothers' names—or at least their Web nicknames. "There seemed such a friendship that we'd never seen before," Krawcyzk noted. "These guys wanted to be known. They wanted to be known as the guys that run this place—and don't mess with them."

Two days after the Toronto cops had entered the secret chat room, an international connection to another case kicked the WinMX investigation into high gear. While Krawcyzk and Purches were roaming through WinMX, at a nearby desk on the third-flood squad room Det. Const. John Menard had been keeping up his forays into the Freenet. Back in August, he had come across a collection of eighty-three explicit abuse photos of a six-year-old known as the Ellen* series. There were enough clues in the pictures to indicate that they were from the U.K., so on a trip to Europe in early October for some Interpol training, Scott Purches passed on the images to Paul Griffiths.

As Griffiths started going through the series, he suddenly stopped when he got to the tenth picture. "I see an ashtray, and it is actually from a brewery that's about ten miles from my house in Manchester," he said. The pictures were recent, and the girl was young enough to be in primary school, so police began circulating a cropped photo of her to school officials in the area. On the first morning of their canvassing, one headmaster immediately recognized her, and it was not long before police were banging on the door of her father's home.

The case could have ended there as just another example of improving police work if not for the intervention of Toronto's Child Exploitation Tracking System (CETS). By now the database software program that had been developed by Microsoft was already in operation in eight RCMP branches across Canada, at the provincial police forces in Ontario and Quebec and at nineteen municipal police forces. So on November 30, it was a matter of course for the Toronto squad to enter in the details of the U.K. bust. Det. Const. Warren Bulmer was keying in some of the details of words that had been found on pieces of paper that had been placed next to the naked girl in the Ellen series when CETS found a match.

"Wait a second, this is the same thing," he said out loud to the room.

"What?" asked Paul Krawcyzk, as he made his way over to Bulmer's screen.

In one of the pictures, next to the girl's genitals, a piece of paper read "KiddyPics & KiddyVids 2005." There were also photos of the girl asleep, holding a message to someone named Chevman. In other images of her, wearing just her underwear, the name Chevman was on her right thigh, the abbreviation MOH on the left.

"Holy shit!" Krawcyzk exploded when he saw the pictures. "Those guys are from the chat room we just logged in to a couple of days ago."

CETS had connected the Web pictures of the six-year-old girl being abused in England with the WinMX room that the Toronto police were monitoring. "CETS made a link that was significant from otherwise innocuous clues, and from that moment on the case moved forward," said Det. Sgt. Paul Gillespie, who had been instrumental in getting Microsoft on board with the police.

"This put it up a notch, because now we knew for certain that people in that room were creating child porn series on demand with real kids," concluded Krawcyzk. "This was more than your average chat room. We started covering it 24/7."

There were conference calls and strategy sessions with police across the country—the Toronto unit, Wickins in Edmonton, the Ontario Provincial Police and the RCMP's NCECC. As always once a project took on serious legs, they needed a name: someone suggested Wickerman, inspired by a cult horror movie from the 1970s about a detective who tracks down an abducted girl, and Project Wickerman was officially under way.

The KiddyPics & KiddyVids chat room was difficult to infiltrate, run by a tightly knit group of administrators. Each member used a nickname and a complicated system to shield the digital signature of his IP address.

"We were racing against time because the chat room could go down any minute," said Paul Krawcyzk. When they first entered the room, it was hosted by an erratic and unstable man who went under the name TK. "He was a crack addict, very hyper and very easy to annoy," Krawcyzk said.

Fortunately for the investigators, leadership fell into the more efficient hands of a top administrator named GOD—an acronym for Galactic Overlord Duplicate. He was assisted by another thirty-one administrators, including Chevman, Master of Horsemen and—if the handle was any indication—at least one woman, who went under the title of the Honourable Duchess. Other regulars were Acidburn, Lumberjack and Lord Vader.

Their chat was riddled with the usual slang for their child porn viewing habits—"surfing and jerking," as they called it—and there was plenty of sick humor that could be dismissed as locker room banter if the WinMX members were not so deadly serious about their young targets.

"I had lots of fun, went Boxing Day shopping today," Lord Vader wrote one day. "Lots of youngin's at the mall

"Perv?" said another WinMX member.

"Thanks for the compliment," Vader shot back.

But what they were trading and doing was anything but funny: an image of an eighteen-month-old girl with her genitals exposed; a nine-minute video showing a girl about ten forced into sexual acts; a five-minute video depicting two girls enduring physical abuse. The police faced a delicate dilemma: if they moved too soon against a major WinMX player—and they could hardly stand by if they knew he was actively abusing a child—would they lose the chance to arrest the others and save more children?

It was clear that this was one of the most security-conscious groups the authorities had ever seen on the Web, but that could also play into the hands of the cops. Nobody apparently knew the real-life identities of their online conspirators. Langham's arrest and subsequent disappearance had not created any waves, but he was not a senior leader. Thankfully, the arrest of his Webcam partner from Manchester also went unnoticed, since the U.K. man had not been active in the room for months.

But how much longer could the police go on, picking off members of the WinMX crowd, before suspicions were raised? The Kiddypics regulars were constantly trading security tips and technical know-how. Lord Vader, for example, explained the arsenal of sophisticated Web weapons he had amassed that would baffle most ordinary Internet users: a 128MB encrypted router, Ghost Surf Pro and Cryptainer. Another WinMX user boasted that he had put a shotgun bullet inside his hard drive and rigged it to explode if he suspected police were at the door.

The administrators for the "KiddyPics & KiddyVids" chat room were skilled computer geeks. They would host the room on their computers, but if they spotted trouble or were worried about infiltration, they could quickly move the entire room—with all its chat and participants—to another server without anyone knowing. What really stumped the police was the ability of the WinMX software to hide or mask the IP addresses of its users. Normally, when undercover cops chat with child porn collectors, exchange files or look at Webcam feeds, they can read the telltale IP address of the person on the other end. But in WinMX, only the room's administrators could see the IP address of the other club members.

Try as they might, the cops could not crack the code. "We put the top forensic police experts on it," said Krawcyzk. "But everybody told us they were impossible to trace. You just couldn't do it."

Krawcyzk figured that if he couldn't find the suspects through their IP addresses, he would have to do it the good old-fashioned way. He focused on Chevman, one of the administrators who kept bubbling to the surface because of the large number of his postings. On a large whiteboard in the Toronto office of the Sex Crimes Unit, Krawcyzk began to write down every clue he could glean from Chevman's messages—"the trail of breadcrumbs," as he called it. Krawcyzk had spotted a note by Chevman that he "wish[ed] TiVO was in Canada," which narrowed down the country. He made enough references to snowy weather and going for supper around 6 P.M.—when it was already 8 P.M. in Toronto—that Krawcyzk was fairly certain his target was in Alberta. The cops knew about Chevman's cars, about the exact time, date of birth and weight of his daughter's premature baby and about his wife's heart surgery.

"We knew more about him than he knew about himself," Krawcyzk joked.

Chevman and the other administrators reveled in their sense of invincibility. "There's no way they can catch us," the chat room's administrators said in one posting to each other.

What Chevman and his WinMX buddies didn't know was that the cops were reading their chat as they typed it . . . and getting ready to pounce in different countries around the world.

From the start, the Canadians had farmed out leads to their colleagues in the U.K., Australia and the U.S.

One of the first tips found its way to the Chicago branch of Immigration and Customs Enforcement—a stroke of luck, because that city happened to have the largest cyber-crimes ICE field office in the country. Ron Wolflick, a veteran Customs agent who had spent over two decades working everything from drugs to money laundering, headed the seventeen-person unit.

In early December 2005, Wolflick and his team got word from the Canadians that Langham's buddy list indicated that there were three or four potential suspects in the Kiddypics room from the Midwest. One online acquaintance of Langham's, known to him only as Acidburn, had sent him videos of his assault on an infant girl.

For the Chicago investigators, those were chilling deeds. "Somebody may be molesting an eighteen-month-old girl," said Wolflick. "We had to figure out where this gentleman was."

Because Langham had been in touch with Acidburn outside of the WinMX room and in less secure instant-messaging programs, the police had a good lead with an IP address. A check with the local Internet company gave them a street address. The ICE team used phone records and information from other databases to pinpoint the suspect as a twenty-nine-year-old resident of Bartlett, a Chicago suburb, who was in a custody battle with his estranged wife.

Much as they wanted to, the ICE team could not simply burst through the door and arrest him. They first had to gather all the necessary evidence; they had to be sure he was not with the child to avoid his harming her; and if possible they had to grab him when he was not online in the WinMX room to prevent him from warning the others.

Wolflick's team mounted an elaborate operation. They arranged a conference call with Langham from his prison cell—Randy Wickins had to catch the warden late one night at home to authorize the unusual setup—to gather more insight into Acidburn. They applied to the courts and got what is known as a Title 3 Internet intercept—in effect a wiretap on the suspect's computer via his ISP. "As he was surfing, everything he was doing was coming up in our office," said Wolflick.

Next they set up surveillance cameras outside the target's home. They saw that Acidburn took regular smoke breaks in his garage—a convenient moment for an arrest, but a narrow opportunity: he was a fast smoker and finished puffing in three or four minutes.

The takedown was finally scheduled for Sunday, January 8. At 4 P.M., as Acidburn stepped into his two-car garage for a smoke, the Special Response Team deployed and tackled him on the garage floor. "He was not emotional, he wasn't crying, he wasn't screaming," said Wolflick, who stood over the suspect, struck by the fact that the only fuss Acidburn made was about the stereo headphones he was wearing. "He was more concerned about the headphones than the handcuffs."

From Acidburn, the ICE team got the name of one other WinMX member in the Chicago area, whom they arrested immediately, plus leads on about a dozen other people across the country. What the police still could not figure out was how the WinMX software was blocking the users' IP addresses. The challenge of solving that mystery fell to a young cyber investigator named Brian Bone.

By his own admission, Bone was "a natural at computers." His father had been an accountant who got into computers early; Bone even recalls visiting his dad's office and seeing the old punchcard machines. "I was lucky, because even as a really young kid I've always had a computer at my house," he said. Bone had started working as a patrol officer in the sheriff's office when he was twenty-one; his boyish looks meant that he was often used as a decoy in sting operations to nab online predators who showed up for "dates" that they had arranged with what they thought were young victims. But Bone soon graduated to computer forensics and transferred as a detective to the Lake County State Attorney's Office where, at twenty-nine, he assisted the Chicago ICE team in their probes.

In most popular peer-to-peer trading software programs, computers "talk" to each other to exchange files. In that process, it is not hard for one user to read the IP address of the person sending the files; after all, the computer doing the downloading has to know where the computer uploading the files is. But WinMX somehow scrambled the IP code so that only the high-level administrators could see it. "It was hidden somehow through that WinMX connection—that's what was so neat about the system," Bone said with the admiration only a programmer could muster for a worthy opponent. "They thought the cops could never find out what it was, and to a large degree that was true."

When the Toronto cops Paul Krawcyzk and Scott Purches went to Chicago to assist in the takedown of Acidburn, they explained to their American colleagues how crucial it would be to get a fix on one of the room's administrators, like Chevman. "If we could find him, we would be able to break the case," Krawcyzk said.

All day the investigators huddled over the computers. "There had to be some way to do it," Bone insisted. "My computer had to know who I was communicating with. The IP address was in there—we just had to find it."

At 10 P.M., they finally called it a night.

"If you can figure this out, I'll buy you a beer," said Krawcyzk as a parting shot.

Once at home, Bone got on his own computer and started playing with the program. One of the things he soon noticed was that no matter how many times he logged on or off from the WinMX room, the hexadecimal digits after his user nickname—a numeral system in mathematics and computer science that uses the symbols 0 to 9 and A to F—remained the same.

"The hex code stood for something and didn't change," he concluded. "Somehow the hex code was matching the IP."

Bone did some Web searches and eventually found a page in German that seemed to explain some of the WinMX patches. He clicked on one of the Web's instant, if not always reliable, computer translation tools to read the text in somewhat garbled English. It was enough for him to decipher an important clue: the last four digits of the hex series represented the port number—the entry point the user's computer used to communicate with the Internet.

That was crucial because it cleared away some of the clutter in the hex code. Bone tried playing with the remaining digits but still could not get an IP number. Then he realized that the numbers—grouped in a series of four separated by a decimal point—might be backward, with the least significant data first. If he reversed the order and read them right to left, then converted the hex code into regular digits— bingo, he had the IP address.

The next morning, January 12, Bone walked into the office on just a few hours' sleep.

"You owe me a beer," he said to a disbelieving Krawcyzk.

"No way," said the Canadian cop.

Bone was still not entirely sure about his formula; he had tested it only on his own terminal at home. So the police logged on to WinMX from various computers in their office, and each time it worked. Then they tried it on the code coming up after Chevman's name.

If the Canadian cops were surprised by the American investigator's success in cracking the code, they couldn't help smiling at what the code revealed. The IP address for Chevman indicated that the administrator they had been after all this time lived in the city where the case had first started.

"It came full circle back to Edmonton," said Randy Wickins, who shook his head in disbelief when he heard the news.

Chevman, it turned out, was a forty-nine-year-old clerk named Carl A. Treleaven whose wife worked in a local daycare.

By January 14, the police were able to run an IP trace through the Shaw Internet provider in Alberta to come up with a street address. On January 25, Paul Krawcyzk and Scott Purches flew out to Edmonton to help Wickins with the arrest. At seven-thirty the next morning, it was still dark as the officers waited in a surveillance van parked just outside the man's simple bungalow. The stakes were high because the police did not want to simply arrest Treleaven; they wanted to take over his identity so they could infiltrate the group as a top administrator. To do that, they needed to nab him during those brief moments when he was online but temporarily away from his computer.

"We knew what we could get—if the computer was still on," said Wickins.

In the van, they had a partial view inside Treleavan's home through a front window. They were also on the phone to John Menard back in Toronto; he was monitoring Chevman's live online chats.

As Chevman typed in a message on his keyboard, Menard read it over the phone and Scott Purches repeated it out loud in the van: "Be right back—coffee time."

That was the cue they were waiting for—a few precious minutes when Chevman was away from his screen.

"Okay, go. He's in the kitchen!" Randy's excitement crackled over the police radio to the troops outside. Quickly, a decoy officer ran to the front door and rang the bell. The cops figured that Treleaven had two choices: answer the door, or run for the computer. Either way, the SWAT team was standing by.

"As soon as he opened the door, his life changed forever," said Wickins.

The cops burst in. Krawcyzk rushed for the computer. At his doorstep, Treleaven was shaken, visibly distraught and sobbing.

"I just look at pictures," Treleaven told officers tearfully. "I don't want to hurt anybody." Chevman was being disingenuous at best: his criminal record included convictions in 1986 and again in 1993 for indecent assault and gross indecency for attacks on young girls. Now, standing in his open doorway in the cold Alberta winter morning, Treleaven could feel his world come crashing down around him.

"I know why you're here,' he said, still sobbing, to the arresting officer.

"Why am I here today?" the cop asked.

"To put me in jail forever," said the avid WinMX predator somewhat melodramatically. In Canada, he was looking at only a handful of years behind bars since there was no evidence—this time—that he'd committed any hands-on abuse. On his computer in the WinMX chat room, police found over ninety people waiting to download the more than twenty gigabytes of child abuse images that Treleaven had stored.

While Chevman cried to the arresting officers, a few feet away Paul Krawcyzk was crouched over the man's computer, hoping to pull off an updated, online version of the "bait and switch" con: he had to convince the hundreds of WinMX underlings—and, more important, the other top chat room administrators—that he was Chevman. "He was probably the most trusted person in the chat room," Krawcyzk said.

In Toronto and in Chicago, where the code cracker Brian Bone and other members of the ICE team were monitoring the room, they waited nervously, knowing that the next time Chevman logged in, it was one of their officers typing in the words. "There was probably a good five minutes between Chevman's departure and when Paul started typing, so it was one of those hold-your-breath moments," said Bone.

"We had to make sure that once we took Chevman down, there wasn't widespread panic in the room," explained ICE's Ron Wolflick. "We're waiting with our fingers over the phone buttons, because if things went badly, we needed to make sure we got people deployed." Deployed and ready to make arrests of the known targets in WinMX.

But there was no need to panic. In a few minutes, "Chevman" returned; his WinMX buddies assumed he had finished his coffee break, and no one raised any doubts. Later that day, Treleavan gave the police a four-hour interview—and also gave up his password as the room administrator. Over the next few hours, then days and weeks, Krawcyzk kept going in as the Chevman administrator, unchallenged. "It was such as seamless takeover of him; there was no hiccup," Krawcyzk said. "I had been studying him for so long that we were able to take over and be him. All we had to do was run with it."

It was the turning point in the investigation, and in many ways a reflection of how far investigators had come in a few short years. In Landslide, they were buried by the overwhelming evidence, in subsequent cases, they found themselves constantly playing technological catch-up with the savvy online predators. Now, the police were in a position where they could infiltrate a major child abuse operation at the highest levels. It was the online equivalent of penetrating a major drug cartel: you had to have enough luck, skill and insider information to get away with it.

"It blew the door off the next stage of the investigation," Randy Wickins pointed out. "We were right in there. It was the motherlode."

Up to that point, the police had been just lurking in the WinMX room and, thanks largely to Langham's original buddy list, they were able to make a few arrests. But now, as Chevman, the cops had access to everyone's IP address—in effect, the membership records of the "KiddyPics & KiddyVids" club. When someone entered the room—at any given time there were usually between thirty to sixty people online—the undercover cops could see their nickname, their IP address and how many files they were sharing.

From January 26 until March 6—when the major takedown took place—Krawcyzk and his team kept up the ruse. As police officers they were not allowed to offer child pornography, so they had to come up with an excuse why Chevman was suddenly not in the trading business anymore. "Chevman" told his online pals that he had just repartitioned his hard drive and did not have easy access to his collection; he was waiting for tax return money to buy a new drive.

"Chevman gave us a huge break," said Krawcyzk. "He came with the status. It was like purchasing the key to the room." It was a key that would eventually help put dozens of people in jail not just in Canada and the United States, but also in the Netherlands, Germany, Scotland, Denmark and Sweden.

The Toronto cops had sent a lead about one suspect called Blue Dragon to Det. Acting Insp. Jon Rouse of the Queensland Police Service. "Just by his conversations online, we knew that he was a significant member of the network and that he had a fairly large collection of images that he was sharing," said Rouse. Det. Const. Warren Bulmer, who was coordinating international leads for the Toronto Sex Crimes Unit, kept the Australians apprised of any progress through Groove, the secure information-sharing network that the police had been operating for several years.

As Chevman, the Toronto cops were able to establish an IP address for Blue Dragon. Unfortunately, the IP address led to a university with over forty thousand students: the suspect could have been anybody—a student, a professor, even an administrator. Working closely with the university's IT department, the Australians had Toronto do several IP traces with Blue Dragon in a short period of time. After three positive hits on one IP address, they knew they had the right person.

He turned out to be a thirty-eight-year-old Australian university student from the inner western Brisbane suburb of Ashgrove. Equally disturbing, he possessed what is known in Queensland as a Blue Card, issued after a background check to anyone who works or volunteers by the Office of the Commissioner for Children and Young people. Blue Dragon was a registered teacher, though not practicing at the time of the operation. "Still, our concern rose to the point where we put surveillance on him to see what he was doing," said Rouse.

Thanks to Toronto's undercover work as Chevman, they also had Blue Dragon under surveillance online. The police could track his chat with a WinMX buddy nicknamed Knight Rider, as he boasted about taking everything off his computer and hiding it on his new toy, an MP3 player:

> Blue Dragon: It's the size of a cigarette packet (lol) [laughing out loud].
> Knight Rider: iPod for CP [child pornography].
> Blue Dragon: Heh-heh.
> Knight Rider: What if the cops fall from the sky in 100

helicopters and your HD [hard drive] is
found?

Blue Dragon: Best part is this thing imitates an MP3
player—heh heh—it's so tiny i could crush
it with one hand.

The police didn't need helicopters when they arrested Blue Dragon.
"When our team went through his dorm, he was quite cocky, very
cocky, that nothing would be found," said Jon Rouse. Until the police
went straight for his MP3 player. Then his face blanched. Blue Dragon
eventually pleaded guilty to possessing child exploitation material.

Back in Canada, Chevman's powers to screen and monitor members
allowed Det. Const. Krawcyzk to track down the pompous Lord Vader
whom he had been monitoring for so many months. Krawcyzk had
used some pretty innovative snooping techniques to figure out a lot
about the WinMX diehard who had once boasted there were "no cop-
pers coming to visit me." When the rock band Mötley Crüe was coming to visit Lord Vader's hometown, he was eager to buy tickets. So
eager, in fact, that he told his WinMX pals on December 3 that tickets were going on sale on the Ticketmaster Web site "in one hour." It was
12:08 P.M. on Krawcyzk's watch in Toronto, and he knew that
Ticketmaster opened up its sales at 10 A.M., so that meant Vader lived in
a time zone three hours behind—somewhere on the Pacific Coast. A
quick check on the concert Web site showed that tickets were going on
sale that day for a Mötley Crüe show in Prince George, British Columbia.

Not long afterward, Lord Vader was back in the chat room happily
reporting: "Awesome, I got six tickets, row 9, center stage." Krawcyzk
contacted Ticketmaster and found only one buyer who matched that
purchase of a half dozen tickets in row 9. A lot of good detective
work, but no pay-off. The lead didn't pan out—Krawcyzk discovered
later that Lord Vader had been over at a friend's house, and they had
used the credit card of his friend's mother.

Now, as Chevman, Krawcyzk had the edge. When Lord Vader
logged on to "Kiddypics & Kiddyvids" on Friday at 5:15 P.M. on
January 27, Krawcyzk used Chevman's administrator privileges to
read the IP address. It was registered to Telus Corporation, a major
provider in the West Coast area. A subpoena eventually got the police

the name and address of the person hiding behind the online mask of Lord Vader: a twenty-eight-year-old from Prince George. He was eventually charged with the possession and distribution of child pornography; his case is still pending.

Slowly but surely, the police in Canada and the United States were rolling up the network. Out of Chicago, Ron Wolflick's team took over coordination of the entire national investigation, which mushroomed to include as many as 147 ICE agents. Wolflick's investigators fielded phone calls, reports and leads from across the country and went out to help other field offices with arrests, interviews and debriefs. Two ICE agents in Chicago also joined the Canadians in undercover work inside the chat room.

By March 6, the Americans were ready to pounce. In the first of a series of sweeps, they arrested fourteen people in Illinois, Tennessee, Michigan, Nevada, Florida, New York, Arizona, Hawaii and North Carolina.

In Clarksville, Tennessee, federal agents knocked on the door of apartment E73 in a quiet dwelling on Madison Street where Royal Raymond Weller, a forty-nine-year-old service repairman, lived. Some of his neighbors found him to be rather odd: one woman would later recall that when she had once caught a glance inside Weller's apartment, she spotted no furniture at all except a new Dell computer on the floor. Weller's mother, though, insisted that her son was a fine boy who had supper every Sunday with his parents and three siblings.

Weller, the dutiful son, was GOD—the Galactic Overlord Duplicate who ran the Kiddypics chat room.

In the small trailer park near Osceola, Iowa, a shabby brown mobile home was suddenly the scene of much commotion as another federal raid targeted Lisa Winebrenner, thirty-six. She shared the cramped quarters with two children. The floor was littered with dirty clothes, garbage, empty cans of Mountain Dew, and excrement. But Winebrenner also had in her possession the latest in technological hardware—four computers. Welcome to the castle of the "Humble Duchess." "In the real world she was nobody," said the Chicago investigator Brian Bone. "In the WinMX room, she would have all these people who thought she was the world."

Winebrenner tried to wipe out any record of her reign in that world by running Evidence Eliminator, a hard-drive-erasing tool, but police still retrieved a handful of child abuse images—and of course, they also had the records of her online activity. Her case is still before the courts.

The WinMX crowd ran the gamut of people and professions so typical of child abusers online: some were grandparents, others had never married. They lived in mobile homes or comfortable suburbs; one was a student, another a lumber salesman. One WinMX member used the telltale name A_School_Teacher. David Perrozi, who had made a fortune in the oil business, did, in fact, teach Sunday school in Buffalo.

Not all the arrests went smoothly. The police found no exploding bullets inside the hard drives of the suspects, but when Perrozi answered the door at his expensive home in Buffalo to see grim-looking federal agents, he quickly slammed it shut, rushed to his computer and typed in a few keystrokes to wipe out his hard drive. "In split seconds he blitzed it," said ICE's Ron Wolflick. "He had implemented his security protocol."

On Wednesday, March 15, 2006, CNN interrupted its regular news coverage to carry a special news conference from Chicago by the U.S. attorney general, Alberto Gonzales, announcing the success of Project Wickerman, with the arrest of twenty-seven people in the States, Canada, the U.K. and Australia. "The behavior in these chat rooms and the images many of these defendants sent around the world through peer-to-peer file-sharing programs and private instant messaging services are the worst imaginable forms of child pornography," said Gonzales. It was the first time the most senior justice official in the country had lent his stature to a child porn bust, a tribute to both the magnitude of the Wickerman investigation and the enhanced public status of Internet crimes against children.

Onstage with the attorney general were the deputy police chief of Toronto and senior ICE officials, but in the audience, beaming with pride, were the front-line officers who had done all the grunt work: Ron Wolflick and his Chicago team; Paul Krawcyzk and Scott Purches from Toronto; and Randy Wickins, who had started it all from Edmonton.

As Gonzales put it, "This investigation is an example of how American law enforcement can and will work side by side with our international law enforcement partners to shut down these rings and protect young, vulnerable victims from the horrors of sexual abuse."

As he watched the broadcast behind his prison bars in Canada, Mark Langham could not believe what he had helped to get started. "My god, I did this!" he remembers saying to himself—and to no one else, as such a boast in jail could be his death sentence. "I thought for once in my life I was doing some good. I actually helped some kids rather than hurt somebody."

A few people watching Gonzales on TV were also typing furiously on their keyboards. In the WinMX chat room, there was a growing sense of doom among the last remaining members. "We were monitoring the whole channel as it went down, and it was like rats running off of a ship," said Australia's Jon Rouse.

This is what those closing chat logs looked like:

—im kinda getting worried, so im out again, cya dudes
—hey, did you guys hear they took down rooms on winmx?
—stop spreading bullshit . . . no one has taken any rooms down on winmx
—for real check CNN, not trying to scare anyone but it's true.
—holy shit
—yep

The room went dead. But not for long.

Like drug addicts, they kept coming back for more, even if they knew of the dangers. "I liken it to the worst horror film, where every day one of the characters would go missing but the rest would still show up to the cabin to get killed," Krawcyzk said with a chuckle. "It was just like that."

In the new WinMX room, Krawcyzk could no longer use the Chevman alias once his cover had been blown by the arrests. A few weeks after the news conference, the Toronto cop assumed another identity and found himself chatting online again with a WinMX member from Denmark named Bastien who had been arrested by Danish police and then let go, only to get his hands on another computer:

Bastien: Trust no one . . . We gotta be careful . . . was
            arrested and police came and took all . . . still
            waiting for answer on all HDs [hard drives]
            but . . . used QuickWipe on all of them, hope-
            fully its gone, but don't know.
Krawcyzk: oh no man that is bad.
Bastien: they track all admins on Chevman's power . . .
            The Canadian police were the ones who sent
            the info over about me.
Krawcyzk: are you shitting me?
Bastien: really . . . don't know when I am back but
            might pop in from time to time, gotta keep
            low profile, am sure you can understand.

But his profile was not low enough. Danish police arrested him
again, thanks to these conversations and to images seized from other
WinMX computers that showed he was abusing his own children.

Four months after the Gonzales news conference in Chicago, the
police had doubled their arrest totals from twenty-seven to fifty-five,
with twenty-two in the States, sixteen in Canada and the remainder
fairly evenly split among Australia, the U.K. and the rest of Europe. In
all, police had identified eighteen children who had been actively
molested by the gang. In Scotland, another suspect named David Sim
had his DNA taken—a standard procedure for almost anyone arrested
in the U.K.—and police found a match for an unsolved sexual assault
of a three-year-old girl. Sim got five years.

The heaviest sentences, as was to be expected, were in the States.
David Perrozi, the part-time Sunday school teacher who managed to
zap his computer of most evidence, still got five years for distribution
and a $55,000 fine. Michael Burns of Reno, Nevada, who helped
administrate the room under the alias Wharfrat got ten years;
CuLeX, an administrator from Florida whose real name was Jason
Wilson, was sent away for twenty years.

In Canada, Carl "Chevman" Treleavan had pleaded guilty to possession and distribution of child pornography, which netted him a
three-and-a-half-year sentence—pitifully short compared with what
the Americans were handing out, but a year longer than any previous

Canadian sentence for distribution of child pornography. Still, his light treatment outraged many, including his younger sister Cindy, who alleged in front of reporters outside the court that Treleaven had sexually abused her when she was a child.

"How many others?" she cried. "Look at those babies he had on his computer! Some of them are literally babies!"

Project Wickerman showed that the police, in a coordinated global effort, had matured in the digital world and could take on the most sophisticated online abuse networks on their own terms.

The technological tools that law enforcement had been developing over the years—Groove to chat securely and share files, and CETS to mine the police databases for important clues—had proved invaluable. Investigators had peeled away a lot of the mystery of the Freenet and could crack the WinMX code that shielded IP identities. And for all the high-tech wizardry, the police could also rely on a powerful informal network that allowed them to pick up the phone and talk to foreign colleagues they had come to know and trust.

For the Edmonton detective who had started it all, it was simply a matter of dogged curiosity paying off. "If you find a thread in an investigation, and you pull on it and it starts to unravel, don't stop pulling until it all unravels," said Randy Wickins.

He never suspected that what would unravel would be one of the most sordid collections of child abuse online police had seen, replete with the live, streaming video torture of children. Wickins's wife once asked him: "How can you look at this stuff? It must be so hard."

It was hard. Wickins took comfort from a passage his wife found online from the writings of South African freedom fighter Alan Bosak:

> . . . We will go before God to be judged, and God will ask:
> "Where are your wounds?"
> We will answer: "We have no wounds."
> God will ask: "Was there nothing worth fighting for?"

Months later, the Wickerman fight was not over. There were still many active members of the "KiddyPics" room whom police had not captured. One of them—the same Knight Rider who had been chatting with BlueDragon about fooling the cops—sent out an online movie to the WinMX crowd shortly after the arrests. "Look what I am doing to my CP [child pornography] and unsafe files," he said. The video then showed him piling boxes and boxes of CDs and pictures in a corner and soaking them with a combustible fluid. He set the collection ablaze, laughing as the yellow flames consumed the evidence. The final shot showed the charred remains being dumped into a garbage truck and Knight Rider's chortles on the soundtrack.

Naturally, the police are analyzing the video for clues. "Knight Rider still has not been identified," Randy Wickins said grimly. "But he has popped up in other places and we're still looking."

The police were also hot on the trail of the new host who had stepped in to replace Raymond Weller, better known to WinMX users as GOD. Seeing how far the once-mighty GOD had fallen, the new WinMX leader was more cautious and cagey, but he had chosen an apt nickname for himself: Son of GOD.

Fifteen

VIRTUAL GLOBAL COPS

This is about us using technology to make the world smaller . . .
If the predators know that no matter what time it is, no matter
where they are, there could be children and police on guard, that
changes the world forever.
—JIM GAMBLE, CHAIR, VIRTUAL GLOBAL TASKFORCE

When Bill Walsh put together the first Crimes Against Children Conference in Dallas, Texas, back in 1989, there were fifty participants and two speakers. By 2006, Walsh was surrounded by twenty-six hundred delegates from over twenty-four countries.

"We've come of age in the fight against child abuse," said Walsh, the former Dallas police lieutenant who helped lead the Landslide investigation and many other child pornography probes.

The keynote opening address was delivered by Attorney General Alberto Gonzales, who called on the assembled police officers, prosecutors and child rights advocates to "rise up together as soldiers in the army of compassion." Gonzales himself had become increasingly impassioned and outspoken on the issue. A turning point had come a few months earlier when Gonzales visited the offices of Drew Oosterbaan and his team at the DOJ's Child Exploitation section. Oosterbaan took a calculated risk and showed the country's most powerful justice official just a small selection of some of the graphic images prosecutors and police are forced to deal with daily.

In a hushed room, Oosterbaan stood behind Gonzales as he watched in silence while the images streamed by; he could not see his boss's face but he could sense the impact: "You can see something drain out when people watch this," he said. "Nobody who has seen these images is ever the same and you could tell the attorney-general was moved."

"I have seen pictures of older men forcing naked young girls to have anal sex. There are videos on the Internet of very young daughters forced to have intercourse and oral sex with their fathers," Gonzales said later that day in surprisingly graphic public speech. "Viewing this was shocking and it makes my stomach turn," he said, "but if we do not talk candidly, then it is easy for people to turn away."

Certainly, the delegates to the Dallas conference were not turning away from the hard realities of their own battles. They crammed into a hotel ballroom to hear the psychologist Joe Sullivan explain his "spiral of abuse." They filled another conference room to watch the FBI agent Emily Vacher recount how she had used the John Doe warrants and creative detective work to put away James Reigle for life. They listened as the Edmonton detective Randy Wickins and his ICE counterparts from Chicago revealed their high-tech undercover takedown of the WinMX rooms in Project Wickerman.

Around the world, investigators were taking stock of how much progress they had made in the past decade since the Internet had fueled an explosion in child exploitation material. In the U.S., the disparate and often disputing law enforcement agencies were better coordinating their activities. The Department of Justice had expanded funding for forty-five regional Internet Crimes Against Children (ICAC) task forces to provide training and technology so that local, state and federal investigators could team up.

In Australia, Jon Rouse and his Queensland team were pushing police on the state and federal levels to band together to set up a national image database system. In Canada, RCMP Inspector Earla-Kim McColl, the new officer in charge of the National Child Exploitation Coordination Centre, was trying to set countrywide standards and training. The RCMP had created Integrated Child Exploitation units with local police forces in several cities and assumed control of the CETS database initiated by the Toronto Police and Microsoft.

NCMEC was also now one of twenty-five tip lines in twenty-two countries set up to help the public, police and the industry patrol the Web. NCMEC was also now one of twenty-five tip lines in twenty-two countries set up to help the public, police and the industry patrol the Web. In Canada, a similar Cybertip organization was set up, though it operates with a lot fewer dollars and staff than its American counterpart. A small team of four full-time analysts sifts through the 600–700 reports they get each month—a remarkable 43 percent of those get passed on for action by police forces.

Around the world, these groups banded together to form INHOPE, the International Association of Internet Hotlines. Said Lianna McDonald of Canada's Cybertip.ca, "We call ourselves the Neighbourhood Watch of the Internet."

At NCMEC's headquarters in Virginia, Michelle Collins's expanding team bore little resemblance to the small unit she had applied to join on Christmas Eve in 1998.

When Collins had begun to compile an informal tally of rescued and identified victims in NCMEC's early days, she had barely over two dozen. By the start of 2007, NCMEC's list surpassed nine hundred children from almost every corner of the globe. The NCMEC analysts were getting more experienced at zeroing in on the smallest clues in a picture. They also realized that the more eyes, the better. Why restrict the hunt for clues in the pictures to a handful of specialists at NCMEC if there was a safe and secure way to enlist the skills of law enforcement across the country? So NCMEC created a new Victim Identification Lab, with thousands of photos from unsolved cases. Residing on a secure virtual server, it allowed registered law enforcement agents from across the country to log on, analyze the pictures, audio and other clues and contribute to the hunt. NCMEC tested the lab at the Dallas conference. Police and prosecutors from forty-eight states and eleven countries were given access to more than fifty of the most promising files. Over the course of four days, the conference delegates came up with over 560 leads and specific locations for at least five child victims.

For all her successes, the director of NCMEC's Child Exploitation Unit was worried. As the size of computer hard drives keeps expanding and the speed of Internet connections soars, so too has the average size of the seized collections. "They're massive," Collins said. "They're not 100 images anymore, they're 100,000."

As the numbers go up, the age of the victims seems to drop. "I've been doing this for eight years now, and it was not common at the beginning for me to be seeing images of infants and toddlers," said Collins. Nowadays, almost half—39 percent—of the victims of child porn identified by NCMEC are under the age of five. Nineteen percent of the children in these sex abuse images are under the age of three.

Indeed, these days her team is finding a lot more chat among offenders who say they are deliberately going after pre-verbal infants because they are the perfect targets—victims who literally can't speak up. Collins cites the case of one man who was sexually abusing his four-year-old daughter, but then switched to his eighteen-month-old daughter.

"I've got to start early, even though she's young," he wrote, "before my daughter starts talking."

Three years after he wrote his fateful e-mail to Bill Gates that helped change the way police tackle child abuse on the Internet, Paul Gillespie got to meet the Microsoft leader in person.

It happened at a Virginia seminar for government leaders on using technology to fight crime, sponsored by the company in the early spring of 2006. The two men—the cop and the corporate executive/philanthropist—shook hands and chatted briefly. Gillespie was uncharacteristically at a loss for words.

"It was quite remarkable," was all he could say. "It was an honor."

Gates had high words of praise for the cop whose prodding had led to the creation of the Child Exploitation Tracking Systsem (CETS): "He's truly been a leader in protecting the safety of children online and convincing government, law enforcement and the private sector that we all need to work together."

Paul Gillespie could not believe how much—and how quickly—his baby had grown up. "It's pretty overwhelming when you look at where we were a few years ago and where we are now," he said. "You really do have to pinch yourself. It's brilliant because of its simplicity and because it's such an easy concept that people are buying into it."

Buying into it big-time. By mid-2006, there were 182 Canadian police investigators plugged into CETS in twenty-nine sites across the country. The Americans were test-driving CETS in several cities and were considering a pilot deployment. Indonesia became the first major developing country to sign on to the program. "We'll teach the Jakarta police how to be cybercops," Gillespie said. "I'm going to push for more countries to get it as well."

But he was going to do that pushing without a badge. After six years as the head of Canada's best-known—if at times controversial—Child Exploitation Unit, Gillespie announced in June of 2006 that he was resigning from the police force. Not to give up the fight, but to expand it globally in a way that he couldn't as an officer on a local city police force.

"I wanted to go on to a bigger level, and to me the obvious way would be linking up the world," he said. Working with a non-profit group called the Kids' Internet Safety Association, he hoped to set up what he called a world-class training center in Toronto to instruct investigators, especially from the developing world, in the latest police techniques. As a private consultant, he plans to help Microsoft—which in three years had already poured $7 million into the project—to expand CETS around the globe. Italy became the first European country to officially adopt CETS in November 2006, soon followed by Spain. In the U.K. four police forces in England, Wales and Scotland were running pilot programs. Brazil looked like the next country to take it on, and Gillespie wants to expand its reach in Latin America, perhaps South Africa and beyond Indonesia to the rest of Asia. Microsoft calculated that to date Paul Gillespie's dream had assisted with sixty-four arrests and the rescue and identification of forty-three victims worldwide.

As he cleaned up his office on the third floor at Toronto Police headquarters, Gillespie tried to jam into a black binder more than a hundred cards, letters and printed e-mails he has received from rescued victims. On the wall behind his desk is a framed letter from one of the relatives of Burt Thomas Stevenson's victims: "A year ago I did not know your unit existed. Today, I am incredibly grateful it does. The next time you get disgusted with your job, or disheartened with what you see, or wonder if any of what you do makes a difference, know that it does . . . Thank you for not giving up. Thank you and God bless you."

From his stuffed binder, he pulls out another note: "If it helps, I want to assure you that at least some of the victims will go on to have a normal life like me," one woman wrote. "Now I have a baby girl. Please protect her from the kind of people who once harmed me."

Across the Atlantic, Jim Gamble was witnessing one of his long-standing dreams finally come to life with the creation of the Child Exploitation and Online Protection (CEOP—pronounced *see-op*) Centre, a central, unified agency for the U.K. dedicated to fighting child abuse.

"We are here to tell abusers that the Internet is not the Wild West, it's a public place and we police public places," Gamble told the media on the eve of CEOP's launch in April 2006. The sheriff was back in town, only this time he had a posse made up of a wide range of civilian experts and investigators. The idea was to bring together under a single roof not just police but also child welfare workers, educators, psychologists, the Internet industry, financial investigators and even young people themselves in perhaps the world's most ambitious project to fight child abuse online.

For three years since the end of Landslide's Operation Ore, Gamble had been working on restructuring the way police in the U.K. tackled Internet crime in the twenty-first century. He had the good fortune of being able to build something from the ground up, studying what he called "the good and the bad" around the world. Gamble liked the idea of a national center run by police, like the RCMP-led NCECC in Ottawa, but it did not have the breadth and scope of a centralized clearinghouse with numerous partners like NCMEC in the United States. On the other hand, NCMEC's civilian status meant that it lacked the authority and ability to initiate and direct police investigations; NCMEC took in intelligence and processed it but then had to send it out for police to act.

Gamble wanted the best of both worlds—and got it. CEOP is a crime-fighting agency with police in command, but at the same time it is also a broad coalition of civilians, government and industry. Only about half of CEOP's hundred staff members are police officers. Leading children's organizations such as the National Society for the Protection of Cruelty to Children—the biggest children's charity in the U.K.—have lent considerable resources. So have major corporations such as Microsoft, AOL and Visa. Gamble wasn't just looking for extra bodies—he wanted diversity and debate to challenge police procedures. "You see hardened detectives working alongside social workers, educators and industry people, each group with different skills and different visions to shake up our thinking," said Gamble.

CEOP, with a hefty initial budget of £5 million, was first and foremost a police operation, affiliated with Britain's Serious Organised Crime Agency (SOCA), a new FBI-type national police structure. Gamble brought in some of the best and brightest police investigators who had been tackling child abuse for years, such as veteran investigator Paul Griffiths. Police squads that previously had been working separately—such as the Serious Sex Offenders' Unit and the National Crime Squad's Pedophile Online Investigation Team (POLIT), which Gamble had created during the height of Operation Ore—were now merged.

CEOP's reach also extends beyond the U.K.'s borders, with an ongoing offensive against traveling sex offenders. Deeply moved by the firsthand look at the plight of children that he got in Cambodia, Gamble continued to dispatch teams of CEOP experts and advisers there. He hired Aarti Kapoor, the activist who spent several years campaigning for children's rights in Asia, to study the global problem of child trafficking. And he took steps to make sure that British police monitor and flag potential lawbreakers who travel abroad. "If you are a registered sex offender and we get information that you are going to travel, we are going to have a long, hard look at that. This is where I am 'Making Every Child Matter Everywhere,'" he said, referring to the CEOP's motto.

Drawing on his counterterrorism experience in North Ireland, Gamble placed a high priority on intelligence and financial investigations. CEOP aims to track and seize assets of people who trade in child abuse images by directly integrating a financial investigations branch into its daily operations—a first in law enforcement child pornography circles. Gamble even got Visa International to cough up much of the needed cash, spending £450,000 over three years to fund the unit. He took direct inspiration from the Regpay probe in the U.S., meeting with former prosecutor Carlos Ortiz and the IRS's Maria Reverendo to learn from their success. But he wanted to make sure CEOP's work, unlike the takedown of Regpay, was not a one-off bust that stops after the first big case. "Let's take out the people who profit from this," said Gamble. "I want their homes, I want their cars, I want whatever is in their bank accounts."

In early July, just three months after CEOP was announced, the center pulled off its first nationwide sweep, arresting thirteen people who were alleged to have been part of a pay-per-view online network. Like Regpay, this ring was thought to have been run by criminals from Eastern Europe. CEOP investigators were also tracing bank accounts in New Zealand, Norway and North America.

That was just the start. Under an amendment to the Data Protection Act in July 2006, for which CEOP lobbied hard, British police will be able to pass on to banks intelligence on people suspected or convicted of child pornography offenses; the banks will then be allowed to cancel the person's credit cards. "If you're a pedophile, I want to know everything about you," he said. "I want to know where you're spending your money, how you use cash from your bank account, what credit cards do you have, what you're paying for online. We're going to be all over you like a cheap suit."

Jim Gamble had realized early on that it was not just about putting the bad guys behind bars. More than most senior police commanders, he wanted to understand them, help them if they wanted the help—but deter them at all costs.

In some ways Gamble had come full circle. Initially, police had concentrated on simply arresting online traders and offenders. Then came the realization that the pictures held vital clues to real children who needed to be rescued. Gamble's goal was still to save the children, but he wanted to do that as much as possible *before* the pictures get made.

"Until now, our activity was driven largely by finding the images and taking them offline. Well, yes, find the images if that serves to identify the children and protect them, but don't get caught up in images," he said. "The image is a symptom of the crime."

He likens the flood of child abuse images on the Web to a plugged-up bathtub filling with water pouring out of the taps. Police keep trying to keep the tub from overflowing by emptying the water with a bucket. "If I'm lucky, I'm not going to get the floor wet," said Gamble.

"But it will continue to fill up, and if I drop the bucket at any point, I'm in trouble.

"If we want to stop these images from going online, we have to be much more proactive. Blocking images is great, but stopping people from accessing children, from taking the pictures, is the critical area where we need to focus. Our aim is to inhibit them from going online in the first place and to capture them in the real world so that we can turn the tap off."

To do that Gamble named the psychologist Joe Sullivan as CEOP's principal forensic behavior analyst, to help police study the offenders, learn their habits and their tactics, what triggers them to act and what can stop them. He brought in Maggie Brennan, who worked with the University College Cork's Combatting Pedophile Information Networks in Europe (COPINE) project, to coordinate research with the academic world. It was a refreshing approach to a sickness that needs to be tackled with more than just courts and jails.

The CEOP chief also wanted to curb the predators before and not after they acted by changing the balance of forces on the Web. Instead of allowing the Internet to become a treacherous place where parents fear for their child's safety, why not put the offenders on the defensive? Make them nervous about children, instead of the other way around.

For starters, Gamble wanted the major Internet, computer and mobile phone companies onboard in order to make sure their products and services were "safer by design." Vodafone—the world's largest mobile phone company—had been an early backer. There are fifty million mobile phones in the U.K., and almost half of them have Web access. A Vodafone customer who tries to visit one of the tens of thousands of banned sites on the Internet Watch Foundation's list gets this stark message on his screen:

BLOCKED ACCESS
Deliberate attempts to access this or related sites
may result in you committing a criminal offence

CEOP then scored a major coup in August 2006 when Microsoft announced it would feature a distinctive red "report abuse" button on its instant chat programs. With 11.3 million registered users,

Microsoft's software—popularly known as MSN Messenger but soon to be rebranded as Windows Live Messenger—is the largest instant-messenger service in the U.K. Young people chatting online who suddenly feel they are being exposed to suspicious behavior or inappropriate sexual advances can make a report to police with a single click of a mouse.

"Behind the report abuse button will sit police and intelligence officers who have been specially trained to tackle child sex abuse," Gamble explained to the media when the program was launched. "We will tell you how to capture information and how to seize online discussions and then proactively do all we can to track down the perpetrator."

Gamble's actions earned high praise from at least one group that had been sorely neglected in the past—survivors of child abuse and online exploitation. "We didn't stand a chance until CEOP came in," said Shy Keenan, the outspoken leader of the Phoenix Survivors, which works with victims of child sex abuse. She noted that most people know where their local police station is in their neighborhood, but if you get into trouble on the Web, few know where to turn. "Online, if you needed help before, you didn't have a clue. Now CEOP is changing the landscape and the way we use the Internet."

The new CEOP center also became a much-needed home for Gamble's other dream: virtual global cops who can patrol the Web 24/7. The Virtual Global TaskForce (VGT), bringing together the top British, American, Canadian and Australian police forces dedicated to child protection, was now headquartered in CEOP's building.

Gamble implemented his long-standing plans for a "follow the sun" roster so police from each VGT member agency scattered across the world's time zones would be able to visit chat rooms and other Web sites where children might be exposed to risk. The idea was simple: police have to sleep, but the Internet never does. So while it was midnight in London, it was 8 A.M. in Brisbane and 7 P.M. in Washington, D.C. At all times, a police officer working with the VGT could be there to help children or conduct undercover operations, around the clock.

Lee Costi, a twenty-one-year-old media student from England, was the first to feel VGT's bite. Even at his young age, Costi was an accomplished online groomer of lonely underage girls. In 2004 he persuaded a fourteen-year-old girl to meet him at a Swindon hotel; the following year he assaulted a thirteen-year-old he had found online when she showed up to meet him in an alleyway near Waterloo Station in London. By the time he found his third victim in 2006, the VGT had its online police emergency system in operation. Costi reached out to another fourteen-year-old schoolgirl from Nottinghamshire and enticed her to perform sex acts in front of her Webcam. The girl eventually had second thoughts. She had seen the VGT's Web site and contacted them. Her e-mail report was passed on to local police, who traced Costi to his parents' home. He was sentenced to nine years for assaulting his first two victims and for inciting his third victim.

On his computer they found 355 logs of his online chats with other young girls. "Many of those girls are now aware of the threat he presented because one young person went online and made that report," said Gamble. "The more people we get to do that, the more it undermines the confidence of the predators."

Gamble hoped to see the report abuse button expanded to more Microsoft products and other Web software around the world. A young person who clicks the report abuse button gets directed to a Web page that asks what country he or she is from. U.K. visitors get sent to CEOP to file a report; in Canada, it's Cybertip.ca and the RCMP's National Child Exploitation Coordination Centre; in the United States, NCMEC handles the reports; in Australia, it is the Federal Police; and queries from all other countries get fielded by Interpol. By the fall of 2006, the VGT and CEOP had already received more than nine hundred calls for help from the public and another seven hundred reports from industry, watchdog groups and other agencies.

In the UK, CEOP also launched a "Most Wanted" Web site—the first time details of convicted pedophiles had been released nationwide by Britain's law enforcement agencies—late in November, 2006. The site named five offenders who had served their prison time but failed to report their whereabouts to authorities as required after their release. More than eight million people visited the site on its first day and, within twenty-four hours, one of the five men turned himself in to police in Aberdeenshire. Then in early December, a second culprit was arrested at Stanstead airport upon his return from his native Poland.

Four days later, a third British fugitive was picked up by police in northern France after he was spotted by citizens who had seen his mug shot on the CEOP site.

"If you think that you can escape the terms of your conviction by jumping across borders, going into hiding, assuming different identities—then think again," Gamble warned. "You will be caught. There is no place to hide."

He hoped to expand the program worldwide, with the VGT creating a sort of global "Most Wanted" list for child sex offenders on the run.

"This is about us using technology to make the world smaller," Gamble said. "We're trying to change the dynamic by involving the public. If the predators know that no matter what time it is, no matter where they are, there could be children and police on guard, that changes the world forever."

The era of virtual global cops had arrived.

Sixteen

EMPOWER THE CHILDREN

You have to be in control of your surfing. Not other people—not parents, not teachers and not the pedophiles.
—RISHI PATEL, AGE 16,
CEOP YOUTH ADVISORY PANEL

Jim Gamble's impetus to change the dynamic of the battle against the predators came none too soon, because the dynamic of the Web itself—and the abuse it feeds and fosters—was also changing.

At first, in the early days of the Web, offenders had confined themselves to e-mailing each other to exchange a small number of pictures of abuse committed offline. High-speed connections and massive storage drives changed the speed and quantity of the child exploitation material—more pictures and now video—but not the essence of its content. In a second stage, the popularity of chat rooms and instant messaging gave predators a way to use the Web not just as a trading post but as a trap—a place to find and lure new online victims.

But a third stage has allowed those trends to explode with unforeseen ferocity, thanks to the proliferation of so-called social networking Web sites like MySpace and the availability of cheap Webcams and cell phones with cameras. We are witnessing a perfect storm for predators, a disturbing situation in which not only are many more children vulnerable but some of them are even self-producing the images.

Founded in 2004, MySpace shot into the Web stratosphere when the media mogul Rupert Murdoch bought it for $580 million in the summer of 2005; by then it was edging to close to fifty million members; it doubled its size to a hundred million users by August 2006.

It quickly spawned a Web revolution with similar online personal bazaars like Zanga and Facebook. In the U.K., Bebo became the most popular social site in England, racking up twenty-five million members in barely a year and a half. According to the MediaGuardian, an astounding 61 percent of U.K. children age thirteen to seventeen had a personal profile somewhere on a networking site.

Social networking sites allow young people to post pictures of themselves, exchange songs and images, and swap gossip. The obvious attraction for young people is that this was their space without MyParents—a kind of Web shopping mall where they could hang out and chill with their friends. Or at least people who claimed to be their friends—these Web sites have also become a boon to predators. They make the grooming process—that essential stage in the spiral of abuse when the offender breaks down the defenses of his prey—so much easier. Teens often expose the most intimate details of their lives in their personal profiles on these sites: not just their favorite bands but also the name of their schools, their sports teams, their daily schedules, sometimes even an address or phone number.

The casualties soon started mounting. In March of 2006, Connecticut authorities charged two men with what they said were America's first sex abuse crimes involving MySpace. According to court documents, the first man—a thirty-nine-year-old father of two from Pennsylvania—traveled to Connecticut three times to have sex with a fourteen-year-old he had met on MySpace. The second man— a twenty-two-year-old recent college graduate—was accused of sexually molesting an eleven-year-old girl after they had exchanged MySpace chat and Webcam images.

By April, MySpace moved to quiet the growing storm by hiring away from Microsoft their director of child-safe computing, Hemanshu Nigam, and naming him chief security officer. But he was in for a rough ride. In May, the family of a fourteen-year-old girl from Austin, Texas, sued MySpace for $30 million, charging that the Web site has "absolutely no meaningful protections or security measures to protect underage users." The girl alleged she had met a nineteen-year-old who said he was a high school football player; after a brief online courtship, he picked her up after school, took her for a bite to eat and a movie, then drove her to an apartment where he raped her.

The lawsuit claimed MySpace's security measures to prevent strangers from contacting young users are "utterly ineffective." It is still before the courts.

In July, the Toronto Sex Crimes Unit made its first MySpace bust. A twenty-three-year-old man who tried to pass himself off as a "sweet person" lured a thirteen-year-old from a small town in Ontario to perform sex acts for her Webcam. By August, it got even worse for MySpace when a court in Chicago heard testimony that a fourteen-year-old girl had been gang-raped and left unconscious in an alley after meeting two older teens through the popular Web site.

That same month, MySpace's new security chief tried to assure the delegates to the Dallas Crimes Against Children conference that his company was doing everything it could to protect minors, but many remained skeptical. By the end of the year, MySpace announced it would try to identify predators who had signed up as members by cross-referencing information supplied by its million-plus users against databases of registered sex offenders. But by the company's own admission, the system was far from perfect, likely to catch only those offenders foolish enough to use their real names, locations or pictures.

MySpace, like most social networking sites, insists its users be at least fourteen years of age. Members can report "underage users," and the company says it has deleted some 250,000 such profiles. In reality, though, no proof of age is required for anyone to use these Web sites, so the under-fourteen crowd can easily hang out, unsupervised. As for the older teens, there is little protection for them on Web sites that are popular precisely because they are so free-wheeling and explicit.

In fact, NCMEC was now finding that as much as 10 percent of the seized material it was getting from across the country was coming from older children who were taking compromising pictures of themselves. Sometimes it appeared to be a dare gone wrong or older teens acting out. Two Rhode Island girls of sixteen and nineteen were charged with posting sexually explicit pictures of themselves on MySpace. In another incident, a girl sent a revealing picture of herself to a boyfriend, only to discover after a nasty breakup that he had distributed it on the Web.

More often than not, though, these self-made images were the result of what NCMEC's Michelle Collins calls "online enticement": a lonely child manipulated by a "friend" she met on the Web who coaxed her into snapping pictures of her own body. In just one month in the fall of 2006, the FBI's Emily Vacher found herself working on three such cases at once. In one instance, a fourteen-year-old was befriended online by a man who claimed to be just a few years older than she was. He persuaded her to take pictures of herself; when her horrified mother found them on the computer, she called in the authorities. Vacher was able to trace the girl's suitor to find he was a man in his thirties living in a trailer in Kentucky.

"A huge part of the problem is the attitude of these girls—but technology makes them accessible," said Vacher. One girl snapped pictures of herself on her cell phone, then e-mailed the images to her Yahoo account and from there posted them on the Web. "It's a trend and it's scary," the FBI agent said. "Part of being a teenager is being rebellious and curious, but they can't think two steps ahead."

In Washington, D.C., a congressional hearing listened to harsh testimony against the operators of social networking Web sites who "can no longer be allowed to turn a blind eye to the predators who lurk on the playground they created," as one of the witnesses, the Texas attorney general, Greg Abbott, put it. The lawmakers passed an act that requires public schools and libraries to block student access to social networking sites. In the U.K., too, there were sporadic attempts at censorship. A headmaster for a girls' grammar school banned Bebo when she found that more than seven hundred of her students had signed up with service. And one of Edinburgh's top private schools did likewise when the principal found that his pupils were posting personal details that would expose them to stalkers.

It was a typically heavy-handed approach: trying to solve a problem by forbidding it.

CEOP boss Jim Gamble, on the other hand, has a different perspective. "I think the potential good always outweighs the bad when it comes to the Internet. Social networking is positive; it's fantastic," he says with the enthusiasm of a father of three Web-savvy children. "In my view, it's about getting the bad things right."

It fit into Gamble's overall strategy: if the Internet is a public place like any playground or park, the police cannot reduce crime there simply by beefing up patrols in the neighborhood or closing down all the parks; they have to involve the parents, the children and the community.

It comes down to numbers. "Even if every officer went online twenty-four hours a day, we haven't enough police to protect every child on the Internet," said Helen Penn, in charge of CEOP's education program. "You have to give children the power to take care of themselves."

Police tackling online child abuse had always tried to pull off some public education amid all their other investigative duties, but CEOP was the first law enforcement agency to make it one of its essential duties, not an afterthought. CEOP's goal was to reach one million children in one year, using a team of over a thousand police officers, teachers and child protection teams. The target was children between ten and sixteen, the age group most likely to have unrestricted and unsupervised access to a computer, perhaps in their bedrooms or at school. The rock group Oasis allowed CEOP to use one of its hit songs as the soundtrack for a powerful video that tells the story of a young girl who is assaulted by a stranger she meets online. A Web site built around the campaign's main theme, "Think You Know," features tips, stories and an abuse report site.

Penn said the campaign was designed not to talk down to teens or judge them. "Teens are desperate to explore, and these days they'll meet people and explore their sexuality in ways they couldn't if they were not online," she said. She opened her Web browser to a popular youth site called Teenspot. The "flirt" section was filled with 214 people at that moment, with names like RomanceGirl and SexyAngel, openly advertising their willingness to take sexual risks online. But there was also a message from someone who claimed he was not a teen. "I am an older man (27), please add me" to your Webcam list, he asked. And that's not counting the predators lying about their age or intentions.

"We try to tell the teenagers that it's about assessing risk," said Penn. "It's giving back the power to young people: These are the risks—now you have to choose."

As any parent knows, the best way—and often the only way—to

reach young people is through other young people. "Adults are in many ways the visitors when it comes to the Internet," Gamble is fond of saying. "Children and young people are the natives."

So CEOP set up a youth advisory panel to help the adults reach out to the Internet generation. "We wanted to avoid a nagging approach, because the advice given before was all about don't do this or don't do that," said Rishi Patel, a sixteen-year-old student from Ealing, west London, and one of the fifty panel members. "*You* have to be in control of your surfing. Not other people—not parents, not teachers and not the pedophiles."

The explosion of social networking and the self-production of child exploitation images forced Gamble and his colleagues worldwide to reflect more seriously about something that was already beginning to percolate as a major concern for them: how to widen their battle beyond a strictly technological and law enforcement issue.

"We are always reacting to new trends and new tricks that the criminals are using," said Paul Gillespie. "We have been very lucky to somehow stay up with them to some degree. But I don't think chasing them around the Internet is the answer. Technology is always going to leave us in the dust."

That's quite an admission from the Toronto cop who helped revolutionize the way police work by getting the king of computer technology, Bill Gates himself, to lend a hand. And Gillespie would be first to argue for more gizmos, more high-tech tools, more money to help track the offenders. But Gillespie, Gamble and others were coming to the same conclusion: simply put, if police stick to online solutions to fight online crime, they are trapped in a race they cannot win.

Largely ill-prepared when the first assaults like Landslide hit, police scrambled and played technological catch-up. Slowly, as they gained experience and insight on the battlefield, they picked up new tools and skills to help them nail the offenders and rescue hundreds of children. By 2006, in the wake of international successes like Project Wickerman, the expansion of the Virtual Global Taskforce, the establishment of NCECC in Canada, CEOP in the U.K. and NCMEC's financial and technology coalitions with industry in the United States, law enforcement could legitimately say that at least it was on the offensive. But its officers were never going to win this war online alone.

"We are not about high tech. We are about child protection," said Jim Gamble. "I've decided it's absolutely wrong to see this as an 'Internet crime' because that's blaming the technology. Who you are offline, and the interest you have offline, will affect what you do online."

For Gamble, the goals remain the same: "To rescue the child who has been abused. To protect the child who hasn't been abused. That's it. That's how we measure our success—we're not in the business of how many people we've prosecuted."

To accomplish that, police had to widen their perspective to include all fronts in the offline world. In the schools, educating the children so they "patrol" their own cyberspace neighborhoods, protect themselves and help friends who get into trouble. In industry, more "safer by design" products. Alarm and abuse buttons that are as ubiquitous on the Web as smoke alarms and traffic lights are in the real world. Imagine, Gamble pondered, if every computer in the world was sold with a desktop icon that had an automatic link to the VGT or another abuse hotline.

"This is about shifting the debate," he concluded. "Because my own journey from knowing nothing to knowing just a little bit more than nothing has taught me that this is about people, not technology."

If it is about people, Paul Gillespie takes the argument one step further: "Ultimately, society has to address one question: is the use of the public Internet a right or a privilege? Period. It has to come down to that."

A simple question with some very complicated consequences.

"If it is a right, we have to fashion some reasonable way to hold people accountable for their criminal activity on the Internet," Gillespie said.

Gillespie—and he is not the only person in law enforcement to suggest this—thinks there's one way to hold people accountable for what they do on the electronic highway: the equivalent of a driver's license. The idea might sound outrageous but simply posing the question forces us to re-examine how the Internet operates in our lives and we operate on it. Think about it for a moment. We take driver's licenses and traffic law for granted now, but fewer than ninety years ago that was not the case. It was in Europe—in Germany and France—where mandatory licenses to drive vehicles first appeared at the turn of the twentieth century. Only as automobile deaths climbed in North America was there a call for some kind of regulation here: New York State was the first jurisdiction to bring in drivers' permits in 1910 in a limited fashion; by 1913, New Jersey obliged all drivers to pass an exam first. Today with millions of cars speeding along thousands of miles of highways, it is a crime to get behind the wheel without a valid permit. Police departments spend a big chunk of their budget and forces handling traffic and car-related problems.

In just a few short years, the information superhighway of the Internet has become as essential as the paved roads we drive on. How many deaths and broken lives of children will it take before we start changing our attitude toward the Internet?

Gillespie noted that the one thing everyone on the Web has in common is that they have to log on somehow. It's at that entrance ramp to the electronic highway that Gillespie thinks there can be some kind of validation or verification of identity. "People will do things in the electronic world that they would not even think of doing in the real world," he said. "Then, when they get caught, they try to wrap themselves up in the rights offered to them by the real world. You know what? It's going to take a public outcry. At what point does society stand up and say, 'We're not going to take it anymore. If you use the public Internet, you have no expectation of privacy when you commit criminal acts.'"

That's all true. But the idea of some kind of license to surf the Web will never fly. It is a civil liberties affront to most people, and a technological nightmare at any rate: people will always figure out a way to get around a roadblock on the Internet. Gillespie is the first to admit it is a conundrum—much like the way we treat pedophiles. "You can't lock them up forever; you can't let them out to run around forever. So the truth is probably somewhere in the middle, somehow controlling their activities. It's the same for how we control crime on the Internet. I don't have the answer; there has to be some happy medium."

Nobody has the answers, but the hard questions can no longer be avoided. The Internet—with all its joys and wonders and blessings, along with all its crime and horrors and abuse—is not some technological toy like a toaster that we can turn off with a power button. It permeates every aspect of our society and lives. It is in our offices and dens and bedrooms and cars and on our cell phones, in nursery schools and old-age homes.

It is a Web of contradictions: it is one of our most intimate tools, where we share our most private thoughts in our e-mails and yet it is the most public of our public places. The solutions, therefore, must also be a Web of contradictions.

The police need tougher powers, yet the public needs more safeguards against infringements on our rights: if the Internet has become the world's playground, the same rules must apply and the police must be given the same powers—and the same limits and controls on their actions—that we would expect in any park or playground. We need more laws that mete out serious punishment for "only" possessing abuse images and more judges that take the crime seriously; but we also need more treatment for offenders. We need better surveillance and awareness by parents and schools, but we also need more empowered and wary young people who know the limits and risks of life on the Web.

Like any crime-infested neighborhood, the Internet can be cleaned up. In the real world, child molesters don't go away simply by our wishing they would; nor will online predators vanish by our pretending they don't exist or by curtailing children's access to certain parts of the Web. In the face of a massive ongoing public campaign against child abuse online, some offenders, it must be hoped, will seek help. The rest of them will have to live with the prospect and fear that they now stand a better chance of getting caught—and being punished harshly.

Because it is no longer about computers. What happens on the Internet does not stay on the Internet. It has an impact on our real lives. It *is* our real lives. For the children being tortured and abused to produce images for the Web, that *is* their real life and, for some, real death.

Just ask the Jessicas and the Anns and the Mashas and the thousands of other children whose pictures are still out there.

Epilogue

"WHO SAVES ONE CHILD SAVES THE ENTIRE WORLD"

A simple tapestry with those words hangs on the wall on the Child Exploitation section of the Toronto Sex Crimes Unit, a gift from a woman from Charlottetown, Pennsylvania, who had learned of their work on TV. Across the room, on a large whiteboard, there is a seemingly unending list of the latest suspects and court dates; someone has also scrawled a slogan with a black felt pen:

THE HUNT: RELENTLESS
THE CAPTURE: EXQUISITE

But the swamp of abuse and degradation that the police officers sometimes have to wade through to hunt for those children and capture their abusers could sometimes be overwhelming. One morning, Paul Krawcyzk was analyzing a collection of videos that had recently been seized from a suspect—more than 250 gigabytes in size, over one hundred hours of child exploitation.

"Hey, Bill," Krawcyzk called out to Bill McGarry. "Do you know of a series of images that show a baby being abused with a paintbrush?"

"Is it a green paintbrush?" McGarry shot back with hardly a second thought.

"No, it's yellow," Krawcyzk said.

Then they both froze, stunned by the realization of what they had just said so calmly.

"Imagine that I even had to ask a question about what color the paintbrush was because I had seen another series of images with the same sickening thing," McGarry said. "As good as I am at my job, I really hate this shit."

McGarry stepped out to take a walk, got a coffee, called his wife to see how her day was and then came back to work.

Bill McGarry was luckier than most cops. He got to meet and befriend one of the children he helped.

After Masha—the girl known as Angeli or the Disney girl, whom he had been trying to rescue for two years—stepped into the media glare in late 2005, she became an instant symbol of the thousands of victims of online child exploitation who did not have a voice. She made several appearances on TV, complaining about how widespread her pictures of abuse had become on the Web.

McGarry couldn't escape those pictures of her either; they kept turning up on his computer as he delved into other investigations. "She's not leaving my life. I was constantly reminded of her," he said. He watched with fascination as the little girl he had only seen in photos of torture and abuse turned into an engaging TV teen personality. "I've been carrying this for two years, thinking about her. Part of me needed to talk to her; I guess I needed some closure for myself."

McGarry got that chance early in 2006 when Masha—by then thirteen years old—made it to the pinnacle of media attention. One afternoon in January, she took a seat next to Oprah Winfrey on her immensely influential TV show; then the next night she joined Nancy Grace, the fiery CNN host who focuses on criminal justice causes. Grace had also arranged for McGarry to come down to New York to appear on the show and for the first time meet the girl he had tried so hard to rescue.

For all his tough demeanor as a child exploitation cop, the Toronto detective was anxious that day. "I was freaking out: what am I going to say?" he said, not knowing when he first saw Masha if he should just shake hands with the girl or embrace her as he wanted to. He caught sight of her in the makeup room, catching her reflection in the mirror, her feet dangling on the oversize chair, sipping a Diet Coke.

When the thirteen-year-old was introduced to the cop who had tried to save her life, she disarmed him with a simple "Cool."

Then they hugged. McGarry's bottom lip quivered as he let out a deep breath.

"Wow," said the big, burly cop, more nervous than the child. "I just can't believe I'm here."

Everyone laughed, and McGarry had a great time chatting with Masha, telling her how proud he was of the job she was doing. They made small talk about her schoolwork and her new Xbox. He gave her a gift the Toronto squad had bought for her: a white gold necklace with a cameo of an angel and a diamond set as a star in the sky. On the back were inscribed the words "Always watch over me." Masha put it around her neck. "I'll wear it tonight," she said.

On the air, speaking to millions of TV viewers, Masha urged children like her, trapped in a vice of abuse, to come forward. "There are people who can help them. And they should tell somebody, even if they're afraid to talk about it. And they should have courage and be strong about it, because it's not going to last forever."

She told Grace of her pride at seeing Matthew Mancuso, her abusive adoptive father, sent away to jail in chains. "It just feels like he should be afraid of me now, not the other way around."

"Honey," said the CNN host. "I'm sure he is. I am sure he is."

Masha's story attracted the attention of powerful politicians as well. "It was an instant sense of anger and outrage: we have got to do something about it," Senator John Kerry recalled. "Her strength. Her poise. Her confidence and determination to fight this." The Massachusetts Democratic senator got to meet Masha through a child-rights activist in his home state.

"This is just a young woman who was torn apart by what happened to her but doesn't want it to happen to other people," Kerry said. "There is something really noble about that kind of selflessness and courage. It's very inspiring and deserves to be honored by a lot of adults who have to get in and make something happen."

Kerry joined with a Republican senator to sponsor Masha's Law, which would triple civil penalties for child porn downloaders and give adults whose pictures as children are still being circulated grounds to sue their perpetrators. As the law stood, a victim of child exploitation could get civil statutory damages of $50,000, while a copyright holder of a song could go after an illegal downloader for $150,000.

"What does it tell you about Washington's misplaced priorities that the penalty for downloading songs off the Internet is three times the penalty for downloading pornography—child pornography?" Kerry asked.

In May 2006, Masha took her message directly to Congress, testifying before hearings on Capitol Hill. It was one of most powerful condemnations of the crime—and of the unending consequences—of child exploitation over the Internet. She took direct aim at those who insist that looking at pictures of child pornography is a "victimless" crime. "The people who are doing this should be afraid. We know who they are. A lot of the people downloading these pictures are professionals. They are doctors and teachers and ministers," Masha said. "We're going to put THEIR pictures on the Internet and tell people what they are doing."

To adults who found her willingness to be in the spotlight inexplicable, she offered the simple logic of a child justifiably hurt and resentful when grownups did not listen to her: "A lot of people are surprised that I wanted to go public with my story. I've been on the Internet since I was five years old. Going on a television show wasn't going to hurt me. People need to know about this stuff. The adults who let this happen have just tried to cover it up."

Her closing words were like a slap on the face to the adults who ran the courts and the Congress: "You have to do something about the Internet. Some people say we can't control what's on the Internet but that's ridiculous," the girl said bluntly. "If we can put a man on the moon, we can make the Internet safe for kids."

By July, the stiffer regulations in Masha's Law were incorporated into the tougher child protection measures signed into effect by President George W. Bush.

On Bill McGarry's desk at work, right next to the photos of his wife and children, stands a picture of himself, smiling with a proud and confident Masha by his side.

Other children who endured the same kind of abuse as Masha have found their salvation in more private ways.

Ann, the plucky girl from Walt Disney Elementary school in Indiana who confronted her teacher, is now an honor-roll student at her new school and still dreams of becoming a prosecutor. Jessica, the girl located by the Toronto cops and the FBI, sent a drawing to her rescuers. Crayoned in bright colors and broad strokes, it depicts a little girl with curly brown hair wearing a flower on her dress. "Thank you," it says.

The Mashas and the Anns and the Jessicas have to live with the knowledge that somewhere out there, on someone's computer screen, is a picture of their nightmare. "I'm more upset about the pictures on the Internet than I am about what Matthew did to me physically," Masha told Congress about her adoptive father. "Usually, when a kid is hurt and the abuser goes to prison, the abuse is over. But because Matthew put my pictures on the Internet, the abuse is still going on. Anyone can see them."

Even as an adult—and as powerful advocate for victims' rights—Shy Keenan of the U.K.'s Phoenix Survivors still feels like a prisoner to her photographs. "Any other trauma you are allowed to move on and forget it," she said. "Victims of child pornography are not allowed to move on and forget. You are constantly reminded of the degradation and shame."

There are times, she said, when she is walking down a street and suddenly finds herself staring at the men walking by, wondering, Have you just been looking at pictures of me?

What disturbs Keenan even more is the fear—no doubt valid—that an offender might be using her pictures to fuel his fantasy as he plummets down the spiral of abuse. "The images of me being abused as a child could lead someone to hands-on abuse," she said as her voice, usually so expressive of confidence and resilience, began to crack. "I carry a great deal of pain for those pictures. The memory chokes me; it destroys me."

But it is also what drives her on. Her Phoenix group brings together dozens of victims of child abuse and the families of children murdered by sex offenders. They have the fortitude to hound politicians and police forces for stronger action, along with the foresight to also encourage more treatment for offenders; they educate young people about Web dangers and offer support services to those recovering from child sexual abuse.

"I am trying to reclaim myself," said Shy Keenan.

And to help reclaim the lives of thousands of victims like her.

Little Jessica is no longer cowering in a cage but in many ways she and countless other children are still prisoners to their photographs. When Jessica's father was sentenced to his 100 years in jail, the mother of one of his other victims told the court: "My son is too young to remember what happened to him, but I'm his mom, and it will burn in my heart and soul until the day I die. I will never forget."

"Sadly," she said, "neither will the Internet."

ACKNOWLEDGEMENTS

I have written five investigative books on everything from the Ku Klux Klan to the Hells Angels, the justice system and organized crime. For newspapers and television, I have covered wars and conflict in Baghdad, Beirut, Somalia, South Africa, Kosovo and Siberia. This was by far the most difficult subject I have ever had to confront.

It could not have been done without the patience and help of the many police officers and civilian investigators who took me into their confidence and shared their insights, fears and hopes. I am grateful to the staff at NCMEC, the Department of Homeland Security and ICE, the FBI, and the U.S. Postal Service in the United States; CEOP and New Scotland Yard in the United Kingdom; the RCMP, the OPP and the Toronto Police Service in Canada; as well the people at Interpol, the National High Tech Computer Crime Unit in Denmark; Task Force Argos in Australia; and the BKA in Germany. Jamie Zuieback at the DHS, Angela Barnes at the FBI, Bryan Sierra at the Department of Justice and Sandra Johnson of the Dallas Children's Advocacy Center were particularly tireless in easing the way. The corporate leaders at Microsoft, AOL and Vodafone, Visa and MasterCard were equally generous with their time. David Butt in Canada, Drew Oosterbaan and Kevin Gerrity of the Naval Justice School in the U.S, and Elizabeth George in the U.K. were patient enough to explain the laws to me.

I also owe a debt of gratitude to the victims of abuse and their families who shared their stories and their courage.

I thank the jury and the board of the directors of the Michener-Deacon fellowship, without whose support and grant this book would not have been possible.

For research, I had the benefit of some excellent news reporting in the *New York Times, Time* magazine, the *Toronto Star,* the *Globe and Mail,* the CBC and the BBC, as well as transcripts from CNN's Nancy Grace, the *Oprah show* and ABC's *Prime Time.* In particular, the work of Kellie Hudson of CBC Radio on Landslide, Declan McCullagh of CNET News on U.S. laws and corporations, and Cassell Bryan-Low of the *Wall Street Journal* on Regpay were especially useful.

To understand pedophiles and the children they abuse, I consulted the helpful research of Joe Sullivan, Dr. Sharon Cooper, Dr. John Bradford, Andres Hernandez, Dr. Michael Seto, and Dr. David Finkelhor of New Hampshire's Crimes against Children Research Center.

Concordia University journalism graduates Elisia Bargelletti and Tara Fraser did the bulk of the interview transcripts, aided by Adam Robinson, Sondip Chatterjee, Jenny King, Megan Ainscow, Karen Biskin, Stavroula Papadopoulos, Christopher Hazen, Yannis Themelis and Marie Lyne Laliberté. Additional research assistance came from Matt Carter in Toronto and Kendyl Salcito in Vancouver.

This book would never have seen the light of day without the vision of my literary agent, John Pearce, at Westwood Creative Artists, and my publisher, Anne Collins, at Random House of Canada, the two people who from the beginning believed in tackling this controversial topic. Philip Turner, formerly of Carroll & Graf in New York, and Louise Coe of Vision Paperbacks in London shared their commitment. Pamela Murray wielded a masterful scalpel as the editor, and copy editor Alison Reid made me look a lot smarter. Any remaining mistakes are mine.

As I was writing the final drafts of this manuscript, my father passed away after eighty-four years of a rich and full life. From the time he gave me my first John Steinbeck novel when I was eleven years old to the e-mail notes and suggestions he would send me during my travels, he was an inspiration and a guide. Even from his hospital bed, he was always asking me about the progress of my interviews and research, peppering me with questions and making me think harder. He taught me to respect the power of the word and to love the treasures that could be found within the covers of a book.

He did not get to see the finished version of this book, but I hope it would make him proud.

Julian Sher
February, 2007
julian@sher.com

For more information on my books, visit www.juliansher.com

Appendix

WEB RESOURCES FOR SAFER SURFING

The Internet is like any other community: some neighborhoods are safe for children; others are not. Most people are friendly, but some are dangerous.

You can't keep your child locked up in the house and off the streets forever, and you can't keep your children off the Web. All you can do is arm them with the skills and tools they will need to protect themselves. "You just have to give them the knowledge that they need to make their surfing experience safe," said the FBI's Emily Vacher, who spends a lot of time meeting students and parents in schools. "No one piece of technology or trick or tool is going to do it. It has to be about communication between parents and the kids."

That communication is frighteningly lacking. A survey by I-SAFE, a non-profit foundation in America, found an alarming discrepancy between how parents and children perceive their Web activity. Sixty-nine percent of parents said they know a lot about what their kids do online, but 41 percent of children said they don't tell their parents about their Web habits. A confident 87 percent of parents proudly said they had set firm rules for their children's online life, but 36 percent of children insisted that they had no rules about Web use. Indeed, 29 percent of children admitted that their parents would not approve of their Internet activities—if they knew.

A Teen Summit on Internet Safety sponsored by NCMEC revealed that 30 percent of young people were considering an online encounter, while 14 percent have already met in person with someone they met online.

Make a photocopy of the following tips and Web sites. Talk about them in your family. Post them near your computers. And happy surfing! The U.K.'s CEOP offers these **top tips for parents:**

- Know what your children are doing online and whom they are talking to. Ask them to teach you to use any applications you have never used.
- Help your children to understand that they should never give out personal details to online friends.
- Help your children to understand that some people lie online. They should never meet up with any strangers without an adult they trust.
- Always keep communication open for a child to know that it's never too late to tell someone if something makes him or her feel uncomfortable.
- Teach young people how to block someone online and report them if they feel uncomfortable.

For younger children, Netsmartz—one of the best safety sites on the Web—offers these three simple but important rules for online safety:

- I will tell an adult I trust if anything makes me feel scared, uncomfortable or confused.
- I will ask my parents or guardian before sharing my personal information.
- I won't meet in person with anyone I have first "met" online.

For teenagers, especially girls who might hang out at social networking sites or frequent chat rooms, NCMEC and the U.S. Postal Service launched a "Type Smart—Post Wisely" campaign on a Web site called "2SMRT4U." It features as a teen spokesperson Hayden Panettiere, a cover girl for Neutrogena and a star on various soap operas and popular TV shows. "Having your own webpage or blog and using Instant Messenging may put you in touch will all your friends. But it could also put you in touch with online predators," the site warns. "Seventy-one percent of teens receive messages online from someone they don't know. Would you know what to do?"

Among the tips to teens about what NOT to do online, the 2SMRT4U lists:

- Don't post your cell phone number, address, or the name of your school.
- Don't post your friends' names, ages, phone numbers, school names, or addresses.
- Don't add people as friends to your site unless you know them in person.
- Don't give out your password to anyone other than your parent or guardian.
- Don't make or post plans and activities on your site.
- Don't post photos with school names, locations, license plates, or signs.
- Don't post sexually provocative photos.

The following list of Web resources are not exhaustive but offer a good place to start to make sure your children's Internet experience can be as rewarding, exciting and fun as it should be.

TO REPORT ABUSE:

WORLDWIDE:
Virtual Global Taskforce
   www.virtualglobaltaskforce.com

UNITED STATES:
National Center for Missing and Exploited Children
   www.missingkids.com

CANADA:
Cybertip.ca
   www.cybertip.ca

UNITED KINGDOM:
Child Exploitation and Online Protection (personal abuse)
   www.ceop.gov.uk
Internet Watch Foundation—IWF (Abusive content)
   www.iwf.org.uk

SAFETY TIPS—FOR PARENTS AND CHILDREN

UNITED STATES:
Netsmartz
   www.Netsmartz.org
   www.netsmartzkids.org

CANADA:
Be Web Aware
   www.bewebaware.ca

UNITED KINGDOM:
Think U Know
   www.thinkuknow.co.uk
Childnet's Kidsmart Project
   www.kidsmart.org.uk

OTHER USEFUL SITES

Get NetWise
   www.getnetwise.org
Chat Danger
   www.chatdanger.com
Child Safe International
   www.childsafe.com
Protect Your Kids
   www.protectyourkids.info
SafeKids
   www.safekids.com

SafeTeens
   www.safeteens.com
WiredKids
   www.wiredkids.org
Wired Safety
   www.wiredsafety.org

CAST OF CHARACTERS

UNITED STATES:
FBI—INNOCENT IMAGES PROGRAM:
  Emily Vacher, special agent
  Brooke Donahue, special agent
  Arnold Bell, unit chief

NATIONAL CENTRE FOR MISSING AND EXPLOITED CHILDREN:
  Ernie Allen
  Ruben Rodriguez
  Michelle Collins
  Jennifer Lee
  Christine Feller
  Cristina Fernandez
  Steve Loftin

IMMIGRATION AND CUSTOMS ENFORCEMENT (ICE):
  Perry Woo
  Susan Cantor
  Betsy Perino
  Claude Davenport
  Ron Wolflick

U.S. POSTAL INSPECTION SERVICE:
  Ray Smith, assistant inspector in charge of the
    Child Exploitation Unit

OTHER INVESTIGATORS:
  Brian Bone, Lake County State Attorney's Office, Illinois
  Mike Casida, Clovis Police, California

Mitch Kajzer, St. Joseph County Prosecutors Office, Indiana
Lt. Bill Walsh, Dallas Police Department

STATE PROSECUTORS:
Ken Cotter, Indiana
Jeffrey Dort, California
Rachel Mitchell, Arizona

DEPARTMENT OF JUSTICE
CHILD EXPLOITATION AND OBSCENITY SECTION
    (CEOS):
Drew Oosterbaan, Chief
Jim Fottrell, High Tech Investigative Unit
Lam Nguyen, High Tech Investigative Unit

FEDERAL PROSECUTORS:
Carlos Ortiz
Andrew Norman

INDUSTRY:
Don Colcolough, AOL, director, Investigations and
    Law Enforcement Affairs
Robert Alandt, Visa International, vice president,
    Global Acceptance Compliance Programs
John Brady, MasterCard

U.S. CONGRESS:
Senator Richard Shelby
Senator John Kerry

CANADA:
TORONTO POLICE SEX CRIMES UNIT:
Det. Sgt. Paul Gillespie
Det. Ian Lammond
Det. Const. Bill McGarry
Det. Const. Paul Krawcyzk
Det. Const. John Menard

Det. Const. Scott Purches
Det. Const. Lori Haggett

ROYAL CANADIAN MOUNTED POLICE:
Insp. Earla Kim-McColl
Corp. Garry Belair

ONTARIO PROVINCIAL POLICE:
Det. Insp. Angie Howe

EDMONTON POLICE SERVICE:
Det. Randy Wickins

CYBERTIP.CA
Lianna McDonald

MICROSOFT:
Frank Clegg, former chairman and CEO
Frank Battiston

UNITED KINGDOM:
CHILD EXPLOITATION AND ONLINE PROTECTION (CEOP):
Jim Gamble, chief executive
Det. Sgt. Paul Griffiths
Helen Penn
Aarti Kapoor

SCOTLAND YARD:
Det. Const. Jim Pearce
Det. Const. Sean Robbie

SURREY:
Det. Sgt. Rod Thompson

INTERNET WATCH FOUNDATION:
Adrian Dwyer

INTERNATIONAL:

INTERPOL
TRAFFICKING IN HUMAN BEINGS SUB-DIRECTORATE:
  Hamish McCulloch, assistant director
  Anders Persson, crime intelligence officer

ECPAT (END CHILD PROSTITUTION, ABDUCTION AND
TRAFFICKING):
  David Butt, general secretary

AUSTRALIA:
TASK FORCE ARGOS, QUEENSLAND POLICE
  Det. Insp. Peter Crawford
  Det. Senior Sgt. Jon Rouse, operational leader

DENMARK:
DANISH NATIONAL HIGH TECH COMPUTER CRIME UNIT
  Lars Underbjerg

GERMANY:
BUNDESKRIMINALAMT (BKA)
  Daniel Szumilas
  Corinna Koch

THAILAND:
  Police Sub-Lieutenant Nathapan Sresthputr

MEDICAL EXPERTS:
  Joe Sullivan, principal forensic behaviour analyst, CEOP
  John Bradford , director, Sexual Behaviours Clinic,
    Royal Ottawa Hospital
  Dr. Peter Collins, manager, OPP Forensic Psychiatry Unit
  Dr. Sharon Cooper
  Andres Hernandez, director, Sex Offender Treatment
    Program, Butner federal prison, North Carolina

CHRONOLOGY OF MAJOR INVESTIGATIONS

FBI Innocent Images 1995–Present
In the early days of the Web, one of the first discoveries of a network using e-mail to exchange child abuse images leads to the creation of a permanent team of FBI undercover investigators.

Operation Cathedral 1998
International investigators dismantle the "w0nderland club" with 180 members in twenty-one countries.

Landslide 1999–2003
Known as Operation Avalanche in the U.S., Snowball in Canada, Ore in the U.K. and Ascent in Australia.

Operation Mango 1999–2002
One of the first sex tourism investigations by U.S. Customs investigators uncovers an Acapulco hotel where American tourists abuse young boys.

Regpay 2002–2003
First major financial probe targets a multimillion-dollar child pornography ring run out of Belarus with credit card operations based in Florida.

Operation Hamlet 2002–2003
A bust in Denmark leads to a ring of Europeans and Americans who abuse their own and other children.

Endangered Child Alert Program 2004–Present
> The FBI issues John Doe warrants for men whose faces appear in child abuse images. Five of six suspects are arrested.

Project Wickerman 2005–Present
> An undercover investigation by Canadian, American and British investigators leads to the arrest of more than fifty abusers in a secretive chat room.

ABBREVIATIONS

AFP   Australian Federal Police

AOL   America Online

CCRC   Crimes Against Children Research Centre, University of New Hampshire

CETS   Child Exploitation Tracking System

CEOS   Child Exploitation and Obscenity Section, U.S. Department of Justice

CEOP   Child Exploitation and Online Protection, U.K.

CRIS   Child Recognition and Identification Software

CSOM   Center for Sex Offender Management, U.S. Department of Justice

CVIP   Child Victim Identification Program

DHS   U.S. Department of Homeland Security

DOJ   U.S. Department of Justice

ECPAT   End Child Prostitution, Abduction and Trafficking

ICAC   Internet Crimes Against Children, U.S. Department of Justice

ICE	Integrated Child Exploitation unit, Alberta
ICE	U.S. Immigration and Customs Enforcement
ICMECC	International Centre for Missing and Exploited Children, Alexandria, VA
ICQ	Internet chat (I Seek You)
INHOPE	International Association of Internet Hotline Providers
IP	Internet Protocol (as in IP address)
IRC	Internet Relay Chat
IWF	Internet Watch Foundation, Cambridge, U.K.
NCMEC	National Center for Missing and Exploited Children, Alexandria, Virginia (abbreviation is pronounced NICK-MICK)
NCECC	National Child Exploitation Coordination Centre, run by the RCMP in Ottawa
NCS	National Crime Squad, U.K.
OPP	Ontario Provincial Police
POLIT	National Crime Squad's Pedophile Online Investigation Team, London, U.K.
RCMP	Royal Canadian Mounted Police
VGT	Virtual Global Taskforce

INDEX